F. 6

19/
13

VIKING TALES OF THE NORTH.

THE SAGAS OF

THORSTEIN, VIKING'S SON, AND FRIDTHJOF THE BOLD.

TRANSLATED FROM THE ICELANDIC

BY

RASMUS B. ANDERSON, A.M.,

PROFESSOR OF THE SCANDINAVIAN LANGUAGES IN THE UNIVERSITY OF WISCONSIN, AND HONORARY
MEMBER OF THE ICELANDIC LITERARY SOCIETY,

AND

JÓN BJARNASON.

ALSO,

TEGNÉR'S FRIDTHJOF'S SAGA,

TRANSLATED INTO ENGLISH

BY GEORGE STEPHENS.

CHICAGO:

S. C. GRIGGS AND COMPANY.

LONDON: TRÜBNER & CO.

1877.

KNIGHT & LEONARD, PRINTERS, CHICAGO.

Electrotyped by
A. ZEESE & CO., CHICAGO.

TO

WILLARD FISKE, LL.D.,

PROFESSOR OF NORTH-EUROPEAN LANGUAGES IN CORNELL UNIVERSITY,

THIS VOLUME IS REVERENTLY DEDICATED

BY

RASMUS B. ANDERSON

AND

JÓN BJARNASON.

The Legend of Fridthjof the Valiant is the noblest poetic contribution which Sweden has yet made to the literary history of the world.—HENRY WADSWORTH LONGFELLOW.

No poetical work of modern times stands forth so prominently and peculiarly a representative of the literature of a race and language as the Fridthjof's Saga of Esaias Tegnér.—BAYARD TAYLOR.

In der Fridthjof's Sage verehrt das schwedische Volk seine lieblischste und berühmteste National-dichtung.—GOTTLIEB MOHMIKE, in the preface to the ninth edition of his German translation of the poem.

PREFACE.

ICELANDIC SAGAS are but little known to the American public, and this being the first volume of saga-translations ever published in this country, we trust it will not be found out of place to give a short sketch, first of the Icelandic saga-literature in general, and then of the special interest attaching to the sagas contained in this volume.

The Icelandic word saga (saying) implies anything presented in narrative prose, and is a term used in reference to strictly historical records of persons and events of the past, but it also includes a large amount of half-fabulous and purely fictitious tales which are told in the same narrative form as the genuine historical sagas.

The composition of Icelandic literature in general and the writing of sagas began about the close of the eleventh century, soon after the complete introduction of Christianity in that country (A.D. 1000). Priest Are Thorgilsson the Learned. who was born in the year 1067 and died 1148, has the honor of being the father of Northern history and Icelandic saga-writing. He is the Herodotos of the North, and his "Icelander Book" (Íslendingabók) is the oldest literary monument in the Norse language, excepting the runic inscriptions that are found risted on stone and wood in great numbers throughout the Scandinavian countries of the continent and occasionally in Great Britain and elsewhere. Of these runic inscriptions a large number date back to a time far earlier than that of the birth of Are the Learned;

but runes are not known to have been used in writing books. With Are's saga-works, which embraced a general history of the Northern peoples and a special history of Iceland down to the time of the author, the foundation was laid of the saga-literature; and henceforth, during the twelfth, thirteenth and fourteenth centuries, one work after the other was produced, forming together a collection which, both as regards quantity and quality, has been looked upon with wonderment by the scholars of all lands who have turned their attention to Icelandic studies, and which is admitted to be an achievement so remarkable as to be without a parallel in the literary history of the world.

The writings of Are the Learned are not extant in their original form, with the exception of his "Íslendingabók," which is a compend, prepared by himself, of his large saga-work on Iceland. But they are far from being wholly lost, for the famous Heimskringla (home-circle) of Snorre Sturlasson (Snorri Sturluson), who died in the year 1241, and probably also the history of the Jomsvikings (Jómsvíkinga Saga) and of the Knytlings (Knytlinga Saga), embracing a history of Denmark, by Olaf Thordsson Kvitaskald, and also, so far as Iceland is concerned, the "Landnámabók" (Book of Land-Taking; comp. the Eng. Domesday Book,) are based on Are's great historical works. The saga-writers, especially the older ones, preserved the historical records of the past without stripping them of that popular and colloquial form in which oral tradition, from grandsire to grandson, had preserved them,—a form which had so naturally been given to them by the creative power of the people's imagination. The form of the oldest Icelandic sagas is in this respect not unlike the writings of Herodotos, and thus history repeats itself. Its chief characteristics are the same in the frozen North as beneath the genial rays of a Southern sun. Thus it also happens that even the best of these old sagas have more or less superstition interwoven with the historical facts, and that historical persons sometimes have their characters embellished with supernatural traits. Without impairing the historical value of these sagas, the peculiarity just mentioned serves in a pleasing and naïve manner to enhance their artistic value, making, as it does, an historical drama out of every one of them. Examples of this kind are Njal's Saga, Laxdæla Saga, Grettis Saga, Egil Skallagrimsson's Saga, etc. Some of the events that became the subject of Icelandic saga-writing took place, so to speak, under the very eyes of the saga-man, so that he had an opportunity to investigate the facts; while others had existed a much longer time in popular tradition, and the circumstances upon which they were originally based were so remote as to be almost or entirely beyond the reach of the historical eyes of the saga-man on account of the mystic cloud in which they had become enveloped by tradition. Thus two distinct kinds of sagas were produced. The one was the *strictly historical* and the other the *fabulous*, of which the latter, though often of little or no historical value, may, in other respects, be considered just as genuine as the former.

But as soon as historiography was fairly established in Iceland, historical criticism also was developed, and to a perfection that can scarcely anywhere be found more conspicuous than in the masterly works of Snorre Sturlasson.

After the writing of semi-mythical, semi-historical sagas had acquired a thoroughly artistic form, and when the material for them had been well nigh exhausted, the composition of fictitious sagas took their place. In these the subject was wholly a creation by the author's fancy, and was in no respect based on popular tradition. Still, these fictions adhered very strictly to the form of the other sagas, and the colloquial, dramatic form of the latter was generally very successfully imitated.

In the present volume we offer our readers an English version of two old Icelandic sagas, viz., the saga of Thorstein Vikingsson and the saga of Fridthjof the Bold.

The saga of Fridthjof the Bold belongs to the *fabulous* class mentioned above. The persons figuring therein *may* have existed at some far-off time, which it is impossible to determine; and while the dramatic adventures related *may* have an historical basis, still the mythical element is decidedly the predominating and more conspicuous of the two. It is a mooted question whether the myths of the Eddas may not, in addition to impersonating the forces and phenomena of nature, to some extent be connected with, or even based upon, historical characters and events. We believe the cycle of myths embraced in the second half of the *Elder Edda* may have a real historical foundation, and so far as this is true the legend presented in Fridthjof's Saga must be classed with them. Thus myths may be divided into two classes: the primary myths, in which the thoughts and feelings and actions of the Divine are presented in their most human form; and the secondary myths, in which human ideas and aspirations find their divinest expression. Fridthjof's Saga will then be classified as a secondary myth. Fridthjof and Ingeborg, the two most prominent characters in it, may really have existed in some far-off time, but in our story they serve as representatives of the highest and most godlike type of male and female character, according to heathen conceptions of men and women in the Teutonic North; while Balder and Freyja, for instance, in the purely mythological portion of the Eddas, in an ethical sense, represent attributes of the Supreme God, elaborated in such a manner as to adapt themselves somewhat to the longings of the human soul.

Who the author of Fridthjof's Saga is is not known. The same is true of a large majority of Icelandic sagas. The saga-writers did not, as a rule, attach their names to their literary works. With Íslendingabók, for instance, it is a matter of mere accident that a statement is found in it showing that Are the Learned is its author. And, as has already been indicated, the individuality of the writer is scarcely noticeable in most of the sagas. The old Icelanders seemed to care but little for personal fame as authors. It was their custom to present all ancestral nar-

ratives in the name of the whole people, and not in the name of
a single individual or author. In spite of this fact, it is evident,
when we compare the various sagas one with the other, that the
saga-man was not, as has sometimes been asserted, a mere *trans-
scriber* of popular traditions, but he was an *author*, and as such
would rank favorably with Herodotos or Livy. The great superiority of some sagas over others in respect to the form of narrative
will convince any one, who will take pains to look into the matter, of the correctness of this view, and it becomes especially appar-
ent in cases where the same tradition is found recorded in more
than one of the sagas. In one we may find it presented in an
easy, natural and unaffected manner, while in another the same
story may be told in a clumsy, dull and dry style, with more
or less affectation.

Nor can the time when Fridthjof's Saga was put in writing
be fixed with precision. All we can say of it is, that it is
usually ascribed to the twelfth or thirteenth century.

The Saga of Thorstein Vikingsson is very intimately connected
with Fridthjof's Saga. The latter may be regarded as a contin-
uation of the former, the principal characters treated in Thorstein
Vikingsson's Saga being the ancestors of those figuring in the
saga of Fridthjof the Bold. In another sense Thorstein's Saga
may be considered as an introduction to Fridthjof's Saga, for
while the latter is a genuine semi-mythological story based on
some popular tradition, the former belongs to the class of purely
fictitious viking romances which became so fashionable in the
latter part of the saga-period in Iceland. It dates from the fourteenth century, and represents an average tale of the medieval
North. The most prominent characters in it purport, as already
explained, to be the forefathers of the heroes in Fridthjof's Saga;
but aside from this nominal relation they differ widely in their
general character, and belong to two distinct saga-classes.

The Icelandic originals of both these sagas are found in volume II of the "Fornaldarsögur" (Copenhagen, 1829), and Frid-

thjof's Saga is also found in Dr. Dietrich's "Altnordisches Lese-
buch."

We beg the reader not to look upon the famous poem of the
great Esaias Tegnér as a mere appendix to our work. Our saga-
translations should rather be regarded as two introductory chapters to the poem.   These two sagas are the source from which
the celebrated Swedish poet got his material, and we fear that
many would fail to appreciate the natural and unadorned 'poetry
of the original, were it not brought out in bold relief by Tegnér's
artistic poem; and hence we repeat, that this gem among modern
poetical productions should be looked upon as the interpreter and
illuminator of the original.   Tegnér has shown by this poem
that our old northern paganism enshrines poetical material of a
character profound and sublime enough to be worthy of the
attention of the master poets of a Christian age. Tegnér's Fridthjof's Saga is the very heart of Scandinavian poetry,—a heart
which, though it belongs to the icy North and strikes its deepest
roots far down into the traditional legends of ancestral paganism,
still has enough of warmth and beauty to delight the readers of
the most varied climates and nationalities.   It has been translated into nearly every European tongue, and into some of them
many times.   Thus there are no less than eighteen or nineteen
versions of this poem in English,* and a few years ago the
Icelandic skald, Matthías Jochumsson, gave ·his countrymen a
splendid and truly classical translation.

The English version which is found in the present volume is by
Professor George Stephens, of Copenhagen, Denmark, that famous
Northern scholar and runologist who has done so much to call
attention to the wealth stored up in our own old literary monuments. Professor Stephens has generously granted us permission
to make use of his work; and his reputation as a scholar, coupled
with Tegnér's most flattering testimony that the translator has
succeeded in reproducing the very spirit of the original, will be to

* In reference to the first American translation of the whole poem, see
page 361.

all who may chance to pick up this book a sufficient guarantee that the translation of Tegnér herewith presented is both accurate and excellent.*

Professor Stephens' translation of Fridthjof's Saga forms altogether a book of more than three hundred pages, octavo. Lest our ·volume should become too large, we have been compelled reluctantly to omit a considerable portion of his valuable introductory chapters, notes, etc. On the other hand, we have added a few paragraphs to the excellent sketch of Tegnér's life, written by F. M. Franzén (a countryman of the poet), so as to bring it down to the poet's death. We hereby tender our thanks to the venerable George Stephens for his kindness in permitting us to make use of the fruits of his toil; and we also beg his generous indulgence if he should find that, for reasons above indicated, we have abbreviated, selected, rejected and added in our appropriation of his introduction and notes, in a manner that reminds him but too forcibly of the ancient vandals.

Of our own translation of the two sagas others must be the judges. The first one of the two has appeared twice before in English; once in 1839, by George Stephens, as a part of his work mentioned above; the second time in 1875, after we had nearly completed our translation, by those heroic workers among the old sagas, Eírikr Magnússon, and William Morris, of Cambridge, England. We make no pretensions, and humbly ask forgiveness of the reader, where he thinks he could have performed the task better. Of course a criticism as to the *accuracy* of our translation must be based on some acquaintance with the originals in the Icelandic tongue.

It should have been stated before, that in addition to the Icelandic Fridthjof's Saga, which we have made use of, there

---

* In 1838 Bishop Tegnér wrote a letter to George Stephens, wherein he says:

"*I am of opinion that no one of all the translators, with whom I have had an opportunity of meeting, have penetrated so deeply into the fundamental spirit of the original, and have so much respected its northern characteristics, as — yourself.*—Es. TEGNÉR."

exists another much shorter one, which may be found in the same volume of "Fornaldarsögur" as the other.

Hoping the time may soon come when the saga-literature may gradually become known and appreciated in this Western world, and wishing for this inestimable heritage from our fore-fathers the fostering care of abler hands, we send these vikings out among the dwellers of Vinland the Good as pioneers to make way for their brothers and friends. Give them a bench at your firesides and let them relate their adventures!

R. B. ANDERSON,

JÓN BJARNASON.

CONTENTS.

CONTENTS.

HERE BEGINS THE SAGA OF THORSTEIN,

VIKING'S SON.

I.

THE beginning of this Saga is, that a king named
Loge ruled that country which is north of Norway.
Loge was larger and stronger than any other man in that
country. His name was lengthened from Loge to Haloge,
and after him the country was called Halogeland (Háloga-
land, *i. e.* Haloge's land). Loge was the fairest of men, and
his strength and stature was like unto that of his kinsmen.
the giants, from whom he descended. His wife was Glod
(Glöð, glad), a daughter of Grim of Grimsgard, which is
situated in Jotunheim in the north; and Jotunheim was at
that time called Elivags (Elivágar in the north). Grim was
a very great berserk; his wife was Alvor, a sister of Alf
the Old. He ruled that kingdom which lies between two
rivers, both of which were called Elfs (*i. e.* Elbs), taking
their name from him (Alf). The river south of his kingdom, dividing it from Gautland, the country of King Gaut,
was called Gaut's Elf (*i. e.* Gaut's River, the river Gotha in
the southwestern part of the present Sweden); the one
north of it was called Raum's Elf, named after King Raum,
and the kingdom of the latter was called Raum's-ric. The
land governed by King Alf was called Alfheim, and all his

offspring are related to the *Elves*. They were fairer than any other people save the giants. King Alf was married to Bryngerd, a daughter of king Raum of Raum's-ric; she was a large woman, but she was not beautiful, because her father, king Raum, was ugly-looking, and hence ugly-looking and large men are called great "raums." King Haloge and his wife, queen Glod, had two daughters, named Eisa (glowing embers) and Eimyrja (embers). These maids were the fairest in the land, on account of their parentage, for their father and mother were both very fair. But as fire and light make dark things bright, so these things took their names from the above-named maids. There lived with Haloge two jarls, named Vifil and Vesete, both of whom were large and strong men, and they were the warders of the king's land. One day the jarls went to the king, Vifil to woo Eimyrja and Vesete to woo Eisa; but the king refused both, on which account they grew so angry that they soon afterward carried the maids off, fleeing with them out of the land, and thus putting themselves out of his reach. But the king declared them outlaws in his kingdom, hindered them by witchcraft from ever again becoming dwellers in his land, and, moreover, enchanted their kinsmen, making these also outlaws, and deprived them of the benefit of their estates forever. Vesete settled in an island or holm, which hight Borgund's holm (Bornholm), and became the father of Bue and Sigurd, nicknamed Cape. Vifil sailed further to the east and established himself in an island called Vifil's Isle. With his wife, Eimyrja, he got a son, Viking by name, who in his early youth became a man of great stature and extraordinary strength.

II.

THERE was a king who hight Ring, who ruled a fylke of Sweden. With his queen he had an only child, a daughter, by name Hunvor, a maiden of unrivaled beauty and education. She had a magnificent bower, and was attended by a suite of maidens. Ingeborg hight the maiden, who was next to her in position, and she was a daughter of Herfinn, jarl of Woolen Acre. Most people said that Ingeborg was not inferior to the daughter of the king in any respect, excepting in strength and wisdom, which Hunvor possessed in a higher degree than all others in the land. Many kings and princes wooed Ingeborg, but she refused them all. She was thought to be a woman of boundless pride and insolence, and it was also talked by many that her pride and insolence might some day receive a check in some way or other. Thus time passed on for a while. There was a mountain back of the king's residence so high that no human paths traversed it. One day a man — if he might be so called — came down from the mountain. He was larger and more fierce-looking than any person that had before been seen, and he looked more like a giant than like a human being. In his hand he held a bayonet-like two-pointed pike. This happened while the king was sitting at the table. This "raum" (ugly-looking fellow) came to the door of the hall and requested to be permitted to enter, but the porters refused to admit him. Then he smote the porters with his pike and pierced both of them from breast to back, one being pierced by one point of the pike and the other by the other: whereupon he lifted both of them over his head and threw their corpses down upon the ground

behind him. Then, entering the door, he approached the
king's throne, and thus addressed him: As I, king Ring,
have honored you so much as to visit you, I think it your
duty to grant my request. The king asked what the request might be, and what his name was. He answered :
My name is Harek, the Ironhead, and I am a son of king
Kol Kroppinbak (the humpback) of India; but my errand is
that I wish you to place your daughter, your country, and
your subjects in my hands. And, I think, most people will
say that it is better for the kingdom that I rule it instead
of you, who are destitute of strength and manhood, and,
moreover, enfeebled by age. But, as it may seem humili-
ating to you to surrender your kingdom, I will agree, on
my part, to marry your daughter, Hunvor. But, if this is
not satisfactory to you, I will kill you, take possession of
your kingdom, and make Hunvor my concubine. Now
the king felt sorely perplexed, for all the people were
grieved at their conversation. Then said the king: It
seems to me that we ought to know what she will answer.
To this Harek assented. Then Hunvor was sent for, and
the matter was explained to her. She said: I like the
looks of this man very well, although he seems likely to
treat me with severity; but I consider him perfectly worthy
of me, if I marry him; nevertheless, I wish to ask whether
no ransom can be paid and I be free. Yes, there can,
answered Harek. If the king will try a holm-gang with
me within four nights, or procure another man in his stead,
then all powers shall be surrendered to the one slaying the
other in the duel. Certainly, answered Hunvor, none can
be found who is able to subdue you in a duel; nevertheless,
I will agree to your proposition. After this, Harek went
out, but Hunvor betook herself to her bower, weeping bit-

terly. Then the king asked his men if there was nobody
among them who regarded his daughter Hunvor a sufficient
prize for which to risk his life in a holm-gang with Harek.
But, although all wished to marry her, yet nobody was
willing to risk the duel, looking upon it as certain death.
Many also said that this fate was deserved by her, since she
had refused so many, and marrying Harek would be a check
to her pride. She had a man-servant, by name Eymund, a
fellow faithful to her and to be trusted in all matters.
This man she sent for straightway on the same day, saying
to him: It will not prove advisable to keep quiet; I want
to send you away; take a boat and row to the island, which
lies outside of Woolen Acre, and is called Vifil's Isle. On
the island there is a byre (farm, farm-house); thither you
must go and arrive there to-morrow at nightfall. You are
to enter the western door of the byre, and when you have
entered you will see a sprightly old man and an elderly
woman; any other persons you will not see. They have a
son by name Viking, who is now fifteen years old and a
man of great ability, but he will not be present. I hope he
will be able to help us out of our troubles; if not, I fear
there will scarcely be any help for us. You must keep out
of sight, but if you happen to see a third person, then throw
this letter on his lap and hurry home. Without delay,
Eymund, with a company of eleven men, went on board a
ship and sailed to Vifil's Isle. He goes ashore alone and
proceeds to the byre, where he finds the fire-house and
places himself behind the door. The bonde (farmer) was
sitting by the fire with his wife, and he seemed to Eymund
a man of brave countenance. The fire was almost burnt
out and the house was but faintly lighted by the embers.
Said the woman: I think, my dear Vifil, that it would prove

to our advantage if our son Viking should present himself,
for no one seems to be offering himself for combat, and the
time for the duel with Harek is close at hand. I do not
think it advisable, Eimyrja, answered he, for our son is yet
young and rash, ambitious and careless. It will be nis sudden death if he should be induced to fight with Harek;
nevertheless, it is for you to manage this matter as you
think best. Presently a door opened back of the bonde, and
a man of wonderful stature entered, taking his seat by the
side of his mother. Eymund threw the letter on the lap of
Viking, ran to the ship, came to Hunvor and told her how
he had done his errand. Fate will now have to settle the
matter, says Hunvor. Viking took the letter, in which he
found a greeting from the king's daughter, and, moreover,
a promise that she would be his wife if he would fight with
Harek, the Ironhead. At this Viking turned pale, observ-
ing which, Vifil asked him what letter that was. Viking
showed him the letter. This I knew, said Vifil. and it
would have been better, Eimyrja, if I had decided this
matter myself, when we talked about it a little while ago,
but what do you propose to do? Says Viking: Would it not
be well to save the princess? Replied Vifil: It will be sudden death to you if you fight with Harek. I will run the
risk, answered Viking. Then there is no remedy, says
Vifil, but I will give you an account of his family and of
himself.

III.

TIRUS THE GREAT was king of India. He was an excellent ruler in every respect, and his queen was a very superior woman, with whom he had an only daughter, who hight Trona. She was the fairest among the fair, and, unlike the majority of her sex, she excelled all other princesses in wisdom. The Saga must also mention a man by name Kol, of whom a great many good things are told: first, that he was large as a giant, ugly-looking as the devil, and so well skilled in the black art that he could pass through the earth as well as walk upon it, could glue together steeds and stars; furthermore, he was so great a ham-leaper* that he could burst into the shape of various kinds of animals; he would sometimes ride on the winds or pass through the sea, and he had so large a hump on his back that, although he stood upright, the hump would reach above his head. This Kol went to India with a great army, slew Tirus, married Trona, and subjugated the land and the people. He begot many children with Trona, all of whom were more like their father than like their mother. Kol was nicknamed Kroppinbak (*i. e.* Humpback). He had three rare treasures. These were: a sword so mighty that none better was wielded at that time, and the name of this sword was Angervadil; another of the treasures was a gold ring, called Gleser; the third was a horn, and such was the nature of the beverage contained in the lower part of it that all who drank therefrom were attacked by an illness called leprosy, and became so forgetful that they remembered nothing of the past; but

---

* Ham-leaper, one who is able to change his shape.

3

by drinking from the upper part of the horn their health
and memory were restored. Their eldest child was Bjorn,
the Blue-tooth. His tooth was of a blue color, and ex-
tended an ell and a half out of his mouth; with this tooth
he often, in battles or when he was violently in rage, put
people to death. A daughter of Kol was Dis. The third
child of Kol and Trona hight Harek, whose head at the
age of seven was perfectly bald, and whose skull was as
hard as steel, wherefore he was called Ironhead. Their
fourth child hight Ingjald, whose upper lip measured an
ell from the nose, whence he was called Ingjald Trana (the
snout). It was the pastime of the brothers when at home
that Bjorn the Blue-tooth cut his tooth into the skull of his
brother Harek with all his might without hurting him.
No weapon could be made to stick in the lip of Ingjald
Snout. By incantations Kol the Hump-back brought it
about, that none of his offspring could be killed by any
other weapon than by the sword Angervadil; no other iron
can scathe them. But when Kol had become old enough
he died a horrible death. At the time of his death Trona
was pregnant, and gave birth to a son, called Kol after his
father, and he was as like his father as he was akin to him.
One year old, Kol was so ugly to children that he was
nicknamed Kol Krappe (the crafty). Dis married Jokul
Ironback, a blue berserk. She and her brothers divided
their father's heritage betwixt themselves, so that Dis got
the horn, but Bjorn Blue-tooth the sword, Harek the
ring, Ingjald the kingdom, and Kol the personal property.
Three winters after the death of king Kol, Trona married
jarl Herfinn, a son of king Rodmar of Marseraland, and
the first winter after they were married she bore him a
son, named Framar, who was a man of great possibilities

and unlike his brothers. Now it seems to me, continued
Vifil, that you ought not to risk your life in a duel with
this Hel-strong man, whom no iron can scathe. Not so,
answered Viking; I shall run the risk, whatsoever may be
the result. And Vifil, seeing that Viking was in real
earnest when he insisted on fighting with Harek, said:
I can tell you still more about the sons of Kol. Vesete
and I were wardens of king Haloge's country; during the
summer seasons we used to wage wars, and once we met
Bjorn Blue-tooth in Grening's Sound (the present Gronsund,
between the Isle of Man and Falster in Denmark), and in
such a manner did we fight that Vesete smote Bjorn's hand
with his club, so that the sword fell from his hand, and
then I caught it, flung it through him, and he lost his life.
From that time I have worn the sword, and now I give it
to you, my son. Vifil then brought forth the sword and
gave it to Viking, who liked it very much. Viking then
prepared himself, went on board a boat, and came to the
hall of the king on the day appointed for the duel. There
everything was sad and dreary. Viking went before the
king and greeted him. The king asked him his name.
Viking told him the truth. Hunvor was sitting on one
side of the king. Then Viking asked her whether she had
requested him to come. She replied in the affirmative.
Viking asked what terms he offered him for venturing a
holm-gang with Harek. Replied the king: I will give you
my daughter in marriage, and a suitable dowry besides.
Viking gave his consent to this, and then he was betrothed
to Hunvor; but it was the common opinion that it would
be certain death to him if he should fight with Harek.

IV.

THEN Viking went to the holm, accompanied by the king and his courtiers. Thither came Harek, too, and asked who was appointed to fight with him. Viking stepped forward and said: I am the man. Whereto Harek made reply: I suppose it will be an easy matter to strike you to the ground, for I know it will be the end of you if I smite you with my fist. But I suppose, answered Viking, that you consider it no trifling matter to fight with me, since you tremble at the very sight of me. Harek replies: Not so, and I must save your life, since you go willingly into the open jaws of death; and do you smite first, according to the laws of holm-gang, for I am the challenger in this duel; but, in the meantime, I shall stand perfectly still, for I am not afraid of any danger. At this time Viking drew his sword, Angervadil, from which lightning seemed to flash. Harek seeing this, said: I would never have fought with you had I known that you were in possession of Angervadil, and most likely it will turn out as my father said, namely, that I and my brothers and my sister would all be short-lived, excepting the one bearing his own name, and it was a great misfortune that Angervadil passed out of the hands of our family. At this moment Viking struck Harek's skull and split his trunk from one end to the other, so that the sword stood in the ground to the hilt. Then the men of the king burst out in loud triumphant shouting, and the king went home to his hall with great joy. Now they began to talk about preparing the wedding-feast, but Viking said he was not willing to be married yet; she shall remain betrothed, he

said, and not be wedded till after three years, meanwhile
I am going to wage war. So was done, and Viking went
abroad with two ships. He was very successful, gaining
victory in every battle; and after having spent two years
as a viking, he landed at an island in the autumn at a time
when the weather was fair and very warm.

V.

THE same day as Viking landed at the island, he went
ashore to amuse himself. He turned his steps to a
forest and then he grew very hot. Having come to an open
place in the forest, he sat down, and saw a woman of exquisite beauty walking along. She came up to him, greeted
him very courteously, and he received her very kindly.
They talked together a long time, and their conversation
was very friendly. He asked her her name, and she said it
was Solbjort (sun-bright). She then asked him if he was
not thirsty, as he had walked so far, but Viking said he was
not. She then took a horn, which she had kept under her
cloak, offered him a drink from it, and he accepting it, and
drinking therefrom, became sleepy, and bending his body
into the lap of Solbjort, he fell asleep. But when he woke
up again she had entirely disappeared. The drink had
made him feel somewhat strange, and his whole body was
shivering; the weather was gusty and cold, and he had forgotten nearly everything of the past, and least of all did he
recollect Hunvor. He then went to his ship and departed
from that place, and now he was confined to his bed by the
disease called leprosy. He and his men frequently sailed
near land, but were unwilling to go ashore and remain

there. After having suffered twelve months from this sickness it grew still more severe, and his body was covered with many sores. One day sailing to land, they saw three ships passing the harbor, and at their meeting they asked for each other's names. Viking told his name, but the other chieftain said his name was Halfdan, and that he was a son of Ulf. Halfdan was a large and strong-looking man, and when he had learned the condition of Viking he went on board his ship, where he found him very weak. Halfdan asked him the cause of his illness, and Viking told him everything that had happened. Halfdan answered: Here the ham-leaper, Dis, Kol's daughter, has succeeded in her tricks, and I think it will be difficult to get any assistance from her in righting this matter, for she undoubtedly thinks she has avenged her brother, Harek Ironhead. Now I will offer you foster-brotherhood, and we will try whether we cannot revenge ourselves on Dis. Answered Viking to this: Owing to my weakness, I have no hope at all of being able to kill Dis and her husband, Jokul Ironback, but such is my opinion of you, that even though I were in the best circumstances, your valor makes your offer very flattering to me. And thus it was agreed that they should become foster-brothers. Halfdan had a great dragon, called Iron-ram; all of this ship that stood out of the water was iron-clad; it rose high out of the sea, and was a very costly treasure. Having spent a short time there they left the place and went home to Svafe. Then Viking's strength diminished so that he became sick unto death. But when they had landed, Halfdan left the ships alone and proceeded until he came into an open space in a forest, where there stood a large rock, which he went up to and knocked at with his rod, and out of the rock there came a dwarf, who lived there and hight Lit (color), a warm friend of Halfdan, whom the dwarf greeted kindly and asked what his errand was. Replied Halfdan: It is now of great importance to mě, foster-father, that you do my errand. What is it, my foster-son? asked Lit. I want you to procure for me the good horn of Dis, Kol's daughter, said Halfdan. Risk that yourself, said Lit, for it will be my death if I attempt it; and even the sacrifice of myself would be in vain, for you know there does not exist such a troll in the whole world as Dis. Replied Halfdan: I am sure you will do as well as you can. Upon this they parted, Halfdan returning to his ships and remaining there for some time.

VI.

NOW it must be told of king Ring that he and his daughter Hunvor dwelt in his kingdom after the slaying of Harek Ironhead, which seemed to all a deed of great daring. This event was heard of in India, and Ingjald Snout was startled by the tidings of Harek's death. He began to cut the war-arrow, and dispatched it throughout the whole country, thus collecting an army containing a crowd of people, among whom there were many of the rabble, and with this army he marched toward Sweden. He came there unexpected, and offered the king battle. The challenge was accepted without delay, although the king had but a few men, and the result of this battle was soon decided. King Ring fell, together with all his courtiers; but Ingjald took Hunvor and Ingeborg and carried them away to India. Jokul Ironback went to seek after the foster-brothers, wishing to revenge the death of his brother-in-law, Harek.

Now the story goes on to tell about Viking and Halfdan staying at Svafe.   Seven nights had passed away
when Lit met Halfdan and brought the horn to him.   This
made Halfdan very glad, and he went to Viking, whom
almost everybody then thought to be not far from death.
Halfdan put a drop of fluid from the upper part of the
horn on Viking's lips.   This brought Viking to his senses;
he began to grow stronger and was like unto a person
awakening from a slumber; and the uncleanness fell from
him as scales fall from a fish.   Thus he, day by day, grew
better and was restored.   After this they got ready to
depart from Svafe, and directed their course north of
Balegard-side.   There they saw eighteen ships, all of large
size and covered with black tents.   Said Halfdan: Here
I think Jokul Ironback and his wife, the ham-leaper, are
lying before us, and I do not know how Lit has parted with
them, he being so exhausted that he could not speak.   But
now I think there is good reason for going to battle.   Let
everything of value be taken away from the ships, and let
stones be put in instead.   This was done.   Then after a
quick rowing to the strangers, they asked who the chieftains were.   Jokul gave them his name and asked for
their names in return.   They said they hight Halfdan and
Viking.   Then we need not ask what came to pass.   A
very hot battle took place, and the foster-brothers lost more
men than Jokul, for the latter dealt heavy blows.   Then
Viking, followed by Halfdan, made an attempt to board
Jokul's dragon, after which a great number of the crew
of the dragon were slain.   Jokul and Halfdan met and
exchanged blows with each other; but although Jokul was
the stronger, Halfdan succeeded in giving him a blow
across the back with his sword; yet, in spite of his being

without his coat-of-mail, the sword did not scathe him.
Meanwhile Viking came to Halfdan's assistance. He smote
Jokul's shoulder and split his side, thus separating one
arm and both feet, the one above the knee, from the trunk.
Then Jokul fell, but was not yet dead, and said: I knew
that when Dis had been forsaken by luck, much of evil
was in store; the first of all was that the villain Lit betrayed her, and thus succeeded by tricks in stealing the
horn from her and at the same time hurt her, so that she
is still confined to her bed from the encounter; but I should
also be inclined to think that he has not escaped without
some injury himself either. Had she been on foot, the
matter would not have resulted thus. But I am glad
you have not got the princess Hunvor from my brother-
in-law, Ingjald Snout. After this he soon died, and then
a cry of victory was shouted and quarter was given to the
wounded who could be cured. They got much booty there,
and on shore they found Dis almost lifeless from the encounter with Lit. Her they seized, put a belg (whole skin)
over her head, and stoned her to death. Hereupon they
went back to Svafe and cured the wounds of their men.
And having equipped twenty-four ships, all well furnished
with men and weapons, they announced that they were
bound for India.

VII.

INGJALD SNOUT made great preparations, fortifying
the walls of his burg (town, city) and collecting a great
number of people, some of which were rabble of the worst
kind. As soon as the foster-brothers had landed they
harried the country with fire and sword; everybody was in

fear of them, and before Ingjald was aware of it they had made a great plunder. Now he goes against them; they met, and a battle was fought. Halfdan and Viking thought they had never before been in so great danger as in this battle. The foster-brothers showed great bravery, and toward the end of the battle more men began to fall in Ingjald's army. The battle lasted four days, and at last none but Ingjald remained on his feet. He could not be wounded at all, and seemed to move through the air as easily as on the ground. Finally, by surrounding him with shields, they succeeded in getting him captive, put him in chains, and bound his hands with a bow-string. It was then so dark that they did not think it convenient to kill him on the spot, Viking being unwilling to slay a man at night-time. They ran into the burg and carried Hunvor and Ingeborg away to their ships. Here they lay during the night; but in the morning the warders were dead, and Ingjald was not to be found, his chains lying unbroken and the bow-string not untied. No mark of iron could be found on the warders, and thus it was clear that Ingjald had made use of troll-craft. Now they hoisted their sails, left this country, and directed their course homeward to Sweden. Then Viking made preparations for the wedding, and married Hunvor. At the same time Halfdan began his suit and asked for the hand of Ingeborg, the daughter of the jarl. Word was sent to jarl Herfinn of Woolen Acre. He came and gave a favorable answer, and it was agreed that Halfdan should marry Ingeborg. Arrangements for the wedding were made, and the marriage ceremony was performed. The foster-brothers stayed there during the winter. The following summer they went abroad with ten ships, waged wars in the Baltic, and having got great booty they returned home in the fall. Thus they lived as vikings three years, spending only the winters at home; and none were more famous than they. One summer they sailed to Denmark; here they harried and entered the Limfjord, where they saw nine ships and a dragon lying at anchor. They immediately directed their fleet toward these ships, and asked for the name of the commander. He said he hight Njorfe, and added: I am the ruler of the Uplands in Norway, and I have just gotten my paternal heritage; but what is the name of those who have just come? They told him this. Said Halfdan: I will offer to you, as to other vikings, two conditions: the one that you give up your fee, ships and weapons, and go ashore free; and the other, that you fight a battle with us. Answered Njorfe: This seems to me hard terms, and I choose rather to defend my fee, and, if need be, fall with bravery, than to flee feeless and dishonored, although you have a larger army and ships of greater size and number than mine. Said Viking: We shall not be so mean as to attack you with more ships than you have; five of our ships shall therefore lie idle during the battle. Answered Njorfe: This is bravely spoken. And so they got ready for the battle, which then began. They fought with their ships stem to stem. The attack was very violent on both sides, for Njorfe fought with great daring, and the foster-brothers also showed great bravery. Three days they fought, but still they did not seem to know who would win. Asked then Viking: Is there much fee in your ships? Answered Njorfe: No, for from those places where we have been harrying this summer the bondes fled with their fee, and hence but little booty has been taken. Said Viking: Unwise it seems to me to fight only for the sake of outdoing each other, and thus spill the blood of many men;

but are you willing to form a league with us? Answered
Njorfe: It will be good for me to form a league with you,
although you are not a king's son, for I know that your
father was a jarl, and an excellent man; and I am willing
to have a foster-brotherhood formed between us on the
condition that you hight jarl and I king, according to our
birth-right, which must remain unchanged whether we are
in my kingdom or in any other.   During this talk Halfdan
was silent. Viking asked why he had so little to say in this
matter.   Answered Halfdan: It seems to me that it may be
good to make such an agreement betwixt you; but I shall
not be surprised if you should get to feel that some or other
of Njorfe's relatives become burdensome to you.   I will,
however, have nothing to do with this matter — will neither
dissuade nor encourage you.   The result was, that Njorfe
and Viking came to terms and formed a foster-brotherhood,
giving oaths mutually on the terms which have before been
stated.   They waged wars during the summer and took
much booty; but in the fall they parted, Njorfe going to
Norway, and Viking, accompanied by Halfdan, to Sweden.
But soon after Viking had come home, Hunvor was taken
sick and died.   They had a son, who hight Ring.   He was
brought up in Sweden until he was full-grown, and became
a king of that country.   He did not live long, but had a
great many descendants.   The foster-brothers kept on wag-
ing wars every summer and became very famous; during
their warfares they gathered so many ships that they had
fifty in all.

VIII.

IT must be told of Ingjald Snout, that he gathered an innumerable army and went to search for the foster-brothers, Viking and Halfdan. And one summer they met in the Baltic, Ingjald having forty ships. It came straightway to a fight, and they fought in such a manner that it was not easy to see which side would win. At last Viking, immediately followed by Njorfe and Halfdan, tried to board Ingjald's dragon. They made a great havoc, killing one man after the other. Then Ingjald rushed toward the stern of the dragon, with a great atgeir (a kind of javelin) ready for slaughter. Now the foster-brothers attacked Ingjald, and although they fought a large part of the day with him they did not wound him, and when the fight seemed to Ingjald to grow very hot, he sprang overboard, followed by Njorfe and Halfdan, both swimming as fast as they could. Viking did not stop fighting before he had slain every man on the dragon, after which he jumped into a boat and rowed ashore. Ingjald kept swimming till he reached the land, and then Halfdan and Njorfe were drawing near to the surf. Ingjald took a stone and threw it at Halfdan, but he dodged under the water. Meanwhile Njorfe landed, and Halfdan soon after him, in another place. They attacked Ingjald mightily, and having fought thus for a long time, they heard a great crash, and looked thither whence they heard the crash, but on turning their faces back, Ingjald was out of sight, and instead of him there was a grim-looking boar, that left nothing undone as he attacked them, so they could do nothing but defend themselves. When this had been done for some time, the boar

turned upon Halfdan, bearing away the whole calf of his
leg. Straightway came Viking and smote the bristles of
the boar, so that his back was cut in two. Then seeing that
Ingjald lay dead on the spot, they kindled a fire and burned
him to ashes. Now they went back to their ships and
bound up the wounds of Halfdan. After this they sailed
away from this place north to an isle called Thruma, and
ruled by a man who hight Refil a son of the sea-king
Mefil. He had a daughter who hight Finna, a maid of
surpassing fairness and accomplishments. Viking courted
her, and with king Njorfe's help, and Halfdan's bravery, the
marriage was agreed to. Then the foster-brothers ended
their warfaring. King Njorfe established himself in his
kingdom, and Viking took his abode with him and became
his jarl, but Halfdan was made a great herser and dwelt on
his byre, called Vags. His land was separated by a mountain from that which was ruled by jarl Viking. They held
to their friendship as long as they lived, but it was more
cold between Halfdan and Njorfe.

IX.

A KING, hight Olaf, ruled Fjord-fylke (the county of
the fjords). He was a son of Eystein and a brother
of Onund, who was the father of Ingjald the Wicked.
They were all unsafe and wicked in their dealings. King
Olaf had a daughter who hight Bryngerd, whom Njorfe
married, took her with him, and got with her nine sons:
Jokul hight the eldest of these brothers; the rest hight
Olaf, Grim, Geiter, Teit, Tyrfing, Bjorn, Geir, Grane and
Toke. They were all promising men, though Jokul far sur-

passed them all in all accomplishments. He was so haughty
that he thought everything below himself. Olaf stood next
to him, as a man skillful in all deeds; but he was of a
noisy, troublesome and overbearing temperament, and the
same might be said of all his brothers, and they boasted
very much. Viking had nine sons, the eldest of whom
was Thorstein, and the others hight Thorer, Finn, Ulf,
Stein, Romund, Finnboge, Eystein and Thorgeir. They
were hopeful men, of great skill in action, though Thorstein held the highest rank among them in everything.
He was the largest and strongest of men; he was popular, steadfast in his friendship, faithful and reliable in
all things. He could not easily be provoked to do harm,
but when attacked he revenged himself grimly. If he
was insulted, it could scarcely be seen in his daily life
whether he liked it or not, but long afterward he would
act as if he had just been injured. Thorer was of a
most sanguine and vehement temperament; if injured or
affronted he would suddenly be seized by an irresistible
rage, and, no matter whom he had to do with, or what
the result might be, he never hesitated to do whatsoever
came into his mind. He was a most adroit man in all
kinds of games, and a man of uncommon strength. He
was second only to his brother Thorstein. These young
men grew up together in the kingdom. In the mountain separating Viking's and Halfdan's lands, there was
a chasm of fearful depth and of a breadth of thirty ells
at the narrowest, so that it was perfectly impassable for
human beings, and hence the mountain was not crossed
by any paths. It had been tried by king Njorfe and jarl
Viking and Halfdan how easily they might leap over the
chasm. The result was, that Viking had leaped over it

in full armor, Njorfe had done it in his lightest clothes,
but Halfdan had only done it by being received on the
other side by Viking. Now they all kept quiet for a
long time, and the friendship of jarl Viking and king
Njorfe remained unimpaired.

X.

NJORFE and Viking became old, and their sons were
rapidly advancing in growth. Jokul became in all
things a violent and restless man. The sons of Njorfe
were of nearly the same age as the sons of Viking, the
youngest ones being at this point of our Saga about twelve
years old, while Thorstein and Jokul were at the age of
twenty. The sons of Njorfe used to play with the sons of
Viking, and the latter were in no way below the former.
This made the sons of the king very jealous, and in their
jealousy, as in all other things, Jokul surpassed all; and it
was easy to see that Thorstein yielded to Jokul in all
things, nor was this any reproach to him. Thorstein far
surpassed all his brothers and all other men known. Jarl
Viking had warned his sons not to vie with the sons of the
king in any games, but rather to spare their strength and
eagerness. One day the king's sons and the sons of Viking
were playing ball, and the game was played very eagerly
by the sons of Njorfe. Thorstein, as usual, checked his
zeal. He was placed against Jokul, and Thorer was placed
against Olaf, and the others were placed in the same manner, according to their age. Thus the day was spent. It
happened that Thorer threw the ball on the ground so hard
that it bounded over Olaf and fell down again far off. At

this Olaf turned angry, thinking that Thorer was mocking him. He fetched the ball; but when he came back the game was being broken up, and the people were going home. Olaf then with the ball-club struck after Thorer, who, seeing it, dodged the blow in such a manner that the club touched his head and wounded it. But Thorstein, together with many other people, hurried betwixt them and parted them. Said Jokul: I suppose you think it a thing of no great weight that Thorer got a bump on his head. Thorer blushed at Jokul's words, and thus they parted. Said Thorer then: I have left my gloves behind, and if I do not fetch them Jokul will lay it to my fear. Answered Thorstein: I do not think it advisable that you and Olaf meet. Nevertheless I will go, said Thorer, for they have gone home. So saying, he turned back at a swinging pace, and when he came to the play-ground everybody had left it. Then Thorer turned his steps toward the hall of the king. At the same moment the sons of the king also came home to the hall, and stood near the wall of the hall. Then Thorer turned toward Olaf and stabbed his waist, so that the spear passed through his body; whereupon he withdrew and escaped out of their hands. They, on the other hand, had a great ado over Olaf's corpse; but Thorer went until he found his brother. Now asked him Thorstein: Why is there blood on your spear, brother? Answered Thorer: Because I do not know whether Olaf has not perhaps been wounded by the point of it. Said Thorstein: You perhaps tell of his death. Quoth Thorer: It may be that Jokul will not be able to heal the wound of his brother Olaf, though he be a very skillful man in almost all things. Answered Thorstein: This is a sorry thing that now has happened; for I

4

know that my father will dislike it. And when they came
home jarl Viking was out-doors, and looked very stern.
Said he: What I looked for from you, Thorer, has now
come to pass, that you would be the most luck-forsaken of
all my sons. This you have shown, as I think, by killing
the son of the king himself. Answered Thorstein: Now is
the time, father, to help your son, although he has fallen
into ill-luck; and that you know means for this purpose I
think you have shown by your being aware of Olaf's death
while nobody had told you of it. Answered Viking: I am
unwilling to sacrifice so much as to break my oaths for the
life of Thorer; for both of us, king Njorfe and I, have
sworn to be faithful and trusty to each other, both in
private and public matters. These oaths he has kept in
all matters. Now I will not, therefore, show myself worse
than he has been; but this I would do if I should fight
against him, for there was a time when king Njorfe was as
dear to me as my own sons, and it needs not be hinted at
that I should give Thorer any help; he must leave, and
never more come before my eyes. Answered Thorstein:
Why should not all of us brothers then leave home? for
we will not part with Thorer, but stand by one another
for weal or for woe. Answered the jarl: That is a matter
that rests with you, my son; but great I must call the
ill-luck of Thorer, if he is to be the cause of my losing
all my sons and my friendship with the king too, who is
the doughtiest man in all things, and besides these, my
life, which is, however, worth but little. But there is one
thing that makes me glad, and that is that it will not fall
to the lot of any one to put you to death, although your
escape will be narrow enough, and this will all be caused
by Thorer's ill-luck; nevertheless, the loss of him will be

felt on account of his valor. Now, my son Thorstein, here is a sword, which I will give to you; Angervadil is its name, and it has always had victory with it; my father took it from Bjorn Blue-tooth at his death. I have no other distinguished weapons except an old kesia, which I took from Harek Ironhead; but I know that nobody is able to wield it as a weapon. Now if you are going to leave home, my son Thorstein, then it is my advice that you go up to a lake named Vener; there you will find a boat belonging to me, standing in a boat-house; go in it to a holm which lies in the lake; there you will find in a shed food and clothes enough to last you twelve months; take good care of the boat, for there are no more ships in the neighborhood. Hereupon the brothers parted with their father. The brothers all had good clothes and armor, which had been given them by their father before this happened. Thorstein and his brothers went until they found the boat. Then they rowed to the holm, and found the shed; here was enough of all things which they needed, and they took up their abode there.

XI.

NOW it is to be told that Jokul and his brothers told of the death of Olaf to their father. Said Jokul: This is the only thing to be done, that we bring together an army and march to the house of Viking and burn him and all his sons alive in their house, and even this would scarcely be vengeance enough for Olaf's death. Said Njorfe: I wholly forbid that any harm be done to Viking, for I know that my son has not been slain by his advice, and no

one is guilty of this but Thorer. But Viking and I have
sworn to each other an oath of brotherhood, and this oath
he has kept better than anyone else, and hence I shall not
wage any war against him, for I do not think Olaf will be
atoned for in the least by slaying Thorer, and thus giving
more grief to Viking. And so Jokul did not get any help
in this matter from his father. Olaf was buried with the
usual ceremonies of olden times, and from this time Jokul
began to keep a suite of men. King Njorfe was already
growing very old, so that Jokul for the most part had to
ward the land. One day it happened that two men went
before Njorfe, both dressed in blue frocks. They greeted
the king. He asked them for their names. One of them
said he hight Gautan, the other said he hight Ogautan, and
they bade the king give them winter quarter. Answered
the king: To me you look ugly, and I will not receive you.
Said Jokul: Have you any accomplishments? Answered
Ogautan: As to that, we have not much to boast of; still
we know many more things than people have spoken to us
about. Said Jokul: It seems best to me then that you enter
my suite and stay with me. So they did. Jokul did well
by them. It had been heard at the king's hall that Viking
had banished his sons. Jokul was unwilling to believe it,
and went to Viking with a large suite. Viking asked what
his errand was, and Jokul asked him what he knew about
the miscreant Thorer. Viking told him that he had banished his sons, so that they did not live there. Jokul asked
to be allowed to search the rooms of the house. Viking
granted this, but said the king would not have thought that
he would deceive him. They then searched the rooms, but,
as might be expected, found nothing; and having done this
they returned home. Jokul did not like that he heard

nothing of the brothers, and so he said to Ogautan and his comrade: Would not you by your cunning be able to find out where the brothers have their dwelling-place? I guess not, answered Ogautan; you are nevertheless to let me and my brother have a house to sleep in, and nobody must come there before you, nor must you visit the house until after three days. Jokul saw that this was done, and a small separate house was assigned for them to sleep in. Jokul positively forbade all people mentioning them, and he threatened the transgressor of his orders with certain death. Early on the day agreed upon Jokul came to the house of the brothers. Said then Ogautan: You are too hasty, Jokul, for I have just awaked; still I can tell you about the sons of Viking. You know, I suppose, where there is a lake called Vener. In it is a holm, and on the holm a shed, and there are the sons of Viking. Answered Jokul: If what you say is so, then I have no hope of their being overtaken. Said Ogautan: In all things you seem to me to act like a motherless child, and I do not think you will be able to do much alone. Now I will tell you, continued Ogautan, that I have a belg (skin-bag) called the weather-belg. If I shake it, storm and wind will blow out of it, together with such biting frost and cold that within three nights the lake shall be covered with so strong an ice that you may cross it on horseback if you wish. Said Jokul: Really you are a man of great cunning; and this is the only way of reaching the holm, for there are no ships before you get to the sea, and nobody can carry them so far. Hereupon Ogautan took his belg and shook it, and out of it there came so fearful a snowstorm and such biting frost that nobody could be out of doors. This was a thing of great wonder to all; and after three nights every water and fjord was frozen.   Then Jokul gathered together men to the number of thirty.   King Njorfe did not like this journey, and said his mind told him it would cause him more and not less sorrow; for in this journey, he said, I will lose the most of my sons and a great many other men.   It would have been better if we, according to my will in the beginning, had come to terms with Thorer, and thus kept the friendship of jarl Viking and his sons.

XII.

NOW Jokul got himself ready for the journey together with his thirty men, and besides them Gautan and Ogautan.   The same morning Thorstein awoke in his shed and said: Are you awake, Thorer?   Answered he: I am, but I have been sleeping until now.   Said Thorstein: It is my will that we get ourselves ready for leaving the shed, for I know that Jokul will come here today together with many men.   Answered Thorer: I do not think so, and I am unwilling to go at all; or have you any sign of this?   I dreamt, said Thorstein, that twenty-two wolves were running hither, and besides them there were seven bears, and the eighth one, a red-cheeked bear, large and grim-looking.   And besides these there were two she-foxes leading the party; the latter were very ugly-looking, and seemed to me the most disgusting of all.   All the wolves attacked us, and at last they seemed to tear to pieces all my brothers excepting you alone, and yet you fell.   Many of the bears we slew, and all the wolves I killed, and the smaller one of the foxes, but then I fell.   Asked Thorer: What do you think this

dream means ? Made answer Thorstein: I think that
the large red-cheeked bear must be the fylgia (follower,
guardian-spirit) of Jokul, and the other bears the fylgias
of his brothers; but the wolves undoubtedly were, to my
mind, as many as the men who came with them; for,
certainly they are wolfishly-minded toward us. But besides them there were two she-foxes, and I do not know
any men to whom such fylgias belong; I therefore suppose that some persons hated by almost everybody have
lately come to Jokul, and thus these fylgias may belong
to them. Now, I have told you this my thought about
the matter, and we will have to act in the manner
pointed out to me in my sleep, and I would that we
might avoid all trouble. Says Thorer: I think your
dream has been nothing but a scare-crow and idle fore-
bodings, still it would not be uninteresting to try our
mutual strength. Quoth Thorstein: I do not think so;
it seems to me that an unequal meeting is intended, and
I should like that we might get ready to go away from
here. Thorer said he would not go away, and it had to
be as he would have it. Thorstein arose and took his
weapons, and all his brothers did likewise, but Thorer
was very slow about it. At the very time when they
had gotten themselves ready, Jokul came up with his
men. The shed had two doors, one of which Thorstein
guarded together with three of his brothers, the other
was guarded by Thorer together with four men. A sharp
attack then began; the brothers warded themselves bravely, but Jokul attacked the door warded by Thorer so
strongly that three of his brothers fell, but one of them
was driven out of the door to the spot where Thorstein
stood. Thorer still guarded the door for a while, being

by no means willing to yield. Then he turned out of the
door and found his way among the enemies down upon
the ice. They surrounded him, but he defended himself
very bravely. Thorstein seeing this, ran out of the shed
together with those of his brothers who were yet alive,
went down onto the ice where Thorer was standing, and
now a fierce combat took place. Thorstein and Thorer
dealt many heavy blows, and at last all the brothers had
fallen excepting Thorstein and Thorer; and all the sons
of Njorfe had also fallen save Jokul and Grim. Then
Thorstein became very weary, so that he was hardly able
to stand. He saw that he would fall; and of the opposite party all had fallen but Gautan and Ogautan.
Now Thorer was both weary and wounded, and the
night was already growing very dark. Just then Thorstein turned against Gautan and stabbed him through
his body with Angervadil, so that he fell to the ground
among the other dead bodies. Then three men, Jokul,
Grim, and Ogautan, arose and searched for Thorstein
among the slain, and they thought they had found him,
but the person they found was Jokul's brother, Finn, for
they were so much like each other that it was impossible to know them apart. Grim said Thorstein was dead.
Said Ogautan: That shall be put beyond a doubt, and he
cut his head off, but of course it did not bleed, for he
was already dead. After this they went home. King
Njorfe asked them how the meeting had turned out, and
learning this, he did not approve it at all, saying that he
now had lost much more than his son Olaf, his seven
sons and many other men having died. Now Jokul kept
quiet.

XIII.

IN the next place it is to be told that Thorstein lay
among the slain so tired out that he was wholly
unable to help himself, but he was but little wounded.
And toward the end of the night he heard a wagon
coming along the ice. Then he saw a man following the
wagon, and he saw that the man was his father. And
when the man came to the field of battle, he cleared his
way, throwing the dead out of his path, but he threw
none with more force than the sons of the king. He saw
that all were dead except Thorstein and Thorer. He then
asked them whether they could speak at all, and Thorer
said that he could. Still Viking saw that he was covered with gaping wounds. Thorstein said that he was
not wounded, but very tired. Viking took Thorer in his
lap, and then it seemed to Thorstein that his father, in
spite of his age, showed great strength. Thorstein went
to the wagon himself and laid himself in it with his
weapons. Then Viking drove on with the wagon. The
weather began to grow dark and cloudy, and it changed
so fast that, in a very little while, the whole ice seemed
to Viking to give way. Just at the time when they had
landed, all the ice had melted out of the lake. Then
Viking went home to his bed-chamber. Close by his bed
was the entrance to an underground dwelling, and down
into it he took his sons; in it was enough of food and
drink, and clothing, and all things that might be needed.
Viking healed the wounds of his son Thorer, for he was
a good leech. One end of the house stood in a forest;
and here Viking very strongly warned his sons never

5

to leave the underground dwelling, for he said it was
sure that Ogautan would straightway find out that they
were alive; and then, added he, we may soon look for a
war. As to this they made good promises. Time passed
on until Thorer became altogether whole again. It was
now talked abroad throughout the country that all the
sons of Viking were dead; but nevertheless, it was talked
somewhat after Ogautan that it was not sure whether
Thorer was dead or not. Then Jokul bade him seek and
try to find out with certainty where Thorer had his dwelling-place. Now Ogautan fell into deep thinking, but still
he did not become any surer about Thorer. One day it
happened that Thorer said to Thorstein: I am getting very
tired of staying in this underground dwelling, now the
weather is fine, and my will is that we take a walk into
the forest to amuse ourselves. Answered Thorstein: I
will not, for we would then break the bidding of our
father. Nevertheless, I shall go, said Thorer. Thorstein
had no mind to stay behind, and so they went to the
forest and spent the day there amusing themselves. But
in the evening, when they were about to go home again,
they saw a little she-fox scenting round about her in all
directions, and snuffing under every tree. Said Thorer:
What Satanic being goes there, brother? Answered Thorstein: I really do not know; it seems to me that I have
once seen something like it, namely, the night before
Jokul's visit to the shed, and I think that we here have
the cursed Ogautan. He then took a spear, which he shot
at the fox, but she crept down into the ground. After
this they went home to their underground dwelling, and
did not let on that anything had happened. Shortly
afterward, jarl Viking came there and said: Now you

have done a bad thing, having broken what I bade you,
by leaving the cave, and thus Ogautan has found out that
you are here. I therefore expect the brothers soon will
come with war upon us.

XIV.

SHORTLY after this, Ogautan had a talk with Jokul
and said: It is indeed true that I am your right and
not your left hand. What is there now about that? asked
Jokul. Answered Ogautan: It is that the brothers, Thorer
and Thorstein, are still alive at Viking's, and are hid by
him. Answered Jokul: Then I will gather together men,
and not give up till we have their lives. Jokul got together eighty men, among whom there were thirty of the
king's courtiers, all well busked as to clothes. In the
evening they were busked for setting out, being about to
leave the next morning. Two young loafers, of whom the
one hight Vott and the other Thumal, had just come there,
and when they had just gone to bed in the evening, Vott
spoke to Thumal: Do you not think it is wise, brother,
that we arise and go to Viking, and tell him of Jokul's
plans, for I know it will be the bane of Viking if they come
upon him unawares, and it is our duty to go and help him.
Made answer Thumal: You are very foolish; do you not
think that the watchmen will become aware of us if we
travel by night, and then we shall be killed without giving
any help to Viking. Said Vott: You always show that you
are a coward; but although you dare not move a step, I will
nevertheless go and tell Viking what is about being done,
for I would gladly lose my life if I could hinder the death

of Viking and his sons, for he has often been kind to me.
Then Vott arose and dressed himself, and likewise did also
Thumal, for the latter had now no mind of staying in
the bed alone. Now they went their way, and came to
Viking's at midnight, and aroused him from his sleep.
Vott told him that Jokul was to be looked for there with
a large number of men. Said Viking: Well have you
done, dear Vott, and your deed surely deserves a reward.
Then Viking called together some men from the neighborhood, so that he had thirty men. Then he went down to
his sons in the cave, and told them the state of things.
Said Thorer: They shall be withstood if they come, for we
will come up out of the cave and fight together with you.
Answered Viking: You shall not! Let us first see how
our fight may turn out, and if it should look hopeless to
me, then I will go to that place below which is your cave
and make a great noise, and then you must come and help
me. Thorstein said he would do so, and so Viking went
away. After daybreak Viking and all his men took their
weapons. He took the kesia called Harek's loom in his
hand; but everybody thought he would not be able to
wield it on account of its weight, he being so old. A
wonderful change then seemed to take place; for as soon
as Viking had put on the armor he seemed to be young
a second time. A large yard was inclosed by a high wall
in front of Viking's byre; it formed a very good vantage
ground, and here he and his men busked themselves for
the battle, and weapons were given to Vott and Thumal.

X V.

NOW it is to be told that Jokul busked himself and
all his army for starting early the next morning,
and he did not halt in his march before he came to the
dwellings of Viking. Viking was standing outside upon
the wall of the yard, and bade Jokul and all his men
come in. Answered Jokul: Quite otherwise have you
deserved than that we should accept your invitation; our
errand here is that you give up those mishap-bringing
men, Thorstein and Thorer. I will not do it, answered
Viking; nevertheless I will not deny that both of them
have been here, but I would sooner give up myself than
them. Now you may attack us if you like, but I and my
men will ward ourselves. They now made a hard attack,
but Viking and his men warded themselves bravely. Thus
some time passed. Then Jokul tried to scale the wall·
Viking and his men slew many men; but now all his own
men began to fall. Then Viking went to the place over
the underground dwelling, struck his shield hard, and
made a fearful noise. This Thorer heard, and said to
Thorstein: We ought to make haste, and for all that we
may be too late, for I think our father has fallen already.
Thorstein said he was quite ready, and when they came out
only Vott and Thumal and three other men were standing
with Viking. Nevertheless Viking was not wounded yet;
he was only very tired. As soon as the brothers came
out, Thorstein turned to the spot where Jokul was standing, but Thorer went where Ogautan and his men stood.
Twelve of king Njorfe's men attacked Viking and his men.
Viking warded himself, and was not wounded by the men

who were against him. Their leader hight Bjorn. In a
short time Thorer slew all the followers of Ogautan, and
stabbed at him with his sword, but Ogautan thrust himself
down into the ground, so that only the soles of his feet
could be seen. Thorstein attacked Jokul. Said Vott: It
is well that you are trying each other's bravery, for Jokul
never could bear to hear that Thorstein was a match for
him in anything. Now there was a very hard battle between Thorstein and Jokul, and it so turned out that
Jokul, scarred with many wounds, bounded back, and fell
down outside of the wall. But when Jokul had gone
away, Viking gave quarter to the men of the king's court
that still were alive, and sent them away with suitable
gifts, begging them to bring his friendly greetings to king
Njorfe. And when Jokul came home, Ogautan was there
already. Jokul blamed him bitterly for having fled before
anybody else. To this made answer Ogautan: It was not
possible to stay in the fight any longer, and truly it may
be said that we there had to do with trolls rather than
with men. But Jokul found that his words rather overdid
the matter. Somewhat later king Njorfe's men, to whom
quarter had been given by Viking and his men, came
home, bringing Viking's greetings to king Njorfe, and
telling him of all the kind treatment they had gotten
from Viking. Said the king: Truly is Viking unlike
most other men, on account of his high-mindedness and
all his bravery, and now, my son Jokul, I speak the truth
when I solemnly forbid any war to be waged against
Viking from this time forward. Answered Jokul: I cannot bear to have the slayers of my brothers in the garth
next to me, and in a word, I declare that Viking and his
sons shall never live in peace so far as I am concerned,

and I shall never cease persecuting them before they are
all sent to Hel (the goddess of death). Answered the
king: Then I shall try and see who of us two is the more
blest with friends, for with all those who are willing to
follow me I will go and help Viking; it seems to me to
be of great weight that you do not become the bane of
Viking, for if that should follow, I would be forced to do
one of two things, either to have you killed, and that
would be the cause of evil talk, or to break my oaths
which I have sworn, namely, that I would avenge Viking
if I should outlive him. And thus he ended his speech.
Viking had a talk with his sons, and said to them: Owing
to Jokul's power I dare not keep you here; but there is
another matter of still more weight, and that is, that I do
not want any discord to arise between me and king Njorfe.
Said Thorstein: What will you then advise us to do?
Answered Viking: There is a man, by name Halfdan, who
rules over Vags; Vags is on the other side of yonder
mountain. Halfdan is my old friend and foster-brother.
To him I will send you, and commend you to his good will;
but there are many dangerous hindrances in the way,
especially two hut-dwellers (robbers), one of whom is worse
to deal with than the other; the name of one of them
is Sam, and the other is hight Fullafle; the latter has
a dog called Gram, with which it is almost as dangerous to deal as with the robber himself. Now I am not
sure that you will reach Vags, though you may escape
both of these robbers, for there is a chasm along the
mountain so deep and broad that I do not know any one
who has passed it but my foster-brothers and myself; but
I should indeed think it more likely that Thorstein might
pass it, whereas I feel less hopeful about Thorer. Shortly

afterward the brothers busked themselves for setting out, having all their weapons with them. Then Viking gave the kesia to Thorer; he handed a gold ring to his son Thorstein, begging him to give it to Halfdan as a token of their old friendship.

Now be patient my son Thorer, says Viking; although Halfdan may be peevish toward you, or does not look much to you or your errand. Then the sons took leave of their father, who was so deeply moved that the tears trickled down his cheeks. Viking looked after them as they were going away, and said: I shall never in my life see you again, and nevertheless you, my son Thorstein, will reach an old age, and become a very distinguished man; and now farewell, and all hail to you both. Then the old man returned home, but his sons climbed the mountain until they reached a hut in the evening. The door was half shut. Thorer stepped over to it, and by using all his strength, he pushed it open; and when they had entered the hut, they saw there a great deal of wares and supplies of all kinds. There was a large bed. And at nightfall the hut-dweller, a man of somewhat frowning look, came home. He said: Are you here, you mishap-bringing men,—you sons of Viking, Thorstein and Thorer, who have slain seven of the sons of Njorfe? And now all their ill-luck shall come to an end, for it will be an easy matter for me to strike you to the ground. Who is that, says Thorer, who so boastingly insults us? Answered the robber: My name is Sam; I am the son of Svart; my brother's name is Fullafle; he is boss in the other hut. Said Thorstein: I see that feyness* calls on us two brothers, if you alone kill both of us, and there-

---

* Feyness (Icel. feigð) means the approach or foreboding of death.

fore I do not hesitate to test our valor, but Thorer shall
stand by without taking any part in our combat. At the
same time Sam ran suddenly under Thorstein with so
great speed, that the latter lost the hold he had gotten, but
still did not fall. Then Thorer ran to Sam, stabbing him
with his kesia in one side so that it came out at the
other side, and thus Sam fell down dead. So they stopped
there during the night and had a good rest, for there
was plenty of food. They made the hut warm, but did
not carry away any fee with them. In the morning they
left the hut, but in the evening of the same day they
came to another hut, much larger than the former one.
There also the door was half shut. Thorer stepped over
to the door, intending to push it open, but he could not.
He used all his strength, but still the door would not
open. Then Thorstein stepped over to the door, and
pushed it until it gave way, and so they went into the
hut. On the one side there was a stack of wares and
on the other one of logs; a bed was placed in the inner
part of the hut, crosswise, and it was so large that they
were surprised at its size. At one end of the bed was
something like a large, round bedstead, and they judged
that it must be the couch of the dog Gram. They then
seated themselves and built a fire before them, and long
after nightfall they heard heavy footsteps outside; presently the door was opened, and a giant of stupendous
stature entered, carrying bound on his back a large bear,
and a string of fowl on his breast. He laid his burden
down on the floor, saying: Fie! here I have the miscre-
ants, the sons of Viking, who, on account of their ill-fated
deeds, are held in the worst repute throughout the whole
land. But how did you escape the hands of my brother

Sam? We escaped in such a manner, said Thorstein, that
he lay dead on the spot. You have taken advantage of
him in his sleep, said Fullafle. By no means, said Thorstein, for we fought with him, and my brother Thorer
slew him. I shall not act as a nithing toward you to-
night, says Fullafle; you shall stay till to-morrow morning, and have what food you want. Then the hut-dweller
cut his game to pieces, took a table and put victuals on
it, whereupon they all took to eating, and after their sup-
per they went to bed. The two brothers slept together
in some marketable cloaks. The dog growled as they
passed by him. Neither party tried to deceive the other.
In the morning both parties arose early. Said Fullafle:
Now, Thorstein, let us try each other's strength, but let
Thorer fight with my dog in another place. Answered
Thorstein: That shall be according to your wish. Now
they went out of the hut and over on the lawn which
fronted it, and suddenly the dog, with his jaws wide open,
leaped upon Thorer. Both Thorer and the dog fought
fiercely, for the dog warded off every blow with his tail,
and when Thorer tried to pierce him with his kesia, he
escaped by biting the weapon at every stab. Thus they
fought for three hours, and Thorer had not yet succeeded in
wounding him. Once Gram suddenly darted upon Thorer
and bit a slice out of his calf. At the same time Thorer
stabbed the dog with his kesia, pinning him down to the
ground, and soon after Gram expired. But of Fullafle
it is to be told that he had a large meker (Anglo-Saxon
mece, a kind of sword) in his hand, and Thorstein had
his sword also. They had a long and severe struggle; for
Fullafle was wont to deal heavy blows, but as Angervadil bit armor no less than flesh, he fell dead, and Thorstein was wholly without a wound.

XVI.

NOW the brothers busked themselves for leaving, and continued their walk until they reached a great chasm, which it seemed to Thorstein it would be very dangerous to pass. Nevertheless, he made himself ready to leap over the abyss, and did it. He was immediately followed by Thorer, but when Thorstein had reached the other side of the chasm and looked round, Thorer had just reached the same side and was falling down into the chasm. Thorstein succeeded, however, in seizing him and pulling him up again. Said Thorstein then: Brother, you always show that you are a dauntless fellow; so you did now, too, for you might know that it would be certain death to you if you should fall into the chasm. It did not happen this time, answered Thorer, for you saved me, as you have so often done before. Then they proceeded on their journey until they came to a large river, which was both deep and rapid. Thorstein said they must look for the ford, but without delay Thorer waded into the river, and not far from the bank the water was so deep that the bottom could not be reached, and therefore he had to sustain himself by swimming. Thorstein not being minded to be standing on the bank, threw himself into the river and swam after him. Thus they reached the other bank, where they wrung their wet clothes. But while they were doing this the weather grew so bitterly cold that their clothes froze hard as a stone, and so they could not put them on. At the same time a fearful snow storm arose, and it was thought that Ogautan was the cause of it. Thorstein asked Thorer what was the best

thing for them to do. Answered Thorer: I think we can
do nothing better than to dip our clothes in the river,
for in cold water things soon thaw out. So they did, and
thereby were able to put on their clothes again. Then
they went on until they came to the byre of Vags. It being
night when they came there, the door of the house was
locked, so they could not enter. They kept knocking at
the door a long time, but nobody came to it. In the
yard lay a beam twenty fathoms long. This they brought
upon the roofs of the houses, and they rode upon it in
such a manner that every timber began to creak, and all
the inmates of the house became so frightened that they
ran each into his corner. Then Halfdan went to the
door and out to the front yard, and the brothers now
went over to him and greeted him. Halfdan gave them
a cold and reserved answer, asking them, however, for their
names. They gave him their names, adding that they
were the sons of jarl Viking, and that they brought greetings from the latter to him. Said Halfdan: I cannot talk
about foster-brothership between us; to me it seems that
many a man keeps his word of foster-brothership but
middlingly well, and no more; and as for you, who have
slain the most of king Njorfe's sons, it also seems to me
that you have not regarded the sanctity of foster-brothership in respect to many of Njorfe's descendants. Still,
you may enter my house, and lodge here to-night, if
you like. Then Halfdan went in at a swinging pace,
followed by the brothers. They entered the stofa (sit-
ting-room), where there were but few persons. Nobody
took the clothes off the brothers, and thus they sat during the evening, till people began to go to bed; then a
dish, containing porridge, and a spoon in each end of it,

was placed on the table before them. Thorer began to
eat the porridge. Said Thorstein then: You are very
inconsistent in regard to your pride; and, so saying,
he took the dish and threw it on the floor in the further part of the room, so that it broke to pieces. Hereupon the people went to bed. The brothers had no
bed, and got but very little sleep during the night.
Early in the morning they got up and busked themselves for leaving. But when they had got outside the
door the old man came to them and asked them: What
did you say last night, or whose sons did you say you
were? Made answer Thorer: What more do you know
now than when we told you we were the sons of jarl
Viking? Said Thorstein: Here is a golden finger-ring,
which he begged me to give you. Said Thorer: I think
he will be the worse off who shows him anything of it.
Made answer Thorstein: Be not so peevish, brother!
Here is the gold ring, as a token that you should receive us in such a manner that we might be comforted
and protected at your house. Halfdan took the ring,
became glad, and said: Why should I not receive you,
and do all the good in my power for you? To do so
is my duty, on account of my relations to my friend
Viking. You seem to be men blest with good luck.
Said Thorer: The adage is indeed a true one, that it is
good to have two mouths for the two kinds of speech.
Last night, soon after we had come to you, you treated
us quite otherwise. I therefore am inclined to think
you a coward, and you everywhere show your slyness.
Said Thorstein: Let us be patient, Halfdan, with my
brother, although he is cross in his words to you, for
he is a reckless man in his words and doings. An-

swered Halfdan: I have heard that you are the most
doughty of men, and that Thorer is hot-tempered and
reckless; still, I think that you are in every respect
a man of more spirit.   Hereupon they went into the
house, their clothes were taken off them, and every
attention was shown them.   They stayed there during
the winter, and enjoyed the most hearty treatment.   But
in the beginning of spring Thorstein said to Halfdan:
We shall now leave this place.   Answered Halfdan:
What is your best advice?   Made answer Thorstein: I
wish you would give me a ship, manned with a crew, for
I intend to set out and wage war and gain booty.   To
this Halfdan gave his consent.   After busking themselves
properly, they sailed to the south, along the coast of the
country, until they met with two vessels, which had been
sent out by their father, and were filled with men and
good weapons.   Now Thorstein sent back the ship which
had been given to him by Halfdan, and sent the crew
with it; but the brothers became skippers, one on each
of the two ships.   They waged wars in many places during the summer, and gained much fee and fame.   In the
fall they landed on an island which was ruled by the
bonde, whose name was Grim.   He bade them stay with
him through the winter, and they accepted his offer.   Grim
was married and had an only daughter, by name Thora,
a tall and fine-looking girl.   Thorer fell in love with her,
and told his brother Thorstein that he wanted to marry
her.   Thorstein talked about the matter to Grim, the
bonde, but the latter flatly refused to give his consent.
Answered Thorstein: Then I challenge you to fight with
me in a holm-gang, and he who wins shall be master of
your daughter.   Grim said he was ready for the holm-

gang. The next day they took a blanket, which they threw under their feet, and then they fought the whole day very bravely, but in the evening they parted, neither of them having received any wound. The second and the third days they fought, but the results were the same as the first day. One day Thorer asked the daughter of the bonde how it came to pass that Grim could not be vanquished. She said there was in the fore part of his helmet a stone, which made him quite invincible as long as it was not taken away from him. This Thorer told to Thorstein; and on the fourth day of their fight Thorstein threw his sword, grasping the helmet of his antagonist with both his hands with so great force that the cords of the helmet were severed. Shortly after he attacked Grim, and now Thorstein's greater strength was shown. He brought Grim down, but gave him quarter. Then Grim asked who had advised him to take the helmet. Thorstein said that Thora had told it to Thorer. Then she wants to be married, answered Grim, and it shall so be. Thus it was resolved that Thorer should marry Thora. In the beginning of spring Thorstein set out to carry on wars, leaving Thorer at home. The newly married couple took to loving each other very much, and they got a son, whom they named Harald. This was their only child. He afterward took his father's kesia, after which he was nick-named and was called Harald Kesia.

XVII.

A KING was named Skate, a son of Erik, who again was a son of Myndil Meitalfsson. Skate was king in Sogn, and with his queen he had two children, a son named Bele, who was a very excellent man, and a daughter who hight Ingeborg. At this time she was not in the kingdom, having been spellbound (and thus removed from the country). Skate had been a berserk and a very great viking, and he had forced his way onto the throne of Sogn. There was a man who hight Thorgrim, and who had to defend the realm against the invasion of foes. He was a great champion and a warlike man, but not over faithful. Between Thorgrim and the king's son, Bele, there was a warm friendship. Bele had great celebrity throughout all lands. It had happened, after king Skate had grown very old, both his children still being young, that two vikings, one named Gautan and the other Ogautan, had landed in his country. They had taken the king by surprise, and offered him two conditions, either to fight a battle with them, or give up his land and become a jarl under them. King Skate, though he had no troops to meet them with, would rather die with honor than live with shame; he would rather fall in his kingdom than serve his foes. He therefore went to battle, having no other troops than his courtiers. Thorgrim escaped with the king's son, Bele, but Ingeborg remained at home in her bower. In the combat with Ogautan, king Skate fell with honor, but those of his men who escaped death in the battle fled to the woods. Now Ogautan took the kingdom into his charge, and had the title of king given to himself. He asked

Ingeborg to become his wife, but she flatly refused, saying she would rather kill herself than marry the bane of her father, and such a villain, too, as Ogautan; for you, she said, are more like the devil himself than like a man. At this Ogautan grew angry, and said: I shall reward you for your foul language, and I hereby enchant you, so that you shall get the same stature and looks as my sister Skellinefja, and the same nature also as she, as far as you may be capable of assuming it; and, spell-bound, you shall inhabit that cave which is on the Deep River, and you shall never escape out of this enchanted state until some man of noble birth is willing to have you, and pledges himself to marry you; still you can never escape until I am dead. But my sister shall wear your looks. Said Ingeborg: I cause you to be so enchanted that you shall keep this kingdom only for a short time, and never have any good of your reign. The spells pronounced by Ogautan proved true, and Ingeborg disappeared. Soon afterward, the king's son, Bele, came thither again, together with Thorgrim and many other men. It was night, and they set fire to the upper story of the house in which the two brothers slept, and burnt it up, together with the people who lived in it, except the brothers, who escaped through an underground passage and fled, without stopping until they came to the court of king Njorfe. Bele took possession of his country again, and Thorgrim remained in his former position as warder of the king's land.

6

XVIII.

A KING, named Vilhjalm (William), ruled over Valland. He was a wise man, and was blest with
many friends. He had a daughter, who hight Olof, and
was a woman of great culture. Now it is to be told that
Jokul, Njorfe's son, after the departure of the sons of
Viking, made Thorstein and Thorer outlaws in every place
within the boundaries of his kingdom. King Njorfe did
not consent to it, for he and Viking kept their friendship
during their whole life. Once Ogautan had a talk with
Jokul, and asked him if he would not like to get married.
Jokul asked him where he saw a match for him. Answered
Ogautan: Vilhjalm of Valland has a daughter named Olof,
and I think a marriage with her would add to your honor.
Said Jokul: Why not then make up our minds as to this
subject? So they busked themselves for the voyage, and
together with sixty men they sailed for Valland. Here
they paid a visit to king Vilhjalm, who received Jokul very
heartily, for his father, Njorfe, was well known throughout
all lands. Now Jokul asked for Olof in marriage, and
Ogautan pleaded with the king in his behalf, but the latter
appealed to his daughter. And straightway after this conversation thirty very brave-looking men entered the hall.
The one who went before them was the tallest and fairest,
and he went up to the king and greeted him. As soon as
Ogautan saw these men his voice fell, his beard sunk, and
he begged Jokul and his other men not to mention his
name so long as they stayed in that land. The king asked
the stately men what they hight, and the chief called himself Bele, and said he was the son of Skate, the king, who

was ruler of Sogn. My errand hither, he added, is to woo your daughter. Made answer the king: Jokul, the son of Njorfe, came here before you on the same errand; now I will settle the matter in this way, that she choose herself which one of the two wooers she will have. Then the king placed Bele on one side of himself, and there was a great banquet. After three nights they took a walk to the bower of the princess, asking her which one of the two wooers, Jokul or Bele, she would marry, and it soon appeared that she would rather marry Bele; but at that moment Ogautan threw a round piece of wood into her lap, whereby her nature was suddenly changed to such an extent that she refused Bele and married Jokul. Then Bele returned to his ships. Jokul and Bele had formerly been on good terms, so that some people say that Bele had got a reward for killing Thorstein and Thorer. Bele did not blame Jokul though the daughter of the king declined to marry him (Bele), for the matter depended upon her decision. Thereupon Bele went home to his kingdom, and after the wedding Jokul also repaired homeward accompanied by Ogautan.

XIX.

NOW our saga must turn to Thorstein at the time when he was returning home from his warfare, bound for Grim the bonde, for his brother Thorer resided in that island. Jokul got news of Thorstein's voyages. He spoke to Ogautan, asking him to try his tricks and by witchcraft bring about a storm against Thorstein, in order that he might be drowned, together with all his men. Ogautan said he would try, no matter what the result might be. Then, with his incantations, he caused so tremendous a storm against Thorstein that his ships were wrecked amid the tumultuous waves, and all his crew perished. Thorstein held out well a long time, but at last he became tired of swimming, and then he had reached the surf and was beginning to sink down. At this moment he saw an old woman, of very great stature, wading from the shore out toward him. She wore a shriveled skin-cloak, which fell to her feet in front, but was very short behind, and her face was very large and like that of a monster. She stepped over to him and, seizing him up from the sea, said : Will you accept life from me, Thorstein ? Answered he : Why should I not, or what is your name? Said she: My name is uncommon; it is Skellinefja; but you will have to make some sacrifice in return for your life. Said he: What is it? Made answer she: That you grant me the favor that I ask of you. Said Thorstein: You will ask nothing from me that will not bring me good luck; but when shall the favor be granted? Answered she: Not yet. Then she bore him ashore, and now he had come to that island which was governed by Grim. She then wrestled with him till he grew warm, whereupon they parted, each wishing the other success. Then she walked on, for she said she had other places to call at. But Thorstein went home to the byre, and his meeting there with his brother was the cause of great joy to both of them; and so Thorstein remained there during the winter, and very much was made of him. Now we must turn to Jokul and Ogautan as they were sailing homeward. One very fine day it happened that their ship was suddenly shrouded in darkness, accompanied by such a biting frost and cold that

nobody on board dared to turn his face against the wind.
They all covered their faces with their clothes; but when
the weather had cleared off again they saw Ogautan hanging
in the hole of the mast-head, and he was dead. Jokul
looked upon his death as a great loss, and returning to his
kingdom he remained quiet. Early the next-spring Thorstein and Thorer busked themselves for a voyage, intending
to visit their father, Viking; and when they came as far as
to Deep River, before they knew of it, Jokul came there to
them with thirty men. A combat between them straightway began. Jokul was very eager in the fight, and so was
his brother Grim. Thorer and Thorstein defended themselves bravely, and a long time passed before these brothers
received any wounds from Jokul and his men, for not only
did Thorstein deal heavy blows, but Angervadil also bit
iron as well as cloth. Thorer defended himself excellently,
although he did not have his kesia, which he had left at
home. He and Grim met, and they fought very bravely:
still the end of the fight was that Grim fell to the ground,
dead. By this time Thorstein had slain eighteen men, but,
as might be expected, he was both tired and wounded, and
so was Thorer. Then the brothers turned their backs together and still defended themselves well. Now Jokul,
with his eleven men, pursued them and made so valiant an
attack that Thorer fell. Then Thorstein defended himself
manfully until there remained no more than Jokul and
three of his men. But then Jokul stabbed Thorstein with
his sword, wounding him in the upper part of the thigh;
and Jokul being a strong man, and bearing on the sword
with all his might while he stabbed him, Thorstein, who was
very tired, and was standing on the very edge of the river-
bank, fell down from the crag, while it was all that Jokul

could do to stop himself so that he did not fall also.
After this Jokul went home, thinking he had slain Thorstein and Thorer; and having come home he remained quiet.
But now it is to be told of Thorstein, that he, having
fallen from the crag, alighted upon a grassy spot among
the rocks; but, being tired and wounded, he was unable
to move, and yet he was in his full senses after he had
fallen. Angervadil fell out of his hand and down into
the river. Thorstein was lying there betwixt life and
death, and expecting soon to breathe his last. But before he had lain thus very long he saw Skellinefja coming; she was clad in her skin-gown, and looked no fairer
than before. She approached the place where Thorstein
was lying, and said: It seems to me, Thorstein, that your
misfortunes will never come to an end, and now you
seem already to be breathing your last, or will you now
grant me the favor upon which we formerly agreed?
Said Thorstein: I do not now find myself able to render
much of any service to you. Made answer she: My request is that you promise to marry me, and then I will
try to heal your wounds. Said Thorstein: I do not know
as I had better make that promise, for to me you look
like a monster. Said she: Still you have your choice between these two things. You must either marry me or
lose your life; and, in the latter case, you break, in the
bargain, the oath which you swore to me when you
pledged yourself to grant my favor after I had saved
you at Grim's Island. Said Thorstein: There is much
truth in your words, and it is better to keep one's
promise; hence I vow that I will marry you, and you
will prove to be my best helper in time of need; still I
should like to stipulate with you that you get me my

sword back, so that I may wear it in case my life is pro-
longed. Says she: So be it. And having taken him up in
her skin-gown, she leaped, as if quite unencumbered, up
over the crags and proceeded until a large cave was before
them. Having entered the cave, she bandaged Thorstein's
wounds and laid him on a soft bed, and within seven nights
he was almost healed. One day Skellinefja had left the
cave, and in the evening she came back with the sword,
which was then dripping wet, and she gave it to Thorstein. Said she: Now I have saved your life twice and
given you your sword back, of which you are fonder than
of aught else; and a fourth thing, which is of great importance to both of us, is that I hanged Ogautan. And yet
you have completely rewarded me, for you have delivered
me from the spell-bound condition into which Ogautan
enchanted me. My name is Ingeborg; I am the daughter
of king Skate and the sister of Bele, but my only means
of delivery from bondage was that some man of noble
birth should promise to marry me. Now you have done
this, and I am freed from bondage. Now you must busk
yourself for leaving the cave and follow my advices, and
you will find my brother Bele and four men with him.
Among the latter will be his land-warden, Thorgrim
Kobbe. From Jokul they have received some money,
offered as a price for your head, and they will begin a
battle with you. I do not care if you do kill Thorgrim
and his companions, but spare the life of my brother
Bele, for I should like to have you become his foster-
brother; and if you have a mind to marry me, then go
with him home to Sogn and woo me. I shall be there
before you, and it may be that I will look otherwise to you
then than now. Then they parted, and he had not gone

far before he met Bele, accompanied by four men, and, at
their meeting, Thorgrim said: It is good, Thorstein, that
we have found each other. Now we shall try to win the
price put upon your head by Jokul. Said Thorstein: It
seems possible to me that you may lose the fee and for-
feit your life too.

XX.

NOW we must tell about Thorstein that he was attacked by Bele and his men, but he defended himself
well and bravely, and the result was that Thorgrim and
three of his companions fell. Then Thorstein and Bele
entered a new contest. Thorstein defended himself, but
would not wound Bele. Bele kept on attacking Thorstein,
until the latter seized him and set him down at his side,
saying: You are wholly in my power, but I will not only
give you your life, but also offer you an opportunity to become my foster-brother. You shall be king and I shall be
herser, and in addition to this I will woo your sister Ingeborg, and get her estates in Sogn as a dowry. Said Bele:
This is no very easy matter, for my sister has disappeared,
so that nobody knows what has become of her. Answered
Thorstein: She may have come back. Said Bele: I do not
see how she could get a doughtier fellow than you are,
and I give my full consent to the proposition. Having
settled this with their words of honor, they went home to
Sogn. Bele soon became aware that his sister had come
back, and that she had not lost any of that blooming beauty
which she had had before in her youthful days. Thorstein
began his suit, and asked that Ingeborg might become his

wife. This was resolved upon. As a dowry she got from
her home all the possessions lying on the other side of
the fjord. The byre where Thorstein resided was called
Framness, but the byre governed by Bele was called Syr-
strond. The next spring Thorstein and Bele set out to
wage wars, having five ships, and during the summer they
harried far and wide, and got enough of booty, but in the
fall they returned home again having seven ships. The
next summer they went out a harrying again, but got very
little booty, for all vikings shunned them; and having
reached the small rocky islands called Elfarsker, they anch-
ored in a harbor in the evening. Thorstein and Bele went
ashore, and crossed that ness (peninsula) toward which
their ships were lying. But having crossed the ness, they
saw twelve ships covered with black tilts. On shore they
saw tents, from which smoke arose, and they seemed to be
sure that these tents must be occupied by cooks. Having
taken on a disguise, they went thither, and having come to
the door of a tent, they both placed themselves in it in
such a manner that the smoke did not find any out-way.
The cooks made use of abusive words, and asked what sort
of beggars they were, as they were guileful enough to
want them burnt alive or smothered. Bele and Thorstein
made an ugly disturbance, and answered with hoarse voices
that they came to get food; or, said they, who is the excellent man who commands the fleet lying here at the shore?
Said they: You must be stupid old men if you have not
heard of Ufe, who is called Ufe the Unlucky, and is the
son of Herbrand the Bigheaded. This Ufe is the brother
of Otunfaxe, and we know there are no men under the
sun more celebrated than these two brothers. Said Thorstein: You tell good tidings. Shortly after, Thorstein and
7

Bele returned to their own men, and early the next morning, having busked themselves, they rowed around the ness and immediately shouted the cry of battle. The others then quickly busked themselves, took their weapons, and a vehement battle began. Ufe had more men, and was himself a most valiant warrior. They fought for a long time in such a manner that it could not be seen which side would gain the victory. But on the third day Thorstein began to board the dragon commanded by Ufe the Unlucky, and he was followed without delay by Bele, and a great havoc they made, killing all who were between the prow and the mast of the ship. Then Ufe came from the poop and attacked Bele, and they fought for some time, until Bele began to get wounds from Ufe, who handled his weapon dexterously and dealt heavy blows. Meanwhile Thorstein came with his Angervadil, and gave Ufe a blow with it. The sword hit the helmet, split the whole body and the byrnie-clad man from head to foot, and Angervadil struck against the mast-beam so forcibly that both its edges sunk out of sight. Said Bele: This blow of yours, foster-brother, will live in the memory of men as long as the North is peopled. Hereupon they offered to the vikings two terms, either to give up and save their lives, or to have a combat. But they preferred to accept a quarter from Thorstein and Bele. The latter gave pardon to all, and they eagerly accepted it. Here much booty was taken, and having stayed three nights, during which time the wounded were healed, they repaired home in the autumn.

XXI.

AT springtime the foster-brothers busked themselves for leaving home, and had fifteen ships. Bele commanded the dragon which had been owned by Ufe the Unlucky. It was a choice ship, its beak and stern being whittled and carved and extensively overlaid with gold. King Bele got the dragon, for it was the choicest part of the booty which they took when they had slain Ufe, it always being their custom to give to Bele the most costly parts of the booty. No ship was thought better than this dragon excepting Ellide, which was owned by Ufe's brother, Otunfaxe. Ufe and Otunfaxe had inherited these ships from their father, Herbrand, and Ellide was the better one of the two in these respects, that it had fair wind wherever it sailed, and it almost understood human speech. But the reason why Otunfaxe and not Ufe had gotten Ellide was, that Ufe had fallen into so bad luck that he had killed both his father and his mother, and it seemed to Otunfaxe that if justice should be done, Ufe had forfeited his right of inheritance. Otunfaxe was the superior of the two brothers on account of his strength, stature and witchcraft. Now the foster-brothers went out a harrying, and waged wars far and wide in the waters of the Baltic, but they found but very few vikings, for everybody, upon hearing of them, fled out of their reach. At this time none were more celebrated for their harrying exploits than Thorstein and Bele. One day the foster-brothers were standing on a promontory, on the other side of which they saw twelve ships lying at anchor, and all of them were very large. They rowed rapidly toward

the ships and asked who was the commander of the warriors. A man who stood leaning against the mast made
answer: Angantyr is my name; I am a son of jarl Her-
mund of Gautland. Said Thorstein: You are a hopeful
fellow; but how old are you? Made answer he: I am
now nineteen years old. Asked Bele: Which do you
prefer, to give up your ships and fee or to fight a battle
with us? Said Angantyr: The more unequal your terms
are, the more promptly I make my choice. I prefer to
defend my fee, and fall, sword in hand, if such be my fate.
Said Bele: Busk yourself then; but we will make the
attack. Then both of them busked themselves for the
battle and took their weapons. Said Thorstein to Bele:
There is very little of noble courage in attacking them
with fifteen ships, as they have but twelve. Said Bele:
Why shall we not lay three of our ships aside? And so
they did. A hard battle was now fought. Angantyr's
warriors dealt so heavy blows, that Bele and Thorstein
declared that they had never been in greater peril. They
fought the whole day until evening, but in such a manner
that it could not be seen which party would gain the
victory. The next day they busked themselves again for
the fight. Then said Angantyr: To me it seems, king
Bele, that it would be wiser not to sacrifice any more of
our men, but let us two fight a duel, and he who conquers
the other in the holm-gang shall be the victorious party.
Bele accepted this challenge; so they went ashore, and
having thrown a blanket under their feet, they fought
bravely until Bele became tired out and began to receive
wounds. Thorstein thought it evident that Bele would
not gain the victory over Angantyr, and it came to pass
that Bele was not only exhausted but also nigh his last

breath. Said Thorstein then: It seems best to me, Angantyr, that you cease your fighting, for I see that Bele is so exhausted that he is almost gone. On the other hand, I will not be mean enough to play the dastard toward you and assist him; but if you become the bane of Bele, then I will challenge you to fight a duel with me; and as to personal valor and strength, I think there is no less difference between me and you than there is between you and Bele. I will slay you in a holm-gang duel, and it would be a great loss if you both die. Now I offer you this condition, that if you spare Bele's life, we will enter into a foster-brotherhood upon mutual oaths. Said Angantyr: To me it seems a fair offer that Bele and I enter into foster-brotherhood; but it seems to me a great favor that I may become your foster-brother. Then this was resolved upon and secured by firm pledges on both sides. They opened a vein in the hollow of their hands, crept beneath the sod,* and there they solemnly swore that each of them should avenge the other if any one of them should be slain by weapons. Then they reviewed their warriors, and two ships of each party had lost all their men. They healed those who were wounded, and thereupon they left the place with twenty-three ships, returning home in the fall. They spent the winter at home quietly, and enjoyed great honor. Now none were thought more famous on account of their weapons than these foster-brothers.

* There was a heathen rite of creeping under a sod partially detached from the earth, and letting the blood mix with the mould. Persons forming a foster-brotherhood would make use of this ceremony.

XXII.

WHEN spring opened, the foster-brothers busked themselves for departing from home, and had thirty ships. They sailed to the east and harried in Sweden and in all parts of the Baltic. As usual, they carried on their warfare in a seeming manner, slaying vikings and pirates wherever they could find them, but leaving bondes and chapmen in peace. On the other hand, it is to be told that Otunfaxe, when he heard of the death of his brother Ufe, thought it a great loss. And of him it is to be related, that for three summers together he searched for the foster-brothers. ✓ Now it is furthermore to be related, that Bele and his men one day laid their ships near some small rocky islands, called Brenner's Isles. They cast anchor and busked themselves well. Hereupon all the three foster-brothers went ashore, and proceeded until they came to a small byre. There stood a man outside the door splitting wood; he was clad in a green cloak, and was a man of astonishing corpulency. He greeted Thorstein by name. Said Thorstein: We differ widely as to our faculty for recognition; you greet me by name, but I do not remember that I have ever seen you before; what is your name? Says he: My name is an uncommon one. I hight Brenner. I am a son of Vifil, and a brother of your father, Viking. I was born at the time when my father was engaged in warfare, and had his home with Haloge. I was raised on this island, and have lived here since. But have you, my nephew Thorstein, heard anything about the viking Otunfaxe? Answered Thorstein: No; or what can you tell about him? Made an-

swer Brenner: This I can tell, that he has been searching
for you during the last three years, and now he lies here
on the other side of those islands with all his fleet; he
wants to avenge his brother Ufe the Unlucky. He has
forty ships, all of which are very large, and he himself
is as big as a troll, and no weapons can bite him. Said
Thorstein: What is to be done now? Made answer Brenner: I can give you no advice unless you have a chance
to meet the dwarf Sindre; and moreover he will least of
all be embarrassed in finding out what ought to be done.
Asked Thorstein: Where can I expect to find him? Made
answer Brenner: His home is in the island which lies
near the shore, and is called the Smaller Brenner's Isle. He
lives in a stone. I scarcely hope that you will be able to
find him, but you are welcome here to-night. Said Thorstein: Something else must be done than to keep quiet.
Then they went to their ships, and Thorstein launched a
boat and rowed to the island. He went ashore alone, and
when he came to a little stream, he saw two children, a
boy and a girl, playing on its banks. Thorstein asked
their names. The boy called himself Herraud, and the
girl Herrid. Said she: I have lost my gold ring, and I
know this will make my father, Sindre, cross, and I think
I may look for punishment. Said Thorstein: Here is a
gold ring, which I will give you. She accepted the gold
ring and was pleased with it. Said she: I will give this
to my father; but is there nothing that I might do that
might be of service to you? Made answer Thorstein:
Nothing; but bring your father here, that I may have a
talk with him, and manage the matter in such a manner
that he may advise me concerning those things which are
of importance to me. Answered Herrid: I can do this

only provided my brother Herraud acts according to my
will, for Sindre never refuses him anything. Said Herraud: You know I take your part in everything. Thorstein unbuckled a silver belt which he wore, and gave it
him; to it was attached a beautifully ornamented knife.
Said the boy: This is a nice present; I shall take all possible pains to promote your wish; wait here until I and
my sister come back. Thorstein did so, and after a long
while the dwarf Sindre came, accompanied by the boy and
his sister. Sindre greeted Thorstein heartily, and said:
What do you want of me, Thorstein? Made answer Thorstein: I want you to give me advice as to how I may
conquer the viking Otunfaxe. Answered Sindre: It seems
to me wholly impossible for any human being to vanquish
Faxe, for he is worse to deal with than anybody else, and
I will advise you not to fight any battle with him, for
you will only lose your men, and hence the best thing
for you to do is to turn your prows away from the island
to-night. Made answer Thorstein: That shall never be;
though I knew it before that I should lose my life, I
would rather choose that than flee from danger before it
has been tried. Said Sindre: I see that you are a very
great champion, and I suggest to you that you unload
all your ships this night, bring all valuable things on shore,
and that you load the ships again with wood and stones.
Then busk yourself early to-morrow morning and come
to them before they wake; thus you may be able to surprise them in their own tents.* You need to do all this
if there shall be any show for you of gaining a victory
over Faxe; for I will tell you this, that so far is common
iron from biting him, that he cannot even be scathed by

* Comb their well-arranged tent-pegs for them.

the sword Angervadil. Here is a belt-dirk, which my
daughter Herrid will give you, and thus reward you for
the gold ring, and I am of the opinion that it will bite
Otunfaxe if you use it skillfully. My son, Herraud, pro-
poses this as a reward for the belt, that you shall name
my name if you seem to be hard pressed. Now we must
part for a while; fare you well, and good luck to you.
By my power of enchanting I promise that my dises
(female guardian spirits) shall always follow and assist
you. Hereupon Thorstein went to his boat and rowed to
his men. Straightway afterward in the night he busked
himself and brought the fee out of the ships, but put
stones in them instead; and when this was done the old
man Brenner came down from his byre, holding in his
hand a large club which was all covered with iron and
large iron spikes, and so heavy that a man with common
strength could scarcely lift it from the ground. Said
Brenner: This hand-weapon I will give you, my nephew
Thorstein. You alone can manage it, on account of its
weight; but yet, it will be rather light for a fight with
Otunfaxe. Now it seems to me that it would be a wise
measure if Angantyr would take the sword Angervadil,
and you fight with this club, for, although it is no handy
weapon, still it will prove fatal to many a man. Now,
my nephew, I would like to be able to help you more,
but I have not the opportunity. Then Brenner went back
from the shore.

XXIII.

WHEN they had made ready they rowed quickly around the ness, and then they saw the place where Otunfaxe and all his naval force was lying. Without delay they sent forth a shower of stones so hard and vehemently that they slew more than a hundred men in their sleep, having taken them by surprise; but from the moment when the warriors awoke they made a powerful resistance. Then a bloody battle was fought. A large number of the men of the foster-brothers fell, for it could almost be said that Otunfaxe shot from every finger. So it went on until night set in; then ten of the foster-brothers' ships were cleared. On the second day the battle began anew, and the slaughter was no less than on the day before. They tried several times to board Faxe's ship, and every time they made great slaughter; but they never succeeded in boarding Ellide, both because Faxe defended her and because her sides were so high. But in the evening all the ships of the foster-brothers were cleared, excepting the dragon called Ufe's naut (gift). On both days they saw that two men came from the island, and that they took their positions one on one crag and the other on another, both shooting with all their might at Faxe's ship. Here they saw the dwarf Sindre, every one of whose arrows brought down a man, and in this manner a great many of Faxe's men lost their lives. The one on the other crag was Brenner, who was shooting more like a bowman out against the ships. It did happen occasionally that stones came flying over the ships, and every stone thrown by

Brenner was inclined to go to the bottom, and, as a consequence of this, many of Faxe's ships sunk. Thus it happened that all his ships, too, had been cleared, excepting Ellide. This battle took place at that time of the year when the nights are bright, and therefore they fought the whole night. Thorstein, together with Angantyr and Bele, tried to board the dragon, but there were many men left on Ellide. Faxe ran forward, against the foster-brothers, Angantyr and Bele, and a good many blows were given and received; but no iron weapons would bite Faxe, and before they had fought very long Angantyr and Bele began to receive wounds. At this moment Thorstein approached, and with his club he smote the cheek of Faxe in the way that it came handiest for him, but Faxe did not even lout the least at the blow. Thorstein smote again, just as hard as before; and now Faxe did not like the blows, but plunged himself overboard into the sea, so that only the soles of his feet could be seen. To both Bele and Angantyr it seemed disgusting to follow him; but Thorstein ran overboard, and swam after the fleeing Faxe, who looked like a whale. Thus a long time passed until Faxe landed; but the foster-brothers fought with those men who still were left, and did not cease until they had slain all on board the dragon. Then they took a boat, and rowed ashore toward Faxe and Thorstein. But Faxe, having landed, seized a stone and threw it at Thorstein just as the latter was swimming toward the shore. He warded off the blow by diving, and swam out of the reach of the stone, which made a great splash as it fell. Faxe took up another stone, and a third one, both of which went the same way as the first one. But meanwhile the fos-

ter-brothers, Angantyr and Bele, approached. When Thorstein sprang overboard, he threw his club backwards, but
Bele had taken it up, and, having now reached the spot
where Otunfaxe was standing, he smote him in the back
part of the head with the club. This he did uninter-
rupted again, while Angantyr at the same time was pelt-
ing him with large stones. Now Faxe's skull began to
ache considerably, and, not liking to receive their blows,
he plunged himself from the crag down into the sea, and
swam from the shore, pursued by Thorstein. Faxe, ob-
serving this, turned against Thorstein, and a wrestle between the two swimming antagonists now took place, in
which there were great, fearful tussles. They were alter-
nately drawn into the deep by each other, and yet Thorstein found out that Faxe's strength was greater than his
own; and it came to pass that Faxe brought Thorstein to
the bottom, and thus he lost his power of swimming.
Now Thorstein, being almost sure that Faxe intended to
bite his throat to pieces, said: How could I ever want you
more than now, dwarf Sindre? And suddenly he observed
that Faxe's shoulder was seized by a grip so powerful
that he soon sank to the bottom, with Thorstein upon
him. Thorstein, who by this time had become very tired
from the struggle, seized the belt-knife which had been
given to him by Sindre, and stabbed Faxe in the breast,
sinking the knife into his body up to the handle, and
then slashing his belly down to the lower abdomen; but
still he found that Faxe was not dead yet, for now said
the latter: A great deed you have done, Thorstein, in
putting me to death, for I have fought ninety battles, and
been victorious in all, excepting this. In duels I have
been the victor eighty times, so that I certainly may say

I have had a holm-gang; but now I am ninety years old.
Thorstein thought it useless to let him go on prattling
any longer if he could do anything to prevent it, and so
he tore away from him everything that was loose within
him. Now the saga goes on to tell about Angantyr and
Bele, that they took a boat and rowed in it out on the
sea, searching for Faxe and Thorstein, but for a long
time they did not find them anywhere. At last they
came to a place where the sea was mixed with blood, and
quite red. They thought it must be that Faxe was at
the bottom of the water, and that he had slain Thorstein,
and after a while they saw some nasty thing floating upon
the surface of the sea. They went nearer, and saw some
large, horrible looking bowels floating there. Shortly
afterward Thorstein emerged from the water, but so
exhausted and outdone that he could not keep himself
afloat. Then they rowed over to him, and dragged him
on board. At this time there was but little hope of his
life, and still he was not much wounded, but the flesh of
his body was almost torn from his bones into knots. They
went away and procured some relief for him, after which
he soon came to his senses. They went back to the
islands, and made a search of the battle-field for the
slain; but only thirty men were found fit to be healed.
Then they went to the old man Brenner, thanking him
for his assistance. Thorstein went to the lesser Brenner's
Isle to call on the dwarf Sindre, to whom he made splendid presents, and thus they parted in great friendship.
Thorstein got the dragon Ellide as his lot of the booty,
while Bele got Ufe's naut, and Angantyr as much gold
and silver as he wished. Thorstein gave his uncle Brenner all those ships which they could not bring away with

them. With three ships they left and went back to Sogn,
where they spent the winter.

XXIV.

IN the spring they set out for warfare again. Angantyr
asked whither they should turn their prows, saying
that he thought the Baltic had already been cleared of
vikings. Says king Bele: Let us then take our course
into the western waters, for we have never been there a
harrying before. So they did, and having reached the
Orkneys, they went ashore, and waged war, destroying the
inhabited parts of these islands by fire and plundering the
fee; and so fearfully did they carry on their depredations
that all living things fled for fear of them. Herraud
hight the jarl who ruled the islands. When he heard of
their depredations he gathered an army to meet them, and
marched by day and by night until he found them at an
island called Pap Isle. Here it came to a battle between
them, and their troops were equal. For two days they
fought in such a manner that it could not be seen which
party would be victorious. At last the slaughter began to
lean to the disadvantage of Herraud, whose ships were
cleared, so that the brothers succeeded in boarding them,
and finally jarl Herraud fell, together with the most of
his men. Hereupon they made expeditions through all
the islands, which they subjugated, and then busked themselves for the home journey. King Bele offered to make
Thorstein jarl of all the islands, but the latter declined,
saying: I would rather be a herser, and not part with you,
than have the name of jarl, and live far away from you.

Then he offered Angantyr the jarlship of those islands, which offer was accepted. The latter became jarl, and was to pay an annual tribute. Afterward they returned home to Sogn, where they stayed the next winter, keeping their men well, both as to weapons and clothes. And now none were thought to be superior to the foster-brothers. Children were granted to them; the sons of Bele hight Helge and Halfdan, and his daughter hight Ingeborg; she was the youngest of the children. Thorstein had a son, who hight Fridthjof. Harald grew up in the island with Grim, but when he had reached the age of maturity he set out a harrying and became a most noted man, although he is not much spoken of in this saga. He kept his nickname, being called Harald Kesia, and a large family is descended from him. Thorstein, Bele, Grim and Harald remained friends as long as they lived.

XXV.

NOW we must return to Jokul, Njorfe's son, who ruled the uplands after the death of Njorfe and Viking. They had preserved their friendship well until their death. Jokul won ships and fee, and was a daring viking, treating his soldiers fairly well, but no better. A few years passed in such a manner that he was the most noted viking, harrying the most of the time in the waters of the Baltic. Thorstein and Bele had not been at home long before they busked themselves for harrying expeditions, and sailing first down along the coast of the country, then through the Sound, they harried in Saxland during the summer, and got a great booty, consisting of gold and silver, and many other costly things. Afterward they intended to sail home, which they did, and having reached the mouth of Lim Fjord, they were overtaken by a violent storm, which carried them out into the sea, and in a short time the ships were separated. Then the sea began to break over the ships from both sides, and all the men were engaged in baling out the water. And it came to pass that this storm drove the dragon Ellide, tossed by the waves, ashore alone at Borgund's Holm. At the same time Jokul also landed there with ten ships, all thoroughly equipped both as to weapons and crews. And now, as might be imagined, Jokul attacked Thorstein and his men. Thorstein was poorly prepared, for he and his crew were very much exhausted from hard work, and from being tossed about on the sea. A severe and bloody battle was fought, and Jokul, being very vehement, kept cheering his men on, telling them that they would never have a better chance to conquer Thorstein; and, said he, it will be an everlasting shame upon us if he escapes now. Then they attacked Thorstein and his men, not letting up until all his men had fallen, so that nobody but Thorstein alone remained standing on the dragon; but still he defended himself bravely, so that for a long time they could not give him a single wound. At last, however, it came to pass that they came so near to him that they could stab him with their spears; but the most of them he cut out of his reach, for the sword Angervadil bit as keenly as ever. Then Jokul made a desperate attack, and stabbed Thorstein with his spear through the thigh. At the same moment Thorstein dealt Jokul a blow, hitting his arm below the elbow, and cutting the hand off. Meanwhile they succeeded in

surrounding Thorstein with shields and capturing him.
But it was near night, so that they thought it was too
late to put him to death, and so fetters were put on
his feet, his hands were tied with a bow-string, and
twelve men were set to watch him during the night.
When all had been brought ashore excepting these twelve
men, together with Thorstein. he said: Which do you
prefer, that you amuse me, or that I amuse you? They
said that he could not care much for amusement now. as
he was to die immediately on the morrow. Now Thorstein, finding himself in close quarters, conceived a plan
of escaping, and in a low, whispering voice he said: At
what other time could I need you more than just now,
my dear fellow Sindre, had not all our friendship already
been broken off? Then darkness came upon the watchmen, and they all fell asleep. Thorstein saw Sindre going along the ship, approaching him, and saying: You
are in close quarters, my dear fellow Thorstein, and it
certainly is high time to help you. He blew open the
lock, then he cut the bow-string off from his hands: and
Thorstein, who thus had become free, now seized his
sword, for he knew where he had left it, and, turning
against the watchmen, he killed them all. Hereupon,
Sindre disappeared, but Thorstein took a boat and rowed
ashore, and went home to Sogn. This meeting with Bele
was a very happy one, and to the latter it seemed as if
he had recovered Thorstein from the domains of Hel
(death). Early the next morning (after the battle) Jokul
awoke, happy in the thought that he was about to take
the prisoner and kill him; but when they came to the
place where they had left him, the prisoner was gone,
and the watchmen dead. This was to them a very great

8

loss. Jokul turned his prows homeward, greatly dissatis-
fied with his voyage, having lost Thorstein, and received
scars that could never be healed. Henceforth he was
called Jokul the One-handed. The foster-brothers, king
Bele and Thorstein, gathered an army and went to the
uplands, sending a message to Jokul, and preparing a
battle-field for him. Jokul gathered men, although, on
account of their friendship with Thorstein, many of his
subjects sat at home, and thus, getting only a few, he
durst not engage in battle, but fled out of his land, and
went to Valland to his brother-in-law, Vilhjalm. The
latter gave him a third part of his kingdom to rule.
King Bele and Thorstein conquered the uplands, whereupon they returned home and kept quiet. Some time
later there came men from Valland to meet Thorstein.
They had been sent out by Jokul. Their errand was to
offer Thorstein, in the name of Jokul, terms of peace.
They were to have a meeting in Lim Fjord, to which both
should come with three ships each, and there they should
settle their dispute. Thorstein was very much pleased
with this offer, confessing that it was contrary to his wish
that he had had troubles with Jokul, saying that he had
entered into them unwillingly on Njorfe's account, and on
account of the latter's friendship with Viking. Now this
was agreed upon. The ambassadors returned home, but in
the summer time Thorstein busked himself for going abroad,
taking with him Ellide and two other ships. To Bele this
voyage did not seem a hopeful one, for he looked upon
Jokul as a treacherous and faithless man. He advised
Thorstein to send spies ahead, and find out whether everything was done faithfully on Jokul's part, and having
found this out, they should return and meet him in the

Sound. They did so, and came back, reporting that Jokul and his party were lying at anchor in Lim Fjord,
and keeping perfectly quiet. So they proceeded on their
voyage till they reached the fjord. Here they held a
meeting in the place agreed upon, and came to mutually
satisfactory terms, on the conditions that the loss of men,
the wounds and the blows, should be considered even on
both sides, but Jokul should get his kingdom back, and
not be tributary to anybody. Thorstein's kingdom in the
uplands should fall to Jokul's lot, in compensation for
the loss of his hand. On these conditions they were to
be fully reconciled. Then Jokul went home to his kingdom, and kept quiet. Thorstein and Bele went home to
Sogn, settled in their kingdoms, and made an end to all
warfares. Ingeborg, Thorstein's wife, had already died,
and Ingeborg, Bele's daughter, had her name. Fridthjof
grew up with his father. Thorstein had a daughter who
hight Vefreyja, who at this point of our saga had reached
the age of maturity, for she was begotten in the cave of
Skellinefja, and there she was born too. In wisdom she
was like her mother. She got Angervadil after the death
of her father, Thorstein, and many excellent men are descended from him. By all, Thorstein was considered the
most distinguished and most excellent man of his time.
With these contents, we now finish the saga of Thorstein, Viking's son, and it is a most amusing one.

HERE BEGINS THE SAGA OF

FRIDTHJOF THE BOLD.

I.

THE beginning of this saga is, that king Bele ruled over the Sogn fylke. He had three children: a son, who hight Helge, another by name Halfdan, and a daughter called Ingeborg, a fair looking woman, of great wisdom, and the foremost of the king's children. On the coast bordering the fjord on the west side there was a large byre, called Baldershage (Balder's Meads). There was a Place of Peace and a great temple inclosed with high wooden pales. Many gods were there, yet none of them was such a favorite as Balder; and so jealous were the heathen people of this place, that no harm should be done therein, either to beasts or to men; and no dealings must there take place between men and women. The place where the king dwelt hight Syrstrand, but on the other side of the fjord was a byre called Framness. There dwelt a man who hight Thorstein, the son of Viking. His byre was over against the dwelling of the king. With his wife, Thorstein had a son, by name Fridthjof, a man taller and stronger than anybody else, and even from his youth furnished with very unusual prowess. He was called Fridthjof the Bold, and so much was he beloved that all men prayed for his welfare. The children of the king were still young when their mother died. Hilding was the name of a good bonde in Sogn. He offered to foster the king's daughter, and so she was brought up in his house well and carefully. She was called Ingeborg the Fair. Fridthjof was also fostered by the bonde Hilding, and thus Ingeborg was his foster-sister, and both of them were peerless among children. King Bele growing old, his personal property began to ebb away from his hands. Thorstein ruled over the third part of his kingdom, and from that man Bele got more aid than from any other source. Every third year Thorstein invited the king to a very costly banquet, while the king, on the other hand, gave a feast to Thorstein the other two years. At an early age Helge, Bele's son, turned to offering to the gods, and yet neither he nor his brother was much beloved. Thorstein had a ship called Ellide, rowed on each side by fifteen oars, furnished with bow-shaped stem and stern, and strong-built like an ocean-going vessel, and its sides were clamped with iron. So strong was Fridthjof, that he, at the bow of the ship, rowed with two oars thirteen ells long, while everywhere else there were two men at each oar. Fridthjof was considered peerless among young men of that time, and the sons of the king were jealous, because he was praised more than themselves. Now king Bele was taken ill, and when he was rapidly approaching death he sent for his sons and said to them: This illness will be my bane, but this I will bid you, that you keep friendship with the friends that I have had, for it seems to me that you are inferior to Thorstein and his son Fridthjof in all things, both in good counsel and bravery. You shall raise a mound over me. Hereupon Bele died. Soon afterward Thorstein also was taken sick, and then he said to Fridthjof: This will I bid you, my son, that you govern your temper and yield to the sons of the king, for this is fitting on account of their dignity, and besides it seems to me that your future promises much good. I wish to be buried in a how opposite the how of king Bele, on this side of the fjord, close by the sea, so that it may be an easy thing to shout to one another about things that are about to happen. Bjorn and Asmund hight the foster-brothers of Fridthjof; both of them were large and strong men. Shortly after this Thorstein died. He was buried in a how according to his request, but Fridthjof took his land and all his personal property after him.

II.

FRIDTHJOF became the most famous man, and the bravest in all dangers. His foster-brother, Bjorn, he valued most, but Asmund served both of them. The best thing he got of his father's heritage was the ship Ellide, and another costly thing was a gold ring, and a dearer one was not to be found in all Norway. So bounteous a man was Fridthjof that he was commonly said to be no less honorable than the sons of the king, excepting their royal dignity. On account of this they showed great coldness and enmity toward Fridthjof, and they could not easily bear to hear him spoken of as superior to themselves; and, furthermore, they seemed to have seen that their sister, Ingeborg, and Fridthjof had fallen into mutual love. Now the time came when the kings had to attend a banquet at Fridthjof's, at Framness, and, as usual, he entertained everybody more splendidly than they were wont to be entertained. Ingeborg was also present at this feast, and Fridthjof frequently talked with her. Said the king's daughter to him: You have a good gold ring. Said Fridthjof: That is true. Hereupon, the brothers went home, and their envy of Fridthjof grew. Shortly afterward Fridthjof became very sad. Bjorn, his foster-brother, asked him what the matter was. Fridthjof answered that he had in mind to woo Ingeborg; for, said he, though my title is less than that of her brothers, still I am not inferior to them in personal worth. Says Bjorn: Let us do so. Then Fridthjof, in company with a few men, went to see the brothers. The kings were sitting on their father's how, when Fridthjof greeted them courteously. Thereupon he presented his request, saying that he prayed for their sister, Ingeborg, Bele's daughter. Said the kings: You do not show great wisdom in making this request, thinking that we will give her in marriage to a man who is without dignity. We therefore most positively refuse to give our consent. Said Fridthjof: Then my errand is quickly done; but this shall be given in return, that hereafter I shall never give you my help, though you may be in want of it. They said they did not care about it at all. Then Fridthjof returned home, and got back his cheerful mind.

III.

THERE was a king, by name Ring, who ruled over
Ring-ric, which also is a part of Norway. He was
a mighty fylke-king, of great ability, but at this time
somewhat advanced in age. Spoke he to his men: I have
heard that the sons of Bele have broken off their friendship with Fridthjof, a man of quite uncommon excellence.
·Now I will send some men to the kings, and offer them
this choice,— either they must become subject and tributary to me, or I will equip an army against them; and
I think it will be easy to capture their kingdom, for they
are not my peers either in forces or in wisdom, and yet
it would be a great honor to me in my old age to
put them to death. Hereupon king Ring's messengers
left, and, meeting the brothers, Helge and Halfdan, in
Sogn, they spoke to them as follows: This message does
king Ring send you, that you must either pay a tribute
to him, or he will come and harry your kingdom. They
made answer that they were unwilling to learn in their
youth that which they had no mind to know in their old
age, namely, to serve him with shame; and now, said
they, we shall gather all the army that we may be able
to get together. And so they did; but, as it seemed to
them that their army would be small, they sent Hilding's
foster-father to Fridthjof, asking him to come and help
the kings. Fridthjof was sitting at the knave-play* when
Hilding came. Said Hilding: Our kings send you their
greetings, and request your help for the battle with king
Ring, who is going to invade their kingdom with arrogance and wrong. Fridthjof answered nothing, but said to

9   * Knave-play, chess.

Bjorn, with whom he was playing: There is an open place there, foster-brother, and you will not be able to mend it; but I will attack the red piece, and see whether it can be saved. Said Hilding then again: King Helge bade me say this to you, Fridthjof, that you should go into this warfare together with them, or you might look for a severe treatment from them when they come back. Said Bjorn then: There is a choice between two, foster-brother, and there are two moves by which you may escape. Says Fridthjof: Then I think it advisable to attack the knave first; and yet the double game is sure to be doubtful. No other answer to his errand did Hilding get, and so, without delay, he went back and told the kings what Fridthjof had said. They asked Hilding what meaning he could make out of those words. Answered he: When he spoke of the open place, he thought, in my opinion, of leaving his place in your expedition open; but when he pretended to attack the red piece, I think he by this meant your sister, Ingeborg; watch her, therefore, as well as you can. But when I threatened him with severe treatment from you, Bjorn considered it a choice between two, but Fridthjof said the knave must be attacked first, and by this he meant king Ring. Then the kings busked themselves for departure, but before they went they brought Ingeborg to Baldershage, and eight maidens with her. Said they that Fridthjof would not be so daring that he would go thither to meet her, for nobody is so rash as to injure anybody there. But the brothers went south to Jadar, and met king Ring in Sokn-Sound. What most of all made king Ring angry was that the brothers had said that they thought it a shame to fight with a man so old that he was unable to mount his horse without help.

IV.

WHEN the kings had gone away Fridthjof took his robes of state, and put his good gold ring on his hand; then the foster-brothers went down to the sea and launched Ellide. Said Bjorn: Whither shall we now turn the prow, foster-brother? Answered Fridthjof: To Balders-hage, and amuse ourselves with Ingeborg. Said Bjorn: It is not a proper thing to do, to provoke the gods. Said Fridthjof: Yet that risk shall now be run; besides, I rate the favor of Ingeborg of more account than that of Balder. Hereupon they rowed over the fjord, walked up to Balders-hage and entered Ingeborg's bower, where she sat, together with eight maidens, and they, too, were eight. But when they came there all the place was covered with cloth of pall and other fine woven stuff. Then Ingeborg arose and said: Why are you so overbold, Fridthjof, that you have come here without the consent of my brothers, and thus provoke the wrath of the gods? Made answer Fridthjof: However this may be, I consider your love of more account than the wrath of the gods. Answered Ingeborg: You shall be welcome here, and all your men. Then she made room for him to sit at her side, and drank his toast of the best wine, and they sat and were merry together. Then Ingeborg, seeing the gold ring on his hand, asked whether he was the owner of that precious thing. Fridthjof said it was his. She praised the ring very much. Said Fridthjof: I will give you the ring if you promise not to part with it, and will send it to me when you no longer care to keep it, and with it we pledge our troth and love to each other. With this pledging of troth they exchanged rings. Fridthjof spent many nights at Baldershage, and every day he went over there now and then to be merry with Ingeborg.

V.

NOW it is to be told of the brothers, that they met king Ring, who had more forces than they; then some people went between them, trying to bring about an agreement, so that there should be no battle. King Ring said he was willing to settle with them, on the condition that the brothers submit to him and give him their sister, Ingeborg the Fair, in marriage, together with the third part of all their possessions. The kings consented to this, for they saw that they had to do with a force far superior to their own. This peace was firmly established by oaths, and the wedding was to be in Sogn, when king Ring came to meet his betrothed. The brothers fared home again with their troops, right ill content with the result. When Fridthjof thought the time had come when the brothers might be expected home, he said to the daughter of the king: Well and handsomely you have treated us, nor has the bonde Balder been angry with us. But as soon as you know that your kings have come home, then spread your bed-sheets on the hall of the goddesses, for that is the highest of all the houses in this place, and we can easily see it from our byre. Said the king's daughter: You have not followed the example of other men in this matter, but we certainly must welcome our friends when you come to us. Then Fridthjof went home, and early the next morning he went out-doors, and when he came in again he sang:

Tell I must,
Our good people,
That our pleasure trips
Wholly are ended;
Men shall no more
Go aboard the ships,
For now are the sheets
Spread out to bleach.

So they went out, and saw that all the hall of the goddesses was thatched with bleached linen. Said Bjorn then:
Now the kings must have come home, and for us I think
there will be but a short peace; to me it seems advisable
that we gather folks together. This was done, and many
men flocked together there. Soon the brothers heard of
the ways of Fridthjof, and of his men and forces. Said
king Helge then: It seems a wonder to me that Balder
must endure every disgrace from Fridthjof. Now I will
send messengers to him, and know what kind of atonement
he is willing to offer us, or else he is to be driven from
the land, for I do not see that we have men enough at
our command now to fight with him. Fridthjof's friends
and his foster-father, Hilding, brought the message to him.
Said they: The kings ask as an atonement from you,
Fridthjof, that you go and collect the tribute from the
Orkneys, which has never been paid since the death of
Bele, for they are in want of the money just now, as
they are about to give their sister Ingeborg in marriage,
and a large amount of wealth with her. Makes answer
Fridthjof: The only thing urging peace between us is
regard for our deceased relatives, but the brothers will
show us no trustiness. But this I will reserve, that all
our possessions shall be left in peace during our absence.

This was promised and bound with an oath. Now Fridthjof made preparations for his voyage, choosing his men
in reference to their bravery and ability to render service.
The company consisted of eighteen men. Fridthjof's men
asked him if he would not before setting out go to king
Helge and make peace with him, and pray Balder to take
his wrath away from him. Says Fridthjof: I make a
solemn vow that I shall never ask for peace from king
Helge. Hereupon he went aboard Ellide, and so they
sailed out of the Sogn-Fjord. But when Fridthjof had
departed from home, said king Halfdan to his brother
Helge as follows: Our rule would be better and greater
if Fridthjof was paid for his misdoings. Let us burn up
his byre, and bring such a storm upon him and his men
that they may perish. Helge said this was a thing to be
done. Thereupon they burnt up the whole byre at Framness, and robbed it of all its fee. Then they sent for two
witch-wives, Heid and Hamglom, and gave them fee to
send upon Fridthjof and his men so mighty a tempest
that they should all be wrecked. So the witches sang
their songs of witchcraft, and ascended the witch-scaffold
with sorcery and incantations.

VI.

BUT when Fridthjof and his men had gotten out of
the Sogn-Fjord there fell upon them a violent storm
and a great tempest, and the sea rolled heavily. The ship
sped on swiftly, for it glided smoothly over the waters, and
had an excellent form for breasting the sea. Sang Fridthjof then:

My tarred horse of the sea
I let swim out of Sogn,
While the maids were drinking mead
In the midst of Baldershage.
The tempest now increases,
Farewell, my brides, I bid you,
Who have a mind to love us,
Though Ellide should be filled.

Said Bjorn: It would be well if you could find something
else to do than to sing about the maids of Baldershage.
Made answer Fridthjof: My songs will not give out so
soon, though. Then they were driven northward to the
sounds near the islands called the Solunds. And now the
storm had reached its highest pitch. Sang then Fridthjof:

High now the sea is swelling;
The waves and clouds unite,
Old spells are the causes
That call forth the breakers;
With Æger shall I not
Contend in the tempest.
Let the ice-clad Solunds
Shelter our people!

Then they stood toward the islands that are called the
Solunds, and intended to stop there; and now the storm
suddenly abated. Then they took another course, and
turned their prow away from the islands, having fair
prospects for the voyage, for they had favorable wind for
awhile; but the fair wind soon freshened into a gale.
Sang Fridthjof then:

In former days
At Framness
I rowed to meet

> My Ingeborg.
> Now I shall sail
> In the tempest cold,
> Making the horse of the wave
> Smoothly speed on.

And when they had sped before the wind far into the
sea the waters began to be violently agitated again, and
a gale blew up, accompanied by so great a snow-storm
that the stem could not be seen from the stern, but the
seas rushed over the ship so that the water had to be
baled out constantly. Sang Fridthjof then:

> The waves are hid from sight,
> For witch-wrought is the weather.
> Heroes we of a well-famed band
> Far out on the sea have come.
> Stand we now all —
> Disappeared have the Solunds —
> Eighteen men a-baling
> And Ellide sustaining.

Said Bjorn: Varied will be his fortunes who fares far.
That is certainly so, says Fridthjof, and sings:

> Helge it is who causes
> The rime-maned waves to swell.
> This is not like kissing
> The bride so fair in Baldershage;
> Otherwise quite does love me
> Ingeborg than the king.
> I know no greater happiness
> Than her wishes to fulfill.

Said Bjorn: Maybe she is looking to something higher
for you than your present position, and this is not un-
pleasant to know. Says Fridthjof: Now is the time to

test good companions, though it would be more agreeable
to be in Baldershage. They busked themselves bravely,
for valiant men had gathered there, and the ship was the
best that ever had been in the Northlands. Sang Fridthjof then this stave:

> The waves are hid from sight,
> Far west in the sea we are come.
> Seems the ocean to me
> Like embers all blazing.
> High dash the breakers;
> Hows are tossed up
> By the swan-feathered billows.
> On the rising ridges
> Now Ellide rides.

Now huge seas were shipped, so that all had to be baling
out water. Sang Fridthjof:

> Much must there now be drunk
> To me by the maid's fair lips
> East, where the sheets lay bleaching,
> If it shall make me sink
> 'Neath the swan-feathered waves.

Said Bjorn: Do you think the maids of Sogn will shed
many tears for you when you are dead? Made answer
Fridthjof: That certainly comes into my mind. Then a
huge sea broke over the bow of the ship, so that streams
of water rushed in; but this saved them, that the ship
was so excellent and the crew so hardy. Sang Bjorn then
a stave:

> It seems not that a widow
> To you does drink,
> Nor that the ring-keeper fair
> Bids you draw near to her.

> Salt are our eyes,
> Soaked in the brine;
> Our strong arms are failing,
> Our eyelids are sore.

Answered Asmund: It does not matter though you do try your arms somewhat, for you did not pity us when we rubbed our eyes every morning when you rose so early to go to Baldershage. Said Fridthjof: Well, why do you not make a stave, Asmund? That shall not be, said Asmund, but still he sang this stave:

> Tight was the tug round the mast,
> When the seas broke over the ship;
> I alone 'gainst eight men
> Within board had to work.
> Better was it to bring
> Breakfast to the maiden's bower
> Than to be baling out Ellide
> Mid the roaring waves.

Said Fridthjof, laughing: You do not speak of your help in lower terms than it deserves, nevertheless you now showed something of the thrall-blood in you, when you were willing to be a table-waiter. The storm still kept increasing, so that the breakers that roared round the ship seemed to the men who were on board more like huge peaks and mountains than like waves. Sang Fridthjof then:

> On cushioned seat I sat
> In Baldershage,
> Singing the songs I knew
> For the king's fair daughter.
> Now am I really
> To Ran's bed going,
> And another shall own
> My Ingeborg.

Said Bjorn: Great fear is now before us, foster-brother,
and your words betoken anxiety, and that is too bad for
such a brave fellow as you are. Says Fridthjof: There is
neither fear nor anxiety, though ditties are made of our
pleasure voyages, but it may be that they are spoken of
oftener than need be, but most men would think themselves nearer to death than life if they were in our place;
and still I will answer you with a stave:

> That did I get to my gain;
> With the maidens eight
> Of Ingeborg did I, not you,
> Succeed in negotiations.
> At Baldershage we laid
> Bright rings together;
> Nor far away was then
> The warder* of Halfdan's land.

Said Bjorn: Such things as are already done, foster-
brother, we must be content with. Now the seas dashed
over the ship so violently that the bulwarks and both the
sheets were broken, and four men were washed overboard
and all were lost. Sang Fridthjof then:

> Broken are both the sheets
> Mid the ocean's great waves;
> Four swains did sink
> In the sea so deep.

Said Fridthjof: Reasonable it now seems to me that some
of our men will go to Ran; but in my opinion we will
not be considered fit to be sent thither unless we may
come there busked like men, and it therefore seems good
to me that every one of us have some gold on him.

* Balder; *i.e.* they were betrothed in the presence of Balder.

Then he cut the ring, Ingeborg's gift, asunder, distrib-
uted the pieces among his men, and sang this stave:

> Before we are lost by Æger,
> Asunder shall be hewed the ring,
> By the wealthy father of Halfdan owned.
> Red as it is,
> Gold shall glitter on the guests,
> If of guesting we have need,
> That will be fitting
> For men of might
> In the midst of Ran's halls.

Said Bjorn then: Now it is not to be looked for with any
certainty that we come there, although it is not unlikely.
At this moment Fridthjof and his men observed that the
ship was gliding over the waves very rapidly, but before
them was a wholly unknown sea, and it was growing dark
on all sides, so that no one could see the stem or stern
from the middle of the ship, and the darkness was accompanied by sea-spray, storm, frost, snow and piercing cold.
Then Fridthjof climbed the mast, and when he came down
again said he to his companions: A wondrous sight I have
seen: a large whale was swimming round the ship, and I
have no doubt we must have come near to some land, and
that this whale intends to keep us from reaching it. King
Helge, I think, does not deal kindly with us, and he has
undoubtedly sent us anything but a friendly messenger.
I saw two women on the back of the whale, and they, methinks, cause this fearful tempest by witchcraft and sorcery
of the worst sort. Now let us try whether our good luck
or their witchcraft is more powerful, and you shall steer
ashore as straightly as possible, but I shall smite these
monsters with beams. Sang he then this stave:

Witches two
On the wave I see,
Has them hither
Helge sent.
Their backs shall Ellide
Cut in twain
E'er she her voyage
Completed has.

It is said that the ship Ellide had by enchantment gotten
the power of understanding human speech. Said Bjorn
then: Now men can see the disposition of the brothers
toward us. Then Bjorn took the command of the ship;
but Fridthjof seized a forked beam, ran to the prow and
sang this stave:

Hail, Ellide!
Leap on the wave!
Break of the witches
The teeth and brow!
The cheeks and jaw-bones
Of the cursed woman,
One foot or both
Of this horrible witch!

Then he shot a fork at one of the ham-leapers (skin-
changers), but the beak of Ellide struck the back of the
other, and the backs of both were broken; but the whale
dove down and swam away, and they saw him no more.
Now the weather grew calmer, but the ship was water-
logged, and then Fridthjof called to his men requesting
them to bale the ship dry. Bjorn said that this work was
not needed. Whereto made answer Fridthjof: Have a care,
foster-brother, and do not fall into despair; it has, you
know, heretofore been the custom of brave men to give

aid as long as possible, no matter what the result may be.
Fridthjof sang this stave:

> My brave men! you need not
> Have fear of death.
> Exult with joy,
> My thanes!
> For this my dreams
> Full well do know,
> That I shall own
> My Ingeborg.

Having then baled the ship dry, and being near land, a
rainy wind still blew against them. Then Fridthjof took
two oars, seated himself in the foremost part of the prow
and rowed rather vigorously. Thereupon the weather
cleared off, and now they saw that they had gotten out of
the sound of Effia, and there they landed. The crew were
very much exhausted, but so stout was Fridthjof that he
bore eight men over the fore-shore; Bjorn bore two, but
Asmund one. Sang Fridthjof then:

> Up to the hearth
> Myself did bear
> My brave men, exhausted
> By the raging snow-storm.
> Now on the sand
> The sail I have brought;
> With the might of the sea
> It's not easy to deal.

VII.

ANGANTYR was in Effia when Fridthjof landed there
with his men. It was his custom when he drank
that some man should sit at the watch-window of his
drinking-hall, and look toward the wind and keep watch
there. This man was to drink from a horn, and whenever
one horn was emptied by him another was filled. He who
was keeping watch at the time when Fridthjof landed
hight Hallvard. Hallvard saw the coming of Fridthjof
and his men, and sang this stave:

> In the violent storm
> I see on board Ellide
> Six men á-baling
> And seven a-rowing.
> The man in the prow,
> Bending over the oars,
> Is like Fridthjof the Bold,
> The valiant in battle.

And when he had drunk from the horn he threw it in
through the window, and said to the woman who gave
him drink:

> Thou fair-walking woman!
> Take from the floor
> The horn turned over,
> Which I have emptied!
> Men I see on the sea,
> Exhausted by storm and rain,
> Who our help may need
> Ere the harbor they reach.

The jarl heard what Hallvard said, and asked for tidings.

Says Hallvard: Some men have landed here; they are quite exhausted, but I think they are good fellows, and one of them is so doughty that he is carrying the other men ashore. Said the jarl then: Go to meet them, and receive them in a seemly manner, if it should happen to be Fridthjof, son of my friend, the herser Thorstein; he is a most excellent man in respect to every accomplishment. Then took up the word the man who hight Atle, a great viking, and said he: Now it shall be found out whether Fridthjof, as it is said, has made a solemn vow never to be the first in praying for peace from anybody. Together with Atle there were ten bad and ambitious men, who often went into berserks-gang. When they met Fridthjof they took their weapons. Said Atle then: Now it seems good, Fridthjof, that you turn this way, for as eagles fight face to face with their claws, so must we also, Fridthjof; and moreover, now is the time for you to keep your word, and not be the first to ask for peace. Fridthjof turned to meet them, and sang this stave:

> Succeed shall you never
> In cowing us down,
> You fainting cowards,
> Dwellers of these isles!
> Rather would I go
> Alone to fight
> With you men ten
> Than sue for peace.

Then Hallvard came to them and said: The jarl desires me to bid you all welcome, and no one shall insult you. Fridthjof said that he heartily accepted this greeting of welcome, and yet he was prepared to take either peace or war. Thereupon they went to call on the jarl, who

received Fridthjof and all his men kindly. They spent
the winter with the jarl, and were held in great honor
by him; the latter frequently made questions about their
voyages. This stave sang Bjorn:

> During ten whole days,
> And eight days more,
> We, fellows so merry,
> Continued a-baling,
> While billows dashed o'er us
> From both sides.

Made answer the jarl: Greatly has king Helge vexed you,
and evil are such kings as do nothing but put people to
death by witchcraft; but I know. Fridthjof, says Angantyr, what your errand hither is; you are sent hither to
gather tribute, and thereto I can speedily give the answer,
that king Helge shall have no tribute from me, but you
may have as much fee from me as you please, and you
may call it tribute or anything else you have a mind to.
Fridthjof said he would accept the fee.

VIII.

NOW it shall be told what came to pass in Norway
after Fridthjof had gone abroad. · The brothers burn
up all the byre at Framness. But while the weird sisters
were performing their spells they fell down from the
witch-scaffold on which they were seated, and both of them
broke their backs. This autumn king Ring came north
to Sogn to have his wedding, and a great feast was prepared for his nuptials with Ingeborg. Says king Ring to
Ingeborg: Whence has come that excellent ring that you
10

wear on your hand? She said her father had been its owner. Answered he: It is a gift of Fridthjof; take it off your hand straightway, for you shall not be in want of gold when you come to Alfheim. Then she handed the ring to Helge's wife, and bade her give it to Fridthjof when he came back. King Ring then went home with his wife, and his love of her was exceedingly great.

IX.

THE next spring Fridthjof departed from the Orkneys, and parted with Angantyr on the most friendly terms. Hallvard went with Fridthjof. But when they came to Norway they learned that his byre had been burnt up, and when Fridthjof came to Framness he said:

> Stout fellows, we
> Formerly did drink
> At Framness
> With my father.
> Now burnt I see
> That same byre;
> Repay must I
> The king's ill deeds.

Then he consulted his men as to what was now to be done, but they bade him look to that himself; whereunto he made answer that he would first hand over the tribute. Afterward they rowed the boat over and came to Syrstrand. There they learn that the kings were at Baldershage, sacrificing to the dises (goddesses). Bjorn and Fridthjof then went up thither; and the latter bade Hallvard, Asmund and the other men break in pieces all the ships, large and

small, that were to be found thereabout. So they did.
Fridthjof and his men then went to the door of Baldershage. Fridthjof wanted to enter. Bjorn bade him go
warily, as he wanted to go in alone. Fridthjof bade Bjorn
remain outside and keep watch while he entered. Sang
he then this stave:

> Alone will I go
> And enter the byre;
> Little help do I need
> The kings to find.
> You shall throw fire
> On the byre of the kings,
> If I do not come
> Back to-night.

Says Bjorn : That stave was well sung. Then Fridthjof
went in and saw that there were but a few people in
the hall of the dises; the kings were there at the time
sacrificing, and sat drinking. Fire was burning on the
floor, and the wives of the kings sat at the fires and
warmed the gods, whereas other women were anointing
the gods and wiping them with napkins. Fridthjof went
before king Helge and said : Here you have the tribute.
Herewith he swung the purse wherein was the silver,
and threw it at his nose so violently that two teeth were
broken out of his mouth, and he fell into a swoon in his
high seat; but Halfdan caught him, so that he did not fall
into the fire. Sang Fridthjof then this stave:

> Take here your tribute,
> King of men!
> Take it with your fore-teeth
> Lest more you demand.

> At the bottom of this belg
> You find silver abounding,
> O'er which have ruled together
> Bjorn and I.

There were but few men in the room, for in another
place there was drinking going on. But as Fridthjof
walked over the floor toward the door, he saw that goodly
ring on the hand of Helge's wife while she was warming
Balder at the fire. Fridthjof took after the ring, but it
stuck fast to her hand, and so he dragged her along the
floor toward the door, and then Balder fell into the fire.
But when Halfdan's wife caught after her quickly, the
god that she had been warming also fell into the fire.
The flame now blazed up around both the gods, as they
had previously been anointed, and thence it ran up into
the roof, so that the whole house was wrapped in flames.
Fridthjof got hold of the ring before he went out. Asked
Bjorn then what had taken place during his visit in the
house. But Fridthjof held the ring up and sang this
stave:

> A blow received Helge;
> Smote the purse the villain's nose;
> Down fell the brother of Halfdan
> In the midst of the high seat.
> Balder had to burn,
> But first got I the ring.
> Then from the fire-place I
> Fearlessly wended my way.

People say that Fridthjof flung a flaming fire-brand at
the roof, so that all the house was wrapped in flames,
and that he then sang this stave:

Wend we our way to the strand!
Then let our aims be high!
For the blue flame is bickering
In the midst of Baldershage.

Hereupon they went down to the sea.

X.

WHEN king Helge had come to his senses he gave orders to follow quickly after Fridthjof and kill him and all of his companions. That man, said he, has forfeited his life, as he has spared no Place of Peace. Now the trumpet was blown, and all the king's men came together; and when they came out to the hall, they saw that it stood in flames. King Halfdan and some of his men went to the fire, but king Helge followed after Fridthjof and his men. The latter had already got on board their ships and were lying on their oars. Helge and his men found that all their ships had been damaged, so they were forced to row ashore again, and lost some men.* Then king Helge grew so angry that he became stark mad. Thereupon, with an arrow on the string, he stretched his bow and intended to shoot at Fridthjof, but he bent his bow with so much force that both ends of it suddenly snapped off. When Fridthjof saw this, he seized two of Ellide's oars and plied them so mightily that both of them broke. Sang he then this stave:

Kissed I the young
Ingeborg,
Bele's daughter,
In Baldershage.

* Hallvard, Asmund and the other men had scuttled all the ships of king Helge while Fridthjof went to Baldershage. See pp. 96 and 97.

> Thus shall the oars
> Of Ellide
> Both be broken
> Like Helge's bows.

After this the wind began to blow out of the inner part of the fjord, so they hoisted the sails and sailed on. Fridthjof said to his men that they might busk themselves not to stay there very long. Afterward they sailed out of Sogn. Sang Fridthjof then this stave:

> Sailed we out of Sogn,
> Here sailed we a short time ago;
> When flames consumed the byre
> My father left to me.
> But now in the midst of Baldershage
> The flames have begun to blaze.
> I now am an outlaw, for sooth
> I know that it has been sworn.

Said Bjorn to Fridthjof: What shall we do now? Foster-brother, said Fridthjof, I shall not remain here in Norway; I will try the life of warriors, and go on viking expeditions. Then they explored islands and skerries during the summer, and thus gained for themselves fee and fame; but in the fall they repaired to the Orkneys, where they were heartily welcomed by Angantyr, and they spent the winter there. But when Fridthjof had left Norway the kings held a thing, and declared Fridthjof an outlaw in all their realms, and made all his possessions their own. King Halfdan settled at Framness, and rebuilt the byre which had been burnt down; and likewise they restored the whole Baldershage, but it took a long time before the fire was put out. That which most touched the heart of Helge was that the gods had been burnt up, and it

cost much to build Baldershage up again as it had been
before. Sat king Helge now at Syrstrand.

XI.

FRIDTHJOF was successful in gaining fee and fame
wheresoever he came; villains and savage vikings he
slew; the bondes and chapmen (merchants) he left in peace;
and he was now a second time called Fridthjof the Bold.
He had gotten by this time a large and well-arrayed army,
and had become exceedingly rich in chattels.   But when
Fridthjof had spent three winters in viking expeditions,
he sailed west and steered up the Vik.* Fridthjof said he
had a mind to go ashore; but you, said he, will have to
go a harrying this winter; for I am growing tired of warfare, and I am going to the uplands to find king Ring,
and have a talk with him; but you shall come back next
summer and get me, and I will be here on the first day
of summer. Says Bjorn: This is no wise plan; however,
your will must prevail; my wish it would be to go north
to Sogn, and kill both the kings Halfdan and Helge.
Makes answer Fridthjof: That is of no use; I prefer to
go and find king Ring and Ingeborg. Says Bjorn: I am
unwilling to run the risk of sending you alone into his
hands, for although he is somewhat advanced in age, Ring
is a wise man and of noble birth. Fridthjof said he must
have his own way; and you, Bjorn, said he, will have to be
the commander of our company in the meantime. They
did as he would have it. So Fridthjof went to the uplands
in the fall, for he was curious to see the love betwixt

* The main part of the present Christiania fjord

king Ring and Ingeborg.   Before he came thither he put
on a large cowled cloak over the other clothes, all shaggy.
He had two staves in his hands, a mask over his face, and
made himself look as old as possible.   Afterward he met
some herd-swains, and going heavily he asked them:
Whence are you?   Made answer they: We have our
homes in Streitaland (Struggle-land), at the king's dwelling.   Asks the old man: Is Ring a mighty king?   Made
answer they: To us you seem to be so old a man that you
ought to know what manner of man king Ring is in all
respects.   The old man said he had been thinking more
about salt-boiling than about the manner of kings.   After
this he went up to the king's hall.   Toward the close of
the day he went in, assumed a very feeble look, and stopping near the door he pulled the cowl over his head and
hid his face.   Said then king Ring to Ingeborg: There
went a man into the hall much larger than other men.
Answered the queen: Such are insignificant tidings here.
The king then spoke to the man-servant who stood before
the table: Go ask the cowl-man who he is, whence he
comes, and where his kinsmen dwell.   The swain then
ran over the floor to the stranger and said: What is your
name, my man? or where were you last night? or where
are your kinsmen?   Says the cowl-man: You ask your
questions rapidly, my fellow; but will you be able to
understand if I tell you about these things?   Certainly I
can, said the swain.   Says the cowl-man: Thjof (thief) is
my name, at Ulf's (wolf's) I spent last night, and in
Anger* (grief) I am brought up.   The swain hastened before the king, and told him the answers of the stranger.

*Angr also means a narrow firth, and in this sense it is still found in
some noted fjord-names on the coast of Norway, as Stavanger (Icel. Stafangr),
and Hardanger.

Says the king: You understood admirably, swain. I know the land called Anger; besides, it may be that this man's mind is not at ease. I think he is a wise man, and a man of great worth. Says the queen: This is a remarkable manner of yours to be so eager to talk with every carle that comes here, whosoever he may be; but so far as this man is concerned, I should like to know of what account he is. Says the king: You do not know any better than I do. I see he is a man that thinks more than he talks, and makes good use of his eyes. Thereupon the king sent a man for him, and the cowled man went to the inner part of the hall before the king; he bent forward somewhat, and greeted the king in a low voice. Said the king: What hight you, my large man? Made answer the cowled man by singing this stave:

FRIDTHJOF (peace-thief) I hight
When I fared with the vikings;
HERTHJOF (war-thief) when
The widows I grieved;
GEIRTHJOF (spear-thief) when I
The barbed shafts threw;
GUNNTHJOF (battle-thief) when I
'Gainst the kings went;
EYTHJOF (isle-thief) when I
The skerries did plunder;
HELTHJOF (death-thief) when I
The babies did toss up;
VALTHJOF (slain-thief) when I
Higher than men was;
But now since then
With salt-boilers about
Have I been wandering;
With needy salt-carles,
Until hither I came.

11

Said then the king: From many things you have taken
the thief's (Thjof's) name; but where were you last night?
and where is your home? Made answer the cowled man: In
Anger (grief) I am born, my mind urged me hitherward,
but my home is nowhere. Says the king: It may be that
you have been brought up in sorrow for awhile, but it may
also be that you were born in peace. You must, I think,
have spent last night in the forest, for there is no bonde
near this place who hight Ulf (wolf); but when you say
you have no home, you undoubtedly mean that you think
your home of little consequence, since your heart drove
you hitherward. Said Ingeborg now: Go thief (Thjof)!
get yourself other night-quarters, or betake yourself to the
guest-chamber! Said the king: I am now old enough to
arrange seats for my guests; come, stranger, put off your
cloak and take a seat at my other hand. Said the queen:
Yea, in your dotage you are, when you ask beggars to sit
down by your side.

Said Thjof: It is not becoming, sir; better is that which
the queen says; I am more accustomed to be among salt-
boilers than to sit by the side of rulers. Said the king:
Do as I will it; for I think my will must prevail this
time. Thjof doffed his cloak, under which he was clad
in a dark blue kirtle, and had a goodly ring on his hand;
a large silver belt was about his waist; down from the
belt hung a large purse full of bright silver coins, and
a sword was girt to his side; but on his head he wore
a large skin cap; his eyes looked dim and his face was
all shaggy. Says the king: Now I dare say that things
look as we would wish to have them; give him, my queen,
a good mantle, and such a one as may be becoming to
him. Answered the queen: Your will shall prevail, my

lord, but I do not like this Thjof (thief) much. Then a
good mantle was given to him, which he donned and sat
down in the high seat beside the king. The queen's face
blushed red as blood when she saw the goodly ring, but
still she was unwilling to converse with him, while the
king was exceedingly cheerful, and said: A goodly ring
you have on your hand, and you must have been boiling salt a long time before you earned it. Made answer
Thjof: This is my whole paternal heritage. Says the
king: May be you have more than that, but few salt-boilers are your equal; so I think, lest it should be that old
age is fast creeping into my eyes. So Thjof spent the
winter here, heartily treated and highly esteemed by all.
He was liberal with his fee and cheerful to everybody.
The queen seldom talked to him, but the king and he
were always happy when they were together.

XII.

THE saga tells that king Ring and his queen and a
large company once were to go to a feast. Said king
Ring then to Thjof: Will you go along, or will you stay
at home? He said he would rather go along. Said the
king: That suits me better. So they started, and had to
cross a frozen lake. Said Thjof to the king: Untrust-
worthy seems to me the ice, and we seem to be going
unwarily. Said the king: It is often to be observed that
you have much forethought concerning us. A little
while afterward all the ice broke down; then Thjof
leaped to the place that was broken, and pulled up the
sled and all that were in it. Both the king and the

queen were sitting in the sled. All these, together with
the horses hitched to the sled, Thjof suddenly pulled up
onto the ice, and then said the king: That was a right
good lift, Thjof; and Fridthjof the Bold, had he been
here, would not have been able to do it with stronger
hands; the doughtiest companions are such men as you.
Now they came to the feast, from which we have no
tidings, and the king fared home loaded with seemly
gifts. Midwinter had passed, and when spring began the
weather grew milder, the forests took to blooming, the
grass to growing, and the ships were able to glide betwixt the lands.

XIII.

IT was one day that the king said to his courtiers: I
want you to go with me to the woods to-day, that we
may amuse ourselves and see how fair is the country; and
so they did, a large number of men rambled out into
the woods with the king. It happened that the king and
Fridthjof were both together in the woods, far from the
other men. Said the king that he was heavy, and would
fain sleep. Answers Thjof: Go home, my lord, for that
is more becoming to a man of noble estate than to lie
out-of-doors. Said the king: I cannot do that. Then he
laid himself down, fell asleep and snored loudly. Thjof
sat near him, drew his sword from the sheath and threw
it far away from him. A little while afterward the king
sat up and said: Is it not true, Fridthjof, that many
things entered your mind? But you dealt wisely with
those thoughts, and henceforth you shall be held in great
honor with us. But I knew you immediately the first

evening when you came into our hall, and you shall not
speedily leave us; and I think a great future lies before
you. Said Fridthjof: My lord, you have treated me well
and friendly, but now I must soon be off, for my troops
are soon coming to meet me, according to a previous ar-
rangement that I have with them. Therewith they rode
home from the woods, and now the king's folk crowded
around them. All went home to the hall and drank
freely. At the drinking it was made known to all that
Fridthjof the Bold had spent the winter there.

XIV.

ONE morning early there was a knock at that door of
the hall where the king, the queen and many others
were sleeping. Asked the king who was calling at the
door. Said he who was outside: Fridthjof is here. I am
now busk and bowne for my departure. Then the door
was opened. In stepped Fridthjof and sang this stave:

> Now must I thank you, ·
> Bountifully you have feasted
> The feeder of the eagle.
> Bowne am I for departure.
> Ingeborg can I ne'er forget
> While to both of us life is granted.
> Fare she well ! and take she
> This costly gift for many kisses.

Therewith he threw the goodly ring to Ingeborg and bade
her accept it. The king smiled at this stave and said :
So, after all, it came to pass that she got more thanks

for your winter quarters than I, and yet she has not been more kind to you than I. The king then sent his servants for drink and food, saying that they should eat and drink before Fridthjof went away. Sit up, queen, he added, and be of good cheer. She said she had no mind to eat so early. Says king Ring: Let us now all eat together, and so they did. But when they had been drinking awhile said king Ring: I wish you might stay here, Fridthjof, for my sons are as yet nothing but children, but I am old and unfit to ward my land, if anybody should seek it for the purpose of harrying. Soon must I be off, my lord; and he sang this stave:

> Live, king Ring,
> Hale and long!
> The highest of kings
> 'Neath the northern skies !
> Guard well, my king,
> Your queen and land.
> Nevermore shall meet again
> Ingeborg and I.

Sang king Ring then:

> Fare not thus from hence,
> My Fridthjof ! dearest
> Son of kings,
>   So sad in mind!
> Your costly gifts
> I shall reward
> Better far
> Than you are aware.

Sang he this too:

> Give I the famous
> Fridthjof my wife,

And therewith all
That belongs to me.

Interrupted him straightway Fridthjof, and sang:

I will not accept
Those gifts from you,
Lest fatal illness
Threatens my king.

Says the king: I should not have given these things to
you had I not thought that this was the case; for I am
sick, and I wish you to enjoy this in preference to all
others, for you are above all men in Norway. I give you
a king's name, too; for her brothers, I think, will be less
willing than I am to grant honor to you and give you
the wife. Said Fridthjof: Accept many thanks from me,
my lord, for your kindness, which is more than I could
ask or even think; but as to my rank, I will take nothing more than a jarl's name. Herewith king Ring, taking
Fridthjof's hand, gave him the government of the kingdom, which he had ruled over, and jarl's name therewith.
Fridthjof was to rule until the sons of king Ring were
old enough to rule their own kingdom. King Ring kept
his sick-bed but a short time, and when he died there
was great sorrow in his kingdom. A how was raised
over him, and, according to his wish, much fee was buried
with him. Then Fridthjof made a great feast, which his
folk came to. At this feast king Ring's funeral and Ingeborg's and Fridthjof's wedding were celebrated together.
Hereafter Fridthjof began to rule this kingdom, and was
thought a most excellent man. He and Ingeborg had
many children.

XV.

THE kings in Sogn, the brothers of Ingeborg, heard these tidings, that Fridthjof had become the ruler of Ring-ric, and that he had married Ingeborg, their sister. Said Helge to Halfdan, his brother, that it was a great shame and an overbold act, that the son of a herser should marry her. So they gathered together much folk and went with them to Ring-ric with a view to slaying Fridthjof and conquering all the kingdom for themselves. When Fridthjof became aware of this he also gathered together folk and said to the queen: A new war has come upon our realm, but, whatever the end of it may be, we do not like to see you in low spirits. Said she: It has now come to this, that we must look to you above all others. Bjorn had then come from the east to aid Fridthjof. They proceeded to battle, and, as he formerly had been wont, Fridthjof was foremost where the danger was the greatest. He and Helge came to a hand-to-hand struggle, and Fridthjof slew king Helge. Then Fridthjof held up the shield* of peace, and thus the battle ceased. Said Fridthjof then to king Halfdan: Two important choices are now in your hands, the one that you surrender everything to me, the other that you get your bane like your brother. It is clear that I am stronger than both of you. Then Halfdan chose to surrender himself and his kingdom to Fridthjof. Now Fridthjof took the rule of the Sogn-fylke, but Halfdan should be herser in Sogn, and pay tribute to Fridthjof as long as he ruled over Ring-ric. The title

* A *white* shield lifted up in the battle was a sign of peace. During the battle the *red* shields of war waved over the contending armies.

of king of Sogn was given to Fridthjof from the time
when he gave up Ring-ric to the sons of king Ring,
and thereupon he added Hordaland by conquest. Fridthjof and Ingeborg had two sons, Gunnthjof and Hun-
thjof. Both of these became men of might. And now.
here ends the saga of Fridthjof the Bold.

FRIDTHJOF'S SAGA:

A LEGEND OF THE NORTH.

BY

ESAIAS TEGNÉR,

BISHOP OF WEXIÖ IN SWEDEN.

―――――――

TRANSLATED FROM THE ORIGINAL SWEDISH

BY

GEORGE STEPHENS,

PROFESSOR OF NORTH EUROPEAN LANGUAGES IN THE UNIVERSITY OF
COPENHAGEN, DENMARK.

―――――――

REVISED AND ILLUSTRATED,

WITH AN INTRODUCTORY LETTER BY THE ILLUSTRIOUS AUTHOR HIMSELF.

―――――――

(PUBLISHED IN THIS VOLUME BY SPECIAL PERMISSION OF GEORGE STEPHENS.)

PREFACE TO FRIDTHJOF'S SAGA.

BY GEORGE STEPHENS. (ABRIDGED.)

TEGNÉR, whom a Swedish author has magnificently denominated "that mighty genie who organizes even disorder," has in no production more distinguished himself than in the work of which the following pages are a translation. If his fame is to be measured by the rule of Madame de Staël, "translations are a present immortality," then it will not soon perish from the records of the great.

Fully aware of the horror every distinguished poet must feel at having mangled versions of his finest lays sent out from distant lands, the translator early resolved not to publish this work unless it met with the approbation of the author himself. This he has been fortunate enough to obtain, accompanied by corrections and communications of the highest value. To the "Introductory Letter" in particular we would refer, as containing explanations indispensable for understanding the original design of the poem. It would be superfluous to add that we express our deepest gratitude for both the kindness itself, which the bishop has hereby shown us, and for *the manner* in which it was done,—to an *unknown* and *undistinguished* student.

As to the "Fridthjof" of Bishop Tegnér, we cannot do

better than quote from a beautiful notice of the bishop's
poem inserted in the " North American Review," No.
XCVI. The author is, we believe, the learned and talented
Professor Longfellow,* whom we remember having seen in
this capital during his northern tour: " We consider the
' Legend of Fridthjof' as one of the most remarkable
productions of the age. It is an epic poem, composed of
a series of ballads. . . . It seems to us a very laudable
innovation, thus to describe various scenes in various metre, and not employ the same for a game of chess and a
storm at sea. . . . The reader must bear in mind that
the work before him is written in the spirit of the past;
in the spirit of that old poetry of the North in which
the same images and expressions are oft repeated, and
the sword is called the lightning's brother; a banner,
the hider of heaven; gold, the daylight of dwarfs; and
the grave, the green gate of paradise. The old skald smote
the strings of his harp with as bold a hand as the Berserk smote his foe. . . . He lived in a credulous age; in
the dim twilight of the past. He was

> The sky-lark in the dawn of years,
> The poet of the morn!

. . . We must visit, in imagination at least, that distant land (Scandinavia), and converse with the genius of
the place. It points us to the past, the great mounds,
which are the tombs of kings. Their bones are within:
skeletons of warriors mounted on the skeletons of their
steeds, and vikings sitting gaunt and grim on the plank-

---

* This interesting essay on Fridthjof's Saga will be found rewritten and
enlarged in Longfellow's prose works, Vol. I (Boston, 1864); and translated
extracts conclusively vindicate the statement that has often been made, that
Longfellow is preëminently the poet who ought to give us a complete translation of Tegnér's poem. (American editors.)

less ribs of their pirate ships. . . . In every mysterious
sound that fills the air the peasant still hears the tramp-
ing of Odin's steed, which many centuries ago took
fright at the sound of a church bell. The memory of
Balder is still preserved in the flower that bears his
name, and Freyja's spinning-wheel still glimmers in the
stars of the constellation Orion. The sound of the ström-
karl's (merman's) flute is heard in tinkling brooks, and
his song in waterfalls. In the forest, the skogsfrun of
wondrous beauty leads young men astray, and tomtgubbe
(little Puck) hammers and pounds away all night long at
the peasant's unfinished cottage. Almost primeval simplicity reigns over this northern land, almost primeval
solitude and stillness."

In translating the work thus commented upon, we have
preserved the same metre and the same number of lines
in twenty-two (or strictly twenty-three, for the second
canto differs little from the Swedish, if printed in four
lines instead of eight) out of the twenty-four cantos.*
Willingly would we have done so in the two remaining
songs also, but found it impossible without sacrificing the
spirit to the form. We wish any future translator better
success. The translation was commenced and almost finished before we met with any one of the versions which
have preceded it; and notwithstanding their general merit, the present pages will perhaps be acceptable to all
who wish to examine Tegnér in faithful echoes, instead

---

* "There are," says Göthe, "two maxims of translation: the one requires that the author of a foreign nation be brought to us in such a manner
that we regard him as our own; the other, on the contrary, demands of us
that we transport ourselves over to him and adopt his situation, his mode of
speaking, his peculiarities." We recognize only one of these maxims of
translation,—the last.

of in a paraphrase; though the latter is, of course, a far
easier task for the versifier.

. . . Lastly, if this work has any merit, let the honor
fall where it is due. It is to my dear and distinguished
brother, the REV. J. R. STEPHENS, THE TRIBUNE OF THE
POOR, that I am indebted for having my attention turned

From sounds to things;

and he it was who recommended to my eager study the
literature of the North in general, and " Fridthjof's Saga "
in particular, which he unrolled before me by an oral
translation, at a time when far away from the shores of
the North, and when the work was altogether unknown
in England.

SKETCH OF THE LIFE AND CAREER

OF THE

AUTHOR OF "FRIDTHJOF'S SAGA."

BY F. M. FRANZÉN,

BISHOP OF HERNÖSUND, SWEDEN.

BEING WRITTEN DURING THE LIFE OF TEGNÉR, IT HAS BEEN BROUGHT DOWN TO HIS DEATH BY THE AMERICAN EDITORS.

THREE of the provinces of Sweden vie with each other in claiming to themselves the name, so glorious for the whole kingdom, so beloved by the whole nation,— TEGNÉR. The first is the iron-veined Wermland, where the great bard was born and grew in years. The second, the fruitful Scania, at whose famed university he suddenly sprang forth an accomplished teacher, instead of what he had been, an extraordinary and for the most part a self-taught pupil, and whence his poetical renown flew through the whole of Sweden, and soon through Europe itself. The pleasant Småland is the third. Here, as the chief of its diocese and the guardian of its educational institutions, he has gained yet greater consideration and yet fresher honors. Indeed, he belongs originally to this bishopric, partly through his father, who was born there, and partly by his name, which his ancestors took from the village of Tegna (Tegnaby), at present a part of the diocese estates.

12

Thus his very name seems to have announced to Tegnér his future station.

His father, who was also called Esaias Tegnér, and who was a good preacher, a cheerful companion and an active agriculturist, had been nominated to the rectory of Milles-vik. It was while he was yet waiting till he could occupy the parsonage, and was living at the house of the assistant minister at Kyrkerud, in the living of By, that his spouse, whose maiden name was Sara Maria Seidelius, bore him on the 13th of November, 1782, his fifth son, Esaias.

While not yet nine years old he lost his father, and for want of means, his elder brothers having all to be supported as students, Assessor Branting, a Småland man, consequently from the same province, and probably also a near friend of his father, took the lad into his office-room. He soon acquired whatever belonged to his employment, and accompanied his foster-father to all the meetings for the collection of the taxes. As the bailiwick was extensive, these journeys taught him to know and admire the beauty with which this province reflects its woods and mountains in its many lakes. A proof of this we find in his fine poem, "To my Home-region," the first which introduced him to the notice of the public.

Tegnér cannot himself remember when he first began to write verse. While yet a child he sang of every event at all remarkable in his uniform life. Nay, he even under-took a considerable poem under the name of "Atle," the subject of which was taken from "Björner's Kämpadater." Thus the same collection of old sagas, in which at a more mature age he found the rough sketch of his "Fridthjof."

The northern sagas were among his first and dearest acquaintances at a time when, ignorant of every language but his mother tongue, he read everything he could meet with, particularly in history and the belles-lettres. He sat with a book in his hand wherever he happened to find himself, sometimes on a stone and sometimes on a ladder; and one day during harvest, when he was to watch a field-gate, he altogether forgot his task, so swallowed up was he in what he was reading, and let the cattle wander through into the yet unmown meadow.

Thus grew he up like a wild apple-tree in the forest, till he was fourteen years of age. Then was it that Branting, who had long remarked his passion for reading, accident-ally discovered the profit he drew from it. One evening, as they were traveling home from Carlstad, and the stars were shining bright above them, his foster-father, who was a pious man of the good old-fashioned school, took occasion to speak of the handiworks of God, and of the evident omnipotence and wisdom he had discovered therein. The boy's answer showed a knowledge of the system of the world, and of the laws for the motions of the heavenly bodies, at which the old man was astonished. How do you know that? he inquired. I have read about it in Bast-holm's "Philosophie för Olärde" (Philosophy for the Un-learned), he replied. Branting was silent; but some days after he observed: You must become a student. How decisive were these words! How important, not only in the life of Tegnér, but in the literature of his country, in which his name has created a new epoch! And how manifold is the good, both in the church and in the schools of Sweden, which must have been lost had it not been for that one sentence! It was on that expression that depended all the renown and pleasure which his works, translated as they have been into so many languages, have excited throughout Europe. Well does the memory of the honorable Branting deserve the distinction to be handed down to posterity conjoined with the name of his immortal foster-. son. But was it his work alone? Though we cannot, it is true, regard it as direct inspiration that he should begin talking about the stars to the simple office-boy, in whose mind lay concealed so great a subject, still, in the whole of this circumstance generally we must acknowledge the guiding hand of Providence,—that hand so evident, but so oft unseen, in the life of the individual, no less than in the history of the world.

To study had long been the secret longing of the boy, but he had not dared to represent his wishes. And even now, however great his joy at this glimpse of unexpected light, he could not help objecting his want of means. God will provide for the sacrifice, answered Branting. You are born for something better than what you can become with me; you must go to your eldest brother, he will guide your studies, and I shall not forget you.

This promise he fulfilled, not only by considerable sums to assist in keeping him at the university, but by a fatherly sympathy in all that regarded him; and this notwithstanding he was now compelled to abandon the hope he had long secretly cherished, of being able in time to leave him his place, together with his youngest daughter.

In the month of March, 1796, Esaias removed to his brother Lars Gustaf, who was then a candidate of philosophy, and was living at Wermland. The latter, a man who had already distinguished himself for uncommon learning, who at the university promotion was a rival of his younger brother, Elof, for the first degree, and who, as many thought, ought to have gained the preference, now became the tutor of the youngest. The wonderful progress which he made is a proof what determined resolution united to commanding talent can accomplish, especially in the warming season of impetuous youth.

After nine months' instruction from his brother, who employed the old solid method of teaching, he was able to study for himself. He now, during the course of 1797, made himself familiar with a multitude of Latin authors, particularly the poets. The latter fixed themselves so firmly in his uncommonly strong memory, that he to this day can repeat large extracts from their works. In Greek also, and in French, he advanced rapidly without any assistance.

So early as the following year, however, when he had not yet completed his sixteenth winter, the youth was compelled to undertake the instruction of others in order to find means for his own further education. The iron master (owner of iron works) Myhrman, who was afterward councilor of mines, invited him to become the tutor of his children. In this also was a special dispensation, which influenced not only his private and immediate circumstances, but also his future happiness. The spot, too, at which he resided was distinguished for a wild but imposing scenery. It belonged to those extensive woodlands to which "Yfvakarl,"* as Karl (Charles) the Ninth is called in this district, summoned his colonists from Finland. The owner of the work was an intelligent and persevering iron founder, but at the same time a man uncommonly educated for his employment. Being himself well versed not only in several modern languages, but also in the Latin tongue, his library contained even

* Karl the Great (Charlemagne).

several Greek classics. Among these was a folio, which
soon became the object of the poetical stripling's most
zealous researches. It was a Homer. Notwithstanding all
the difficulties thrown in his way by the many anomalous
dialects, and by his own still imperfect knowledge of the
language as a whole, and of its various peculiarities, he
was not to be dismayed. Even then the great characteristic of his mind was never to give way; besides which
it exhibited all that energy which distinguishes a great
genius. With Xenophon, also, and with Lucian he became
familiar. But the bard who principally divided his time
and attention with old Homer was his Horace; and here
it was he first became acquainted with his writings. In
the midst of all this he by no means neglected the
literature of France, whose most classical productions
adorned this gentleman's shelves. Thus it was that he
was even now laying the foundation of that independence
with which he afterward withstood all one-sided or nar-
row-minded judgments over the literature both of antiquity and of modern times. But as he did not find a
single German poet in this library, and only learned that
language through the medium of common elementary
books, he acquired a prejudice against it which did not
for a long time become entirely dissipated. With English,
on the contrary, he became poetically acquainted through
McPherson's translation of Ossian. This work produced
such an effect upon his imagination that he learned the
language without any help.

In the usual pleasures and amusements of youth, and
in society in general, he mixed little, if at all. Nor,
indeed, did he miss them, for his books gave him full
employment. He even seldom allowed himself time at

this period to write verses. A report, however, of Bonaparte's death in Egypt occasioned his composing a lyric poem which gave Myhrman, who exceedingly admired the French hero, great hopes of the youthful minstrel. But the production thus grounded on so false a rumor has never yet been published.*

Having now reached his seventeenth year, he repaired to Lund, in the autumn of 1799, and commenced his academic course. His object at first was only to prepare for his entrance into the royal chancery. Still he would give a public proof of his proficiency in the Greek and Roman languages, and accordingly wrote a Latin treatise on Anacreon. Armed with his document he hastened to Dr. Norberg, a scholar famous for his oriental erudition, and to whose professorship the literature of Greece also belonged at that time. This interview produced a never-changing impression on the mind of the young student, not only through the encouraging kindness with which he had received him, but through his whole bearing and manners, which united the charms of original genius with a naive and innocent simplicity. From the beautiful picture which Tegnér has prefixed to the poem dedicated to him, " Nattvardsbarnen " † (the Children of the Sacrament), we may be at least allowed to copy the following features:

Yes! the East's fast friend art thou, the North's proud glory,
A man of fable's vani-h'd days of gold,
And speech and manners hast of patriarchs hoary,
And, wise as eld, the child's pure heart dost hold.

Norberg is one of those men who have had the greatest influence on Tegnér's career. By counseling him to change

* The report of Bonaparte's death, dated Vienna, was published in a newspaper called *Sveriges Posttidningar*, in the issue of Dec. 29, 1798. Tegnér's poem is lost. (American editors.)

† Translated into English by H. W. Longfellow. (American editors.)

his studies at once from the civil official examination to
the degree of master of arts, he kept him at the university, fixed him to literary pursuits, and prepared the way
for him to the station which he now occupies in the pale
of the Swedish church.

Norberg offered him gratis instruction in Arabic. But
the learning of the East had no attractions for the young
skald. The great orientalist was also a perfect master of
the Roman tongue, and contended for the palm with Professor Lundblad, whose Latin school was then in its highest
lustre. The style of the former resembled that of Tacitus
in shortness, expressiveness and antithetic pregnancy of
diction. The latter, on the other hand, who had studied
in Leipzig, and had there formed himself on the model of
Ernesti, had introduced his Ciceronianism into Sweden.
To this school it was that, both by example and by pre-
cept, he strictly kept the young men who were under his
charge. To choose between these two "masters of their
art" was not so easy for a stripling student. Tegnér
decided for the Lundblad party, being induced to take that
step by his brother Elof, who was then reader (docens) at
the university, and was considered one of the very finest
pupils Lundblad had produced.

But it was naturally to be expected that the other professors also should have their attention fixed on a student
of such distinguished qualities. He himself acknowledges
the encouragement he received from Munthe and from
Lidbäck. The former, who was professor of moral philosophy and a zealous Kantian, is represented by Tegnér in
a most charming sketch as one of the noblest men who
have ever adorned any academic chair. With the latter,
who had just been created professor of æsthetics, and had

attempted poetry without any great success, he came into a relation which cannot be better expressed than by the following verses composed by Tegnér:

> . . . He, who latest has left us,
> Gave me his fatherly care, and taught me the scale of the muses,
> While, yet young, I required his counsel. Nor would he grow angry
> If ofttimes I obey'd him but badly; trying, as rash youth
> Will, my pinions in regions not his. Yes! nobly he acted!

In the mathematical sciences he had read little or nothing before he came to the university; but being now engaged in preparing for his degree, his clear understanding enabled him to make rapid progress in this department also, and almost without any assistance. The only lectures he attended were those on physics and on the differential calculus, and his notes on these occasions were afterward a standing loan among his acquaintances, and were highly spoken of for lucidity and precision. Thus at the university, also, he continued to be an αὐτοδίδακτος (self-taught man), although through the medium of books. He commonly worked from eighteen to twenty hours a day, sleeping as little as possible. He seldom partook in the pastimes which belonged to his age, or in the life of a student generally; this gained him the character of a bashful, awkward and singular young man.

Who could believe this of so lively a genius, so cheerful, playfully-witty, and so amiable a society man as at a later time he has been found to be? But this was the only way by which, within so short a time, he could acquire such various and such solid erudition.

Through the assistance of Myhrman and of Branting he had been enabled to pass near a year at the university without being compelled to break off his own studies by instructing others. But his scrupulousness would not

13

permit him any longer to take advantage of their generosity, without some effort to obtain his own subsistence. He therefore applied for and obtained a university private-tutorship in the family of Baron Leyonhufvud, at Yxküll-sund in Småland. His pupil, the Baron Abraham Leyon-hufvud, who has since risen to be president of the high judiciary court, is, of all the individuals he has instructed, the one he has most esteemed and loved. And this feeling has remained unchanged during a course of thirty years. His habits of life at Yxkullsund were the same as at the university — laborious, lonely, and averse to company. But after he had written some French verses, on the occasion of a family fête-day, the awkward and gloomy student began to be remarked with wonder and esteem.

After having passed the summer of 1800 at his seat, he returned to Lund accompanied by his pupil. Here Professor Lidbäck appointed him extraordinary amanuensis to the university library, of which the professor was the manager. To this it is true no salary was attached, but it was an uncommon distinction for a youth of eighteen who had not yet taken his degree.

That he might accomplish this he now prepared himself with increasing zeal, mostly studying philosophy, partly in the dialogues of Plato and partly in the writings of Kant and a few by Fichte. He has himself declared that with his concrete mind he was not disposed for these abstract speculations, and that he grew tired of pursuing a long systematic deduction which allowed no foothold for the fancy. His academic treatises, however, show that he easily penetrated and clearly understood philosophical questions. What more especially drew him to the critical school of Kant was its origi-

nally sceptical nature and its great result, which stops short
at a something — unknown and never-to-be-fathomed.

At the examination for degrees, which he passed in two
divisions, the autumn of 1801 and the spring of 1802, he
obtained "laudatur," the highest certificate, from all the
professors except Norberg. This was altogether unexpected, especially as Tegnér was acknowledged in Greek,
which then belonged to the same professorship as the
oriental languages, to be the most accomplished of all the
promovendi. But Norberg fixed a higher value on the
latter literature, in which also he had gained continental
celebrity.

With such high testimonials, Tegnér was of course the
unopposed *primus* at the promotion, and was to answer
the magister-question. But in the meantime an event oc-
curred which threatened to banish him forever from the
university, to destroy all his prospects there, and to give
his destiny quite another object.

Lundagård is the name of an academic promenade,
shaded by aged trees, beneath whose murmur the students
are accustomed to pass the most innocent of their evening
hours, if not exactly in Socratic dialogues, at least with
somewhat Platonic feelings of the beautiful. One evening,
however, a transaction took place there which was not
altogether so innocent. Without being aware of anything
at all extraordinary, Tegnér, alone as usual, was hasten-
ing thither to refresh himself after the day's hard toil.
He then found assembled there a very large body of students, all armed with branches cut from the old and venerable trees. They, however, had hewed down not a single
bough; it had been done by order of the consistory, to promote the growth of the trees and make their tops more

leafy. This intention the young men misunderstood, supposing that all this maiming foreboded the destruction of their favorite Lundagård, and the more so as they found that whole trees had been felled. These, however, were old and naked trunks, which it was thought ought to make room for younger stems. The rising discontent was principally directed against the university's then officiating Rector Magnificus,* who was by no means loved, and who was believed to have been alone concerned in planning all this ruin. Tegnér, whom the eager crowd surrounded immediately on his arrival with shouts of "Primus must go with us," made representations, but in vain, against the tumult. Clamored down, and armed like the rest with a branch, he was obliged to accompany them. The procession took the route to the rector's house, which was first saluted with the thundering cry of "Pereat rector! vivat Lundagård!" Then all the boughs were thrown in a heap before the entrance, completely blocking up the door. After this, they went tumultuously up the street, giving hurrahs to several of the professors. For the theology professor, Hylander, "vivat" was not shouted, but chanted in chorus. On their return, when the rector was once more saluted with a "pereat," it was very near happening that they proceeded to break his windows also. This, however, was prevented by Tegnér and the magister Wallenberg, afterward bishop of Linkoping, but only by argument that ladies were residing in the rooms that faced the street.

The next morning Tegnér was summoned before him by the rector, to undergo a private hearing, and he there gave a faithful statement of the whole event, without at all denying what was culpable in his own conduct. But

* The rector of a Swedish university is called "Rector Magnificus," or "His Magnificence."

His Magnificence paid no respect to this openness, or to Tegnér's efforts to prevent the uproar. You are already, said he, an officer of this university; you have been nominated primus at the ensuing promotion, and might expect great success in your profession here. All this now is passed. The academic constitutions clearly direct that you must *relegari cum infamia.** Sorry indeed I am that your good fortune should thus be thrown away. Still it might be possible, he added after a pause, that all might be helped and arranged if you would only tell me the names of the ringleaders in the riot. Tegnér, incensed at this question, replied with some warmth that, however it went with himself, he would not play the informer against his own comrades. We were, he concluded, two or three hundred altogether, and there were few among them whom I knew, but these few I never will betray.

In the meantime the whole affair gradually died away, for all the other professors valued too highly the uncommon qualities of the youth, who was also so irreproachable in his manners, not to rescue him from the misfortune with which he was threatened by a man whom even his companions could not esteem.

At this period Tegnér received the sorrowful intelligence that his eldest brother, who was only thirty years of age, had just expired. He was universally lamented as an excellent preacher, and in all respects a pattern for his class. Esaias felt himself at his death again an orphan. Not only was it from him he had obtained the first elements of that learning for which he was now about to receive the laurel-wreath,† foremost among forty; but at

* Be expelled with disgrace.
† The masters of arts, at the Swedish universities, are adorned with a wreath of laurel on the day of their promotion.

his very entrance on the dangerous years of youth it was his brother who had confirmed him in those principles of religion and of morals in which while yet a child he had been instructed, but which he had not enjoyed any opportunity of reducing to practice. Deeply affected by this loss, he made it the subject of an elegy, which was rewarded with a prize by the Literary Society of Gottenburg. This "Lament," together with the before-mentioned poem, "Till min Hembygd" (To my Home-district), which he had composed at the same period, first began to attract the general attention of the people to this rising bard.

After the promotion he traveled in Wermland, on a visit to his mother and to his benefactors, Branting and Myhrman. A virtuous young man can undoubtedly enjoy no greater pleasure from the success of his exertions than that of delighting his parents, and those who have cared for him with a father's or a mother's tenderness. But scarcely less, nay, perhaps, even greater, is their satisfaction when their efforts have been crowned with such results as was now the case.

This visit to Myhrman changed the childish friendship which had already subsisted between his daughter and Tegnér to a serious obligation to which her parents gave their consent. Four years, however, elapsed before circumstances allowed them to enter into the married state.

It was on this journey that, for the first time, he beheld, residing with his father at Ransäter, in Wermland, an individual afterward so famous as a poet, an historian and a thinker — the illustrious Geijer. He was at that time only a student at Upsala, but had even then gained the great prize of the Swedish Academy for his panegyric over Sten Sture. Tegnér himself has made the following observations concerning this acquaintance: "Even at this, our very first meeting, betrayed itself that great divergence in our views of life and literature which time has since only more developed. Our whole intercourse was a continued university act, though without any bitterness or unfriendliness. Even at this early period I learned to value him as one of the most talented and noble natures in our land."[*]

On his return to Lund, Tegnér was appointed by Lidbäck reader (docens) in æsthetics. He was permitted, however, to leave the university for a time and reside in Stockholm, whither he repaired in the beginning of 1803, being received as tutor into the house of the chief director, Strübing. This family lived in first-rate style; but the manners of Tegnér were, as in Lund, retired and for himself. It was there he became acquainted with the poet Choræus, whom he found a cheerful, witty and amiable, but somewhat singular, man. They communicated to each other their poetical efforts; and although Choræus was far inferior to Tegnér in genius, he yet, according to the latter's own statements, could, as older and more experienced in the exercise of "the divine art," assist him with valuable counsel. They corresponded for some time after Tegnér had repaired to Lund, to which place he was accompanied by his pupils.

But having long since been betrothed, he wished to obtain soon some fixed establishment, and therefore applied for the place of gymnasii-adjunct at Carlstad. The consistory did not appoint him, but he obtained the place by appealing to the king, who then resided at Baden. Being shortly afterward, however, appointed adjunct at the University of Lund. he never entered upon his duties at

* Quoted from a letter from Tegnér to George Stephens.

Carlstad. As assistant lecturer (adjunct, vice-professor,) in æsthetics, he was for a whole year at the head of the professorship in this science, during the rectorate of Professor Lidbäck, as well as on many other occasions.

The manner in which he had enabled his hearers to see and understand for themselves all that *beautiful*, of which Lidbäck had only talked and produced the opinions of various critics, made the difference between them only too remarkable. Notwithstanding this, the teacher still preserved the same friendship and goodwill for the pupil by whom he was thrown so much in the shade. For the rest, though it is far from our meaning to undervalue all that was noble in the sentiments of Lidbäck any more than all that was solid in his erudition, we cannot help remarking that Tegnér's peculiar manner of thinking and acting makes his superiority, nay, even his sarcastic witticisms, pleasing and pleasant even to those who are their objects.

There was in Lund another individual who found in Tegnér a dangerous rival. It was Ling, who was not less famous for his northern minstrelsy than for his system of scientific gymnastics. To them both, not less than to Geijer, who harped for us the beautiful "Song of the Viking," and who invoked (living as before!) "The Last Champion" and "The Last Skald" from their ancient barrows, belongs the glory, as Oehlenschläger and Grundtvig had done in Denmark, of having inspired a new life into the Swedish literature, by employing once more the Scandinavian myth and saga. But if the bard of the "Asas" has, like Grundtvig, made us more familiar with the raw force and wild greatness of the olden champions, the chanter of "Fridthjof" has, with Oehlenschläger, attracted more general attention to the forms and images of antiquity by investing them with the milder features of the poetical ideal. Even before that period when the views and efforts of both were developed, Ling and Tegnér could not harmonize. It is curious enough that the gymnastic fencing-master who presented his naked breast to the stabs, not of foils but of the points of swords, possessed a temperament far more irritable and sensitive. But in spite of all their momentary misunderstandings, the honorable true-fast and open-hearted character of both caused them always to retain a firm and mutual friendship, and to acknowledge uninterruptedly each other's worth and merits.

In the year 1806, when he added the office of under-librarian to his assistant-lectureship in æsthetics, besides being notary in the philosophic faculty, he was enabled to complete his nuptial contract with Miss Anna M. G. Myhrman, who added domestic happiness to his literary honors. It was owing to her care and skill as the head of the household, together with his professional industry, that, although his income never exceeded sixty barrels of grain, they still were possessed of a comfortable subsistence.

At this period a number of the younger officers in the university formed a sort of club, called the " Herberge," and of which Tegnér was a member. It had no political tendency, and scarcely any regulations. They conversed on literature in general, and of the government of the university in particular. "Here," writes Tegnér, "was found the pith of views and sentiments which were afterward not without their influence on the university. They played at ball with ideas and witticisms — children of the moment

which might well have deserved to have been more generally known." But among them all, the man who was
most willingly listened to, both for his striking *mots* and
his amiable character, was Tegnér; now no longer compelled to exert himself for his studies, and passing an
agreeable family life, he had become a cheerful and so-
ciable companion. Many of the individuals visiting this
club have gained considerable renown, as teachers at the
university or in the church. Tegnér as a poet and Agardh
as a savan both enjoy foreign celebrity. Three are bish-
ops: Tegnér in Vexiö, Agardh in Carlstad, and Heurlin
in Visby. The last is also acting secretary of state for
ecclesiastical affairs and the department of public instruction. Both Heurlin and Agardh have also distinguished
themselves at the diets, and possess a political importance
which Tegnér, although esteemed for his independence, has
never endeavored to acquire.

Through several lyrical pieces which displayed a genius
of a lofty order, Tegnér had already gained an increasing
reputation as a poet, when his poem "Svea," which received
the great prize of the Swedish Academy in 1811. excited
a universal sensation by its patriotic spirit, no less than
its poetic beauty. Among those things which make this
poem remarkable is the change of form which occurs
toward its close. From Alexandrine, distinguished for
that refined strength, and measured and well preserved
harmony which this kind of verse demands, the skald, in
a sudden transport, is carried away to a dithyrambic
song, whose various tones are in unison with the richly-
varied changes of its subject. This is a poetical vision,
in which the mythological images of the antique poesy
shadow forth what the Swedish nation at the present

moment thought and felt, experienced and hoped. Even although such should not have been the intention of our bard, still the union of these two different styles shows his opinions in reference to the great schism then arising in the Swedish literature.

Without at all degrading the belles-lettres of the older school, he himself was building up the new. But he never went over to our phosphorism, which was so called from "Phosphorus," a literary review which was to announce a new dawn on the Swedish "Parnassos" mount. On this subject he himself writes as follows: "The German theories and the fashionable ' Carbuncle Poetry ' * I could not bear. It is true I thought a change was necessary in our Swedish verse; but it could and ought to be brought about in a more independent manner. The new school seemed to me too negative, and its critical crusade too unjust. I therefore did not mix myself up in the contest, with the exception, perhaps, of a few pleasantries which I wrote or spoke." †

As Lord Byron, in spite of the disrepute into which his enchanting poems brought the older bards, himself did them justice, and among the rest especially valued Pope, just that author whom his own admirers particularly despised: so Tegnér also in the most solemn terms protested against the efforts of the Phosphorists to degrade our older poets, and especially Leopold, whose serious verse rivals Pope's in depth. and whose more playful muse, although she never composed so charming a. song as " The Rape of the Lock," has, notwithstanding, surpassed the English satirist in a flow of light. lively. Voltaire-resembling wit.

* Namby-pamby, glimmer-and-glitter poetry.
† Tegnér's letter to George Stephens.

At the commencement of 1812, Tegnér, during a visit in Stockholm, made the personal acquaintance of Leopold, Rosenstein and other members of the Swedish Academy. Already had he gained their admiration; he now added also their most faithful friendship and esteem.

Besides the Phosphoristic coterie, which could in some respects be compared with "The Poets of the Lake" in England, and among whom Wordsworth may be considered as having some resemblance in depth of thought and feeling to Atterbom, there arose one other literary union under the name of "Göther" (the Goths). Their object was the knowledge and employment of the ancient northern myth and saga in the fine arts. The author of "Svea" was invited .to become a member, and in its magazine, "Idun," first appeared specimens of "Fridthjof," which immediately excited great expectations.

In the year 1812 a new field was opened for the activity of Tegnér, at the University of Lund. It was then that the Greek literature, which had hitherto belonged to the same professorship as the Eastern languages, was erected into a separate chair. The Oriental department remained under the care of Norberg, and it was at his recommendation that Tegnér—as a generally acknowledged Hellenist, without a rival at the university—was proposed by its Chancellor, Von Engeström (then first cabinet minister), and was nominated by His Majesty, without the usual routine, to the professorship of Grecian literature. He received, on his appointment, the living of Stäfje as his prebend.

Thus he entered the ecclesiastical order, and wrote in consequence "Prestvigningen" (the Consecration to the Priesthood), a poem beaming with heavenly beauty. But

as his actual occupation lay within the sphere of the
university, he principally devoted — and that with extraordinary zeal and energy — his time and labor to that
department.   Naturally enough (and the remark is almost
superfluous) he, with his poetical mind, was sure to direct
the attention of his youthful hearers to the beauties of
Greek literature — the surest method to win them over
to the language.   But at the same time, a thing we
should not have expected from a poet, he united thereto
severe demands for a solid acquaintance with its gram-
matical organization, and brought the study of Greek to
a height and splendor hitherto unknown at the University of Lund.

Norberg, who had for his sake resigned this branch
of his public duties, neither showed nor felt (for all that
he felt he showed) any vexation at being thus, perhaps,
surpassed by his successor.   Their friendly relation to each
other was not disturbed for one instant.

In the meantime the fame of Tegnér as a poet was
continually on the increase.   This was partly grounded on
a multitude of lyrical pieces, the one surpassed by the
other, although all were of the most various kinds, and
partly on two more lengthy compositions, which have
also appeared in foreign translations, "Axel" and "The
Young Communicants" (Nattvardsbarnen).   In consequence of this, the Swedish Academy of Eighteen could
not delay summoning him to their body.   He was elected
successor to Oxenstjerna, whose portrait (in Tegnér's in-
auguration -speech) has a beauty inseparable from its
object, but which betrays the coloring of our poet's pencil.

The "Epilogue at the Promotion in Lund in 1829,"
together with many other occasional poems, gave him

individual importance as a liberal-minded, clear-headed and deep-thinking man, who followed with his time without being carried away by its illusions. How well he was able, if he pleased, to imagine and execute even a mystic idea, is proved by his "Address to the Sun" (Sång till Solen), which Leopold, although still less than Tegnér a lover of the mysterious and the fantastic, pronounced the very first of his minor poems, both in the light and lofty flight of its various thoughts, and in a purity of expression and harmony of verse which are kept up in spite of the most difficult of metres. But it is especially "Fridthjof" which has raised Tegnér to the first rank among the bards of modern times; spreading his fame not only around all Europe, but even to other regions and far other climes.

In the same year, 1824, when this admirable poem began to exalt his character as a skald, he obtained unexpected preferment in the bosom of the Swedish church. Although he had enjoyed no opportunity or reasonable occasion of distinguishing himself as a theologian, yet so much had he gained the respect of the clergy of Småland, as a teacher of the academic youth and as a member of the chapter of Lund, that on a vacancy occurring in the bishopric of Vexiö, he obtained, almost unanimously, the first place on the list proposed for appointment. Probably his idyl, "The Young Communicants" (Nattvardsbarnen), had contributed to that confidence in his religious feelings which such a choice presupposes in his brethren. He was appointed bishop in 1824, and immediately justified this promotion by the most zealous guardianship of the educational institutions of his diocese. His speeches on public occasions of importance at the

Gymnasium and the Schools, excited an extraordinary sensation. In them he developed, in the talented manner peculiar to himself, his enlightened views on the questions of the day relative to the reforms proposed in the establishments of education. These speeches have also been spread in foreign lands, by a German translation. How he fulfills his duties as one of the chiefs of the church, we may see in the remarkable document belonging to the assembly of the clergy in Vexiö in 1836. They have not, as usual, been confined within the limits of the diocese, or the *cloth*, but have also attracted the attention of the public at large,* and have convinced all classes that he does not less deserve his consideration as a theologian, a priest, and a guardian of religion and ecclesiastical rule, than as an accomplished and indefatigable guide of all the educational departments.

He has not, it is true, been particularly active at the diets, which he is bound to attend in his capacity as bishop; but as often as he has raised his voice the listening expectation of something at once solid and ingenious has found itself not only satisfied but surprised.

While yet professor he had been adorned with the order of the North Star, which has *now* become a *common* distinction for Swedish literati of merit. But on the breast of one skald far shining from the North, it reminds us of its original signification. Immediately after his advancement to the episcopal chair he was nominated Knight Commander of the same order.

Whether it is that his office, although it has not exhausted all his time, has turned away his attention from the art of the minstrel, or whether the cause may be

---

* They have been translated into German by Mohnike.

that his weak health has somewhat darkened his changingly cheerful and melancholy disposition, true it is that, since the publication of "Fridthjof" he has only occasionally struck the chords of a lyre which has suffered no change in the tones with which it is wont at once to charm and to astonish. We hope, however, that he will yet finish, among other more considerable poems, one which has been long impatiently expected, and of which he has given delightful specimens under the name of "Gerda."* As for himself, indeed, he requires for his glory no more than he already enjoys as one of the most magnificent geniuses of modern times.

The author of this biography will not venture a characteristique of Tegnér as a poet, nor indeed does it necessarily belong to the task he has chosen. But the opinion of that bard himself, as to the causes of his own popularity, must doubly tend to excite our attention, as characteristic both of his muse and of himself. I hasten, therefore, to insert his own observations on this subject:

"The Swede, like the Frenchman, prefers in poetry the light, the clear and the transparent. The profound, indeed, he demands, and values also; but it must be a depth that is pellucid. He wishes that he may see the gold sands at the bottom of the wave. Whatever is dark and muddy, so that it cannot give him any distinct image, let it be as far fetched as it may, he cannot suffer. He believes that

Th' obscurely utter'd is th' obscurely thought,†

and clearness is a necessary condition for whatever shall produce any effect upon him. In this he differs widely

* "Gerda" was never completed. (American editors.)
† Written in Lund in 1890.

from the German, who in consequence of his contemplative nature, not only suffers, but even prefers, the mystical and the nebulous, in which he loves to foresee something deeply thought. He has more 'Gemüth' and gloomy seriousness than the Swede, who is more superficial and more frivolous. This is the source of those mystical feelings and hemorrhoidal sensations (hemorrhoidal-känningarne) in the German poetry, for which we have no taste.

"As regards the spirit itself and the views of the world in the poet's own breast, we love best the life-enjoying, the fresh, the bold, yes, even the overdaring.

"This is also true of the Swedish national character. However weakened, frivolous or degenerate the people may be, a viking-vein still lies at the bottom of the national temperament, and willingly will we recognize it also in the bard. The race of Fornjot* is not yet extinguished. Something Titanic and full of defiance runs through the people like a national feature.

> Northland's strength defies, and never
> Death can conquest from us sever,
> For e'en should we fall at last,
> Life in battle's sport was past.
> Roars the storm — how willing dare we
> Wrestling beard him! Willing bare we,
> Thunder mocking, hairy breast—
> There his arm can strike us best!†

"The proper natural image of the northern disposition is a cold and clear but fresh winter day, which steels and braces all the energies of man, to contend against and to conquer a hard climate and an unwilling soil. Wherever this clear breeze is found, wherever this fresh spirit blows, the nation recognizes its own inward life, and for its sake

* The founder of the giant-race in Norway.
† From "Gerda."

14

pardons other poetic faults. I know no better explanation."

All whom Tegnér's works have made acquainted with his noble genius know, however, another explanation, together with the above, which is undoubtedly both correctly and ingeniously thought, and has a great effect, not only upon his Swedish popularity but also upon his European fame. But notwithstanding all that is northern in the spirit and in the subject of his productions, his poetry has all the richness and luxurious beauty of the South. Indeed, as respects his fresh bright coloring, and the ever springing wealth of his thoughts and images, he may be compared to the verdant crown of an orange tree, whose strong and pure beaming green is adorned with full ripe fruit side by side with the newly opened blossom.

The above sketch by the celebrated Franz Michaël Franzén, the unsurpassed idyllic poet of Sweden, was written before Tegnér's death. We will therefore supplement it with a few words.

Tegnér suffered much from sickness during the last years of his life. In 1833 he went to Bohemia to recruit his health. Here he became acquainted with many distinguished foreign literary men, but his journey did not have the desired effect upon his broken down constitution. He continued growing more and more feeble, and frequently expressed a fear that he might lose the powers of his mind. "God preserve my reason!" we read in one of his letters. "There is a vein of insanity in my family. With me it has hitherto shown itself in the form of poetry, which is a milder type of insanity: but who can vouch for it that it always will vent itself in this man-

ner?" His fears were not unfounded, and, on the advice
of his physicians, he had to submit to being sent to the
Schleswig Insane Asylum, where he remained from the fall
of 1840 until May, 1841. When he returned he was able to
resume the duties of his office, but his strength soon failed
him again, and his last years were spent in increasing
bodily suffering and mental debility. We find him during
this time building wonderful air-castles, planning long
journeys and great national enterprises, and writing
curious letters to his friends. We remember hearing
Longfellow tell us that he received a letter from Tegnér
about this time stating that he was contemplating publishing his works in an edition of one hundred volumes!
One more song did he sing. It was his "Farewell to the
Lyre," a short poem full of strength and pathos. When
these dying strains of the swan of the North had been
sung, his soul burst its prison bars and took its heaven-
ward flight. During his last illness, when the autumn
sun was one day sending its bright rays into his room.
he exclaimed: "I lift my hands to the mountains and
dwelling of God!" These words he afterward frequently
repeated, and they were his last. He died on the 2d of
November, 1846, and on the 17th an exceedingly large
number of people accompanied the corpse to its last rest-
ing-place in Wexiö church-yard, where a white marble
cross, resting on a base of Swedish granite, adorns Tegnér's grave.

To all interested in reading Tegnér's work in the original language. we recommend the Stockholm edition, published in three volumes by Norstedt. In it is to be
found an interesting sketch of Tegnér's life, written by
his son-in-law, Professor C. W. Böttiger.

INTRODUCTORY LETTER

FROM

BISHOP TEGNÉR TO GEORGE STEPHENS,

DATED ÖSTRABO, APRIL 22, 1839.

AT the time when "Fridthjof" was composed, it was commonly enough believed among the literati of Sweden — and I need only mention Leopold as an example — that what was called the Gothic poetry was, notwithstanding the talent it was admitted had been employed on it, altogether and organically unsuccessful. This poesy, it was asserted, rested for fundamental support on a wildness of manners and opinions and an only partial development of the relations of society, impossible to reconcile with the poetry of present times. The latter was, properly enough, regarded as the daughter of modern civilization, and in her countenance it was that the age recognized, though beautified and idealized, the features of itself. And indeed it is quite true that all poetry must reflect the progress and temperament of its time; but still we find those general human passions and circumstances which must remain unchanged in every period, and may be regarded as the foundation of poetry. Even before this, though with various success, Ling had treated several

Northern subjects, for the most part in a dramatic form.
It has been observed that his great poetic talent lay more
in the lyric than the drama, and that he paints exterior
nature far better than the ever changing soul. That the
Northern saga can successfully assume the dramatic form
is, however, abundantly proved by the tragedies of Oehlenschläger. It is with pleasure I acknowledge that his
"Helge" first gave me the idea of "Fridthjof."

It was never my meaning, however, in this poem —
though such seems to have been the opinion of many—
simply to versify the saga. The most transient compari-
son ought to have shown, not only that the whole *dénoue-
ment* is different in the poem and the saga, but also that
several of its parts, such as Cantos II, III, V, XV, XXI.
XXIII and XXIV, have either little, if any, or at least
a very distant, ground in the legend. Indeed it is not in
this one, but in other Icelandic sagas, that we ought to
seek the sources of the incidents I have chosen. My object was to represent a poetical image of the old Northern Hero-Age. It was not Fridthjof, as an individual,
whom I would paint; it was the epoch of which he was
chosen as the representative. It is true that I preserved,
in this respect, the hull and outline of the tradition; but,
at the same time, I thought myself entitled to add or to
take away, just as was most convenient for my plan.
This, as I supposed, was a part of that poetic liberty
without which it is impossible to produce any independent treatment of any poetical subject whatsoever.

In the saga we find much that is highminded and
heroic, and which, equally demanding the homage of every
period, both could and ought to be preserved. But, at
the same time, we meet occasional instances of the raw,

the savage, the barbarous, which required to be either altogether taken away or to be considerably softened down. To a certain extent, therefore, it was necessary to modernize; but just the difficulty here was to find the fitting *lagom.** On the one hand the poem ought not too glaringly to offend our milder opinions and more refined habits; but on the other it was important not to sacrifice the national, the lively, the vigorous and the natural. There could, and ought to, blow through the song that cold winter air, that fresh north wind which characterizes so much both the climate and the temperament of the North. But neither should the storm howl till the very quicksilver froze, and all the more tender emotions of the heart were extinguished.

It is properly in the bearing of Fridthjof's character that I have sought the solution of this problem. The noble, the high-minded, the bold—which is the great feature of all heroism — ought not, of course, to be missing there; and materials sufficient abounded both in this and in many sagas. But together with this more general heroism, I have endeavored to invest the character of Fridthjof with something individually Northern — that fresh-living, insolent, daring rashness which belongs, or at least formerly belonged, to the national temperament. Ingeborg says of Fridthjof (Canto VIII),

> How glad, how daring all, how full of hope!
> His good sword pointing to the norn's own breast,
> "Thou shalt," saith he, "thou shalt give way!"

These lines contain the key to Fridthjof's character, and, in point of fact, to the whole poem. Even the mild, peace-loving, friend-rich old king Ring is not destitute of this great national quality, at least in the manner of his

---

* *Lagom*, a Swedish word, answers to the English "just the thing," "just right," "medium," etc.

death; and it is for this reason I let him "carve himself
with geirs-odd "*—undoubtedly a barbarous custom, but
still characteristic of the time and the popular manners.

Another peculiarity common to the people of the North
is a certain disposition for melancholy and heaviness of
spirit common to all deeper characters. Like some ele-
giac key-note, its sound pervades all our old national mel-
odies, and generally whatever is expressive in our annals,
for it is found in the depths of the nation's heart. I
have somewhere or other said of Bellman, the most
national of our poets:

> And mark the touch of gloom his brow o'ershading,
> A northern minstrel-look, a grief *in rosy-red!*

For this melancholy, so far from opposing the fresh live-
liness and cheerful vigor common to the nation, only gives
them yet more strength and elasticity. There is a certain kind of life-enjoying gladness (and of this, public
opinion has accused the French) which finally reposes on
frivolity; that of the North is built on seriousness. And
therefore I have also endeavored to develop in Fridthjof
somewhat of this meditative gloom. His repentant regret
at the unwilling temple-fire, his scrupulous fear of Balder (Canto XV),

> Who sits in yon sky, gloomy thoughts sending down;
> Ne'er my soul from their sadness is freed!

and his longing for the final reconciliation and for calm
within him, are proofs not only of a religious craving,
but also and still more of a natural tendency to sorrow-
fulness common to every serious mind, at least in the
north of Europe.

I have been reproached (though, I cannot help thinking, without good reason) with having given the love

* The spear-point.

between Fridthjof and Ingeborg, for instance in "The Parting," too modern and sentimental a cast. As regards this I ought to remark, that reverence for the sex was from the earliest times, long before the introduction of Christianity, a national feature of the German peoples. On this account it was that the light, inconstant and simply sensual view of love which prevailed among the most cultivated nations of antiquity was a thing quite foreign to the habits of the North. Song and saga overflow with the most touching legends of romantic love and faith in the North, long before the spirit of chivalry had made woman the idol of man in the South. The circumstances assumed between Ingeborg and Fridthjof seem to me, therefore, to rest upon sufficient historical ground, if not personally, in the manners and opinions of the age. That delicacy of sentiment with which Ingeborg refused to accompany her lover, and rather sacrificed her inclination than withdrew herself from the authority of her brother and guardian, seems to me to find its reason in the nature of each nobler female, which is the same in every period and in every land.

The subjective thus contained in the events and characters demanded, or at least permitted, a departure from the usual epic uniformity in their treatment. The most suitable method seemed to me to resolve the epic form into free lyric romances. I had the example of Oehlenschläger, in his "Helge," before me, and have since found that it has been followed by others. It carries with it the advantage of enabling one to change the metre in accordance with the contents of every separate song. Thus, for instance, I doubt whether "Ingeborg's Lament" (Canto IX) could be given with advantage in any language

15

in hexameters or ten-syllabled iambics, whether rhymed or not. I am well aware that many regard this as opposed to the epic unity, which is, however, so nearly allied to monotony. But I regard this unity as more than sufficiently compensated for by the freer room and fresher changes gained by its abandonment. Just this liberty, however, to be properly employed, requires so much the more thought, understanding and taste ; for with every separate piece one must endeavor to find the exactly suitable form, a thing not always ready for one's hand in the language. It is for this reason that I have attempted (with greater or less success) to imitate several metres, especially from the poets of antiquity. Thus the pentameter iambic, hypercatalectic in the third foot (Canto II), the six-footed iambic (Canto XIV), the Aristophanic anapests (Canto XV), the trochaic tetrameter (Canto XVI) and the tragic senarius (Canto XXIV), were little, if at all, heard of in Swedish previous to my attempts.

As regards the language in itself, the antique subject invited one sometimes to use an archaism, especially where such an expression, without being obscure, seemed to carry with it any particular emphasis. Still this care is at all events lost abroad, and sometimes even at home. It demands, nevertheless, very much prudence. For the great stream of words in a modern poem must, naturally, flow from the language of the day, although an obsolescent word or two may occasionally be employed.

Es. Tegnér.

FRIDTHJOF'S SAGA.

NAMES OF THE PERSONAGES WHO FIGURE IN THE LEGEND OF FRIDTHJOF.

Bele, Fylke-king (independent chief) of Sogn District, in Norway.

Helge,
Halfdan, } his sons, co-heirs to his throne and lands.

Ingeborg, his only daughter, foster-sister and beloved of FRID-THJOF.

Thorstein, a rich and powerful yeoman (bonde), friend, chief stay and brother-in-arms of king BELE.

Fridthjof, his son, lover of INGEBORG, and the hero of the poem.

Hilding, a venerable peasant, the foster-father of FRIDTHJOF and of INGEBORG.

Bjorn, his son, sworn friend and weapon comrade of FRIDTHJOF.

Ring, Fylke-king of Ring-ric, in Norway.

Angantyr, Jarl (Earl, or reigning chieftain) of the Orkney Islands.

Atle, a Berserk, one of his war-men.

Priests, Warriors, Skalds, Peasants, etc.

SCENE—Framness and its neighborhood (in Sogn District), and the Orkneys.

FRIDTHJOF AND INGEBORG.

I.

TWO plants in Hilding's garden fair
  Grew up beneath his fostering care;
Their match the North had never seen,
So nobly tow'r'd they in the green!

II.

The one shot forth like some broad oak,
Its trunk a battle-lance unbroke;
But helmet-like the top ascends,
As heav'n's soft breeze its arch'd round bends.

III.

Like some sweet rose,—bleak winter flown,—
That other fresh young plant y-shone;
From out this rose spring yet scarce gleaneth.
Within the bud it lies and dreameth.

IV.

But cloud-sprung storm round th' earth shall go,—
That oak then wrestles with his foe;
Her heav'nly path spring's sun shall tread,—
Then opes that rose her lips so red!

V

Thus sportful, glad, and green they sprung,
And Fridthjof was that oak the young;
The rose so brightly blooming there,
She hight was INGEBORG THE FAIR.

VI.

Saw'st thou the two by gold-beam'd. day,
To Freyja's courts thy thoughts would stray,
Where bright-hair'd and with rosy pinions,
Swings many a bride-pair—love's own minions.

VII.

But saw'st thou them by moonlight's sheen,
Dance round beneath the leafy green,
Thou'dst say, in yon sweet garland-grove
The king and queen of fairies move.

VIII.

How precious was the prize he earn'd
When his first rune the youth had learn'd!—
No kings could his bright glory reach,—
That letter would he Ing'borg teach.

IX.

How gladly at her side steer'd he
His bark across the dark blue sea!
When gaily tacking Fridthjof stands,
How merrily clap her small white hands!

X.

No birds' nests yet so lofty were,
That thither he not climb'd for her;
E'en th' eagle, as he cloudward swung,
Was plunder'd both of eggs and young.

XI.

No streamlet's waters rush'd so swift,
O'er which he would not Ing'borg lift;
So pleasant feels, when foam-rush 'larms,
The gentle cling of small white arms!

XII.

The first pale flow'r that spring had shed,
The strawberry sweet that first grew red,
The corn-ear first in ripe gold clad,—
To her he offered, true and glad.

XIII.

But childhood's days full quickly fly;
He stands a stripling now, with eye
Of haughty fire which hopes and prayeth;—
And she, with budding breast, see! strayeth.

XIV.

The chase young Fridthjof ceaseless sought;
Nor oft would hunter so have fought;
For swordless, spearless all, he'd dare
With naked strength the savage bear.

xv.

Then breast to breast they struggled grim; —
Though torn, the bold youth masters him!
With shaggy hide now see him laden —
Such spoils refuse — how can the maiden?

xvi.

For man's brave deeds still woman wile;
Strength well is worth young beauty's smile:
Each other suit they, fitly blending
Like helm o'er polished brows soft bending!

xvii.

But read he, some cold winter's night,
(The fire-hearth's flaming blaze his light,)
A song of Valhal's brightnesses,
And all its gods and goddesses, —

xviii.

He'd think: "Yes! yellow's Freyja's hair,
A corn-land sea, breeze-waved so fair; —
Sure Ing'borg's, that like gold-net trembles
Round rose and lily, hers resembles!

xix.

"Rich, white, soft, clear is Idun's breast;
How it heaves beneath her silken vest!
A silk I know, whose heave discloses
Light-fairies two with budding roses,

XX.

"And blue are Freyja's eyes to see,
Blue as heav'n's cloudless canopy!—
But I know eyes to whose bright beams
The light blue spring-day darksome seems.

XXI.

"The bards praise Gerd's fair cheeks too high,
Fresh snows which playful north-lights dye!—
I cheeks have seen whose day lights clear
Two dawnings blushing in one sphere.

XXII.

"A heart like Nanna's own I've found
As tender,—why not so renown'd?
Ah! happy Balder; ilk breast swelleth
To share the death thy skald o'ertelleth.

XXIII.

"Yes! could my death like Balder's be,—
A faithful maid lamenting me—
A maid like Nanna, tender, true,—
How glad I'd stay with Hel the blue!"

XXIV.

But the king's child—all glad her love—
Sat murmuring hero-songs, and wove
Th' adventures that her chief had seen,
And billows blue, and groves of green;

XXV.

Slow start from out the wool's snow-fields
Round, gold-embroider'd, shining shields,
And battle's lances flying red,
And mail-coats stiff with silver thread;

XXVI.

But day by day her hero still
Grows Fridthjof-like, weave how she will,—
And as his form 'mid th' arm'd host rushes,
Though deep, yet joyful are her blushes!

XXVII.

And Fridthjof, where his wanderings be,
Carves I. and F. i' the tall birch-tree;
The runes right gladly grow united,
Their young hearts like by one flame lighted.

XXVIII.

Stands Day on heav'n's arch-throne so fair!—
King of the world with golden hair,
Waking the tread of life and men—
Each thinks but of the other then!

XXIX.

Stands Night on heav'n's arch-throne so fair!—
World's mother with her dark-hued hair,
While stars tread soft, all hush'd 'mong men—
Each dreams but of the other then!

XXX.

"Thou earth!—each spring through all thy bow'rs
Thy green locks jeweling thick with flow'rs—
Thy choicest give! Fair weaving them,
My Fridthjof shall the garland gem."

XXXI.

"Thou sea! in whose deep gloomy hall
Shine thousand pearls, hear love's loud call!—
Thy fairest give me, to bedeck
That whiter pearl—my Ing'borg's neck!"

XXXII.

"Oh, crown of Odin's royal throne,
Eye of the world, bright golden sun!—
Wert thou but mine, should Fridthjof wield
Thy shining disc, his shining shield."

XXXIII.

"Oh, lamp of great Allfather's dome,
Thou moon, whose beams so pale-clear roam!—
Wert thou but mine, should Ing'borg wear
Thy crescent orb among her hair."

XXXIV.

Then Hilding spoke: "From this love-play
Turn, foster-son, thy mind away;
Had wisdom rul'd, thou ne'er hadst sought her—
'The maid,' fate cries, 'is Bele's daughter!'

XXXV.

"To Odin, in his star-lit sky,
Ascends her titled ancestry:
But Thorstein's son art thou; give way!
For 'like thrives best with like,' they say."

XXXVI.

But Fridthjof smiling said: "Down fly
To death's dark vale, my ancestry:
Yon forest's king late slew I: pride
Of high birth heir'd I with his hide.

XXXVII.

"The freeborn man yields not: for still
His arm wins worlds where'er it will;
Fortune can mend as well as mar;
Hope's ornaments right kingly are!

XXXVIII.

"What is high birth but force? Yes! Thor.
Its sire, in Thrudvang's fort gives law:
Not birth, but worth, he weighs above;—
The sword pleads strongly for its love!

XXXIX.

"Yes! I will fight for my young bride,
Though e'en the Thund'ring god defied.
Rest thee, my lily, glad at heart;
Woe him whose rash hand would us part!"

CANTO II.

KING BELE AND THORSTEIN, VIKING'S SON.

I.

In regal hall king Bele stood,
  His sword a staff of light,
And near him lean'd that yeoman good,
  Thorstein, Viking's son hight.
His weapon-brother, old was he,
  A hundred years well nigh,
And scarr'd all o'er as rune-stones be,
  And silver-hair'd on high.

II.

They stood as up and down a hill
  Two off'ring-houses stand;
Once shrines for heathen gods to fill,
  Now ruin'd in the land.
But wisdom's runes, carv'd deep and fast,
  Those broken walls still hide,
And high traditions of the past
  On each arch'd vault reside.

III.

" The shades of ev'ning hasten on,"
  So speaketh Bele now;
" My mead-cup's flavor all is gone,
  The helm weighs down my brow:
My vision fails to trace the lines
  Of human weal and woe,
But nearer, brighter, Valhal shines,—
  My death's at hand, I trow !

IV.

" My children have I call'd; and, friend,
  Thy son is summon'd, too;
For still together should they wend,
  As we were wont to do.
A warning shall they have to-day,
  Those eagles proud and young,
Before all 'counsel sleeps for aye
  Upon the dead man's tongue ! "

V.

Then, as the king's commandments ran,
  Advanc'd they up the hall:
The first was Helge, pale and wan,
  And gloomiest of them all.
He, where yond' altar-circle lies,
  'Mong spaeman* lov'd to stand,

---

* Spaemen — sacrificers, prophets.

And came from groves of sacrifice
    With blood upon his hand.

VI.

Halfdan appear'd the next, a youth,
    With locks as bright as gold:
Noble his features were, in sooth,
    Though womanly their mould.
His sword was belted round about
    For sport, apparently,
And in the guise of hero stout,
    Some girl resembled he.

VII.

But close behind them Fridthjof goes,
    Wrapp'd in his mantle blue;
His height a whole head taller rose
    Than that of both the two.
He stands, between the brothers there,
    As though the ripe day stood
Atween young morning, rosy-fair,
    And night within the wood.

VIII.

"My children," saith the dim-eyed king,
    "Soon sets my ev'ning's sun;
Govern the realm in peace, nor bring
    Discord 'mid union,

For union all in one infolds;
  The ring she likens most
Which grasps the lance;—where no ring holds,
  The lance's strength is lost.

IX.

"Let force stand like a sentinel
  Before the country's gate;
Let peace within the hedg'd land dwell,
  Blooming and consecrate.
The sword defense alone should yield,
  Else is its steel too hard;
Forg'd for a padlock was the shield,
  The peasant's barn to guard.

X.

"His own good land who'd fain oppress
  Is but a simple man;
For kings can do, as all confess,
  But what their people can:
When, on the rocky mountain's side.
  The sapless trunk is dead,
The thick-leav'd crown that was its pride
  Soon. too. is withered.

XI.

"On pillars four of up-heap'd stone
  Stands high heavn's lofty round:

The throne can only rest upon
  Just laws' all-holy ground.
When diets sanction fear'd kings' wrongs.
  Stands ruin near at hand;
But glory to the king belongs,
  And good unto his land.

XII.

"Full well in Disarsal* reside
  The gods, O Helge; but
Not as weak snails, that still abide
  Within their shells close shut;
Far as bright day-light shines on high.
  Far as the voice can sound,
Far as man's thought can upward fly,
  The mighty gods are found!

XIII.

"How oft, in lungs of offer'd hawk,
  Stand faithless token-signs!
And falsely many a rune doth talk.
  Though deeply-grav'd the lines;
But, Helge, on a heart whose lore
  Is sound, glad, upright, just,
Has Odin written runes all o'er.
  Which gods and men may trust.

* The hall of the disee, or goddesses.

16

XIV.

"Firm, but not harsh, my son,—let might
    The touch of mercy feel;
For sword that bends the most will bite
    Most sharply on the steel.
Know, Helge, it becomes a king
    Gentle to be, though bold,
As flow'rs adorn the shield; soft spring
    Brings more than winter cold.

XV.

"A friendless chief, however fear'd.
    However bright his day,
Dies like a trunk in deserts rear'd,
    Its bark all peel'd away;
But whoso claims fast-faithful friends
    Grows like the woodland tree,
Round whose deep roots the streamlet wends,
    Whose branches shelter'd be.

XVI.

"Boast not the fame thy dead sires gain'd.—
    Each hath his own, no more;
Hast thou to bend the bow vain strain'd?
    The bow's not thine,—give o'er.
What wilt thou with that bright esteem
    Which down i' the grave doth sleep?

With own fierce waves, the rushing stream
Flows onward through the deep.

XVII.

"Thou, Halfdan, hear! A pleasant wit
  Is wise men's profiting:
But idle talk can none befit,
  And least of all a king;
Mere honey can no mead afford.—
  With hops 'tis brew'd alway:
Put steel, young man. into thy sword.
  Put earnest in thy play.

XVIII.

"Too much good sense none ever show,
  However wise it fall;
But little enough full many know,
  Who have no wit at all.
An ignorant guest is but despis'd,
  Though seated on the dais;
But clever men's discourse is priz'd,
  However low their place.

XIX.

" Thy true-fast friend is close at hand,
  Thy foster-brother dear,
Although, to reach his welc'ming land,
  The road be not so near;

But Halfdan, far enough away
    That mansion proves to be,
Be short the journey as it may,
    Which holds an enemy.

XX.

"Let not a forward man be made
    Thy bosom counselor;
An empty house stands wide display'd,
    Barr'd is the rich man's door.
Choose one: unnecessary 'tis
    . To seek a second friend;
And the world's secret, Halfdan. is
    What with the third should end."

XXI.

Then upstood Thorstein, and began
    In words like these to speak:
"Not thus, alone, king Bele can
    The hall of Odin seek.
Together have we shar'd. O king.
    The changing scenes of life —
And death, I hope, will never bring
    Occasion for our strife.

XXII.

"Old age. son Fridthjof, in mine ear
    Full many a warning speech

Hath whisper'd soft; list now, and hear
  What wisdom they can teach.
I' the Northland Odin's birds sweep down
  On cairn and hero-mound;
On the old man's lips — ah, sweet renown! —
  Sit wise words, thoughts profound.

XXIII.

" And first, the high gods reverence!
  For good and evil come.
Like storm and sunshine, not from hence,
  But Valhal's shining home.
The heart's most secret vaults they see.
  Though clos'd with fast'nings strong,
And long years' penance shall there be
  For but one moment's wrong.

XXIV.

" Obey the king. With force and skill
  Shall one the scepter sway:
With stars dim night the sky may fill.
  But one eye hath bright day.
Willing the better man will pledge
  The best, glad praise his deeds:
The sword not only wants an edge,
  A good hilt, too, it needs.

XXV.

"Fridthjof, great strength the gods bestow —
　And good it is, my son!
But without wit, mere force we know
　Is soon outspent and done.
By one man slain — the bear can wield
　Twelve men's strength in his paw;
Yes! 'gainst the sword-thrust's held the shield,
　'Gainst violence, the law.

XXVI.

"By few the haughty chief is fear'd,
　Hated he is by all:
And arrogance, by few rever'd,
　Is father to a fall.
How many have I seen high soar,
　Now on a crutch bent low;
Seasons, not men, the harvest pour,
　And heaven's winds fortune blow.

XXVII.

"When down the setting sun hath sunk,
　Then, Fridthjof, praise the day;
Ale may be prais'd, too, when 'tis drunk;
　And, follow'd, counsel may.
Fond youth on many things for aid
　Will trust itself, indeed;

But battle proves the keen sword-blade,
　And want, a friend in need.

XXVIII.

" Trust not to night-old ice, or snow
　Which some spring day may see,
Or slumbering snakes, or words that flow
　Frae th' girl upon thy knee;
For on a wheel that nothing stills
　Is turn'd fair woman's breast;
And 'neath those soft white lily-hills
　Inconstancy doth rest.

XXIX.

" Down to the grave thyself must go,
　And what thou hast, away;
But one thing, Fridthjof, well I know,
　Which never can decay,—
That is, th' unchanging doom decreed
　To every dead man's sprite;—
Will, therefore, every noble deed,
　And do thou every right ! "

XXX.

His warnings thus gave hoary age
　In Bele's kingly hall,
As since the skald whose warnings sage
　Yet sound in Hávamál.

From race to race the proverbs go
    In pithy sentence forth,—
And deeply, from the tomb below,
    Yet whisper in the North.

XXXI.

Thereafter talked the heroes both,
    In many a heartfelt tone,
Of their long friendship's faithful troth
    Through all the Northland known,—
And how their true-fast union,
    In weal and woe the same
(Like two hands firmly grasp'd in one),
    More tight-knit still became.

XXXII.

" Our arms, my son, in danger's path,
    We back to back did wield;
However. then, came the norn's fierce wrath,
    Still struck she 'gainst the shield.
Before you now, with years bow'd down,
    We two to Valhal wend;—
But may our spirits, ye children, crown
    Each wish,—each step attend !"

XXXIII.

And much and long the king talk'd o'er
    The brave young Fridthjof's worth,

And warrior-might, which always more
　　Was priz'd than royal birth.
And much and long doth Thorstein praise
　　The Northland's high-fam'd kings,
And all that glorious fame whose blaze
　　From th' asas-heroes springs.

XXXIV.

" And now, together, as one man,
　　Hold fast, ye children three;
Your over-match — that know I — can
　　Our Northland never see!
For strength, to kingly rank and blood
　　Indissolubly bound,
Is like the dark blue steel-rim good,
　　Which flows the gold shield round.

XXXV.

" My last salute fail not to tell
　　Ing'borg, that rose fresh-blown;
In peace, as it became her well,
　　Her lovely form hath grown.
Hedge round the fair, let no storm-wind
　　Come down, in evil hour,
And to his helmet-bonnet bind
　　My tender blooming flower.

17

XXXVI.

"Helge! be thou her guardian,
　Thyself her father prove!
Ing'borg, my child, my dearest one,
　Oh, like a father love.
Constraint revolts the gen'rous soul,
　But, Helge, softness leads
Woman and man to virtue's goal,
　Just thoughts and noble deeds!

XXXVII.

"Beneath two barrows, in the earth,
　Lay us, ye children dear!
One on each side the billowy firth,
　Whose murmurs we may hear.
For pleasant to the hero's ghost
　Resounds the sea's low song;
Like soft, sad drapas* on the coast,
　The wavelets roll along.

XXXVIII.

"Pouring pale splendors round the hill,
　When bright the moon hath shone,
And midnight dews, all calm and still,
　Fall on the bauta-stone,— †
Then shall we sit, O Thorstein, there
　On our green cairns so round,

---

*Heroic, laudatory poems.　　　　†Grave-stone.

And, o'er the water's rush, declare
  How coming fates astound !

XXXIX.

"And now, ye sons, farewell!—-farewell!
  Hither no more draw nigh.
With great Allfather shall we dwell;—
  We long to be on high,
Like as the wearied flood-streams long
  To reach wide ocean's deep.
And now, Frey guard you, sons, from wrong,
  Thor bless, and Odin keep!"

CANTO III.

FRIDTHJOF SUCCEEDS TO HIS FATHER'S INHERITANCE.

SOFT now in th' earth were laid ag'd Thorstein and
    Bele his sovereign,
Where they themselves had bidd'n; one on each side the
    firth rose their barrows,
Shielding beneath their round two breasts, now death-
    sundered ever.
Halfdan and Helge then, as the people decreed, were
    successors
After their sire in the realm; but Fridthjof divided
    with no one;
Peaceful he heir'd, sole son to his father, and settled in
    Framness.
Far to the right, and the left, and behind his homestead
    ascended
Hills and low valleys and rocks, but its fourth side
    fronted the ocean.
Forests of birch crown'd the mountain-tops, while their
    sides smoothly sloping
Flourish'd with golden corn, and with man-high, bright-
    waving rye-crops.

Lakes full many their glitt'ring mirrors held to the
    mountain,

Held to the woods, too, above, in whose depths had high-
    branching elk-deer

Range as they royally trod, or drank of a hundred fresh
    streamlets.

Pasturing herds were seen in the valleys, cropping the
    greensward,

Or with sleek sides standing, and bags which long'd for
    the milk-pail.

'Mid them were spread, here and there o'er the mead-
    ows, white-woolly sheep flocks,

Wand'ring careless·and free; as (when soft winds herald
    the spring-time)

Heav'n's blue vault small far-scatter'd cloudlets flockwise
    besprinkle.

Rang'd in their stalls, like winds close fetter'd, and
    proud and impatient,

Pawing there stood twice twelve chain'd coursers, sweet
    grasses champing;

Knotted with red were their manes, and their hoofs
    shone brightly with steel shoes.

Wide, and a house by itself, was the drinking hall, built
    of tough heart-fir;

Not five hundred men (though ten twelves went to the
    hundred)

Fill'd that spacious hall, when at Yule they gathered to
    banquet.

Right through the hall's whole length ran the board, of
    scarlet oak timbers,

Polish'd and bright like steel; the two high-seat pillars
    of honor

Stood at its upper end, god-shapes both carv'd from hard
    elm-wood,

Odin with lord-like features, and Frey with the sun on
    his bonnet.

Lately, between them, thron'd on his bear hide, (th' hide
    was all coal-black,

Red like to scarlet its jaws, but the sharp claws shodded
    with silver,)

Thorstein sat there 'mong his friends, hospitality sitting
    with gladness!

Oft, while the moon flew along through the sky, th' old
    chief would tell, cheerly,

Marvels which out in strange lands he had seen, and his
    viking a-rovings

Far o'er the Baltic's waves, and the western seas, and
    in Gandvik.*

Mute sat the list'ng guests, their looks firm fixing on th'
    old man's

Lips, like the bee on its rose; but the skald thought,
    silent, on Brage

* The White Sea.

As, with silvery beard and runes on his tongue, he sits
    calmly

Telling, beneath some thick-spreading beech tree, a saga
    by Mimer's

Fount, whose waves ever murmur, himself a saga un-
    dying.

Midst, on the straw-strewn floor, shot the fire flame cease-
    lessly upward,

Glad in its stone-wall'd hearth; while down through the
    wide-stretching chimney

Heav'nly friends, blue twinkling stars, glanc'd bright on
    the hall guests.

But round the wall, on nails of hard steel, all in rows
    were suspended

Helmet and mail alternate,—while here and there from
    among them

Lighten'd a sword, as in winter ev'nings a shooting star
    lighteneth.

Yet, more bright than or helmet or sword, in the hall
    shone the war-shields,

Clear as the sun's bright orb or the pale moon's silvery
    surface.

Went there at times a fair maid round the board, up-
    filling the mead-horns;

Blush'd she, with downcast eye,—in the mirroring
    shield her image,

Even as she, blush'd too;—how it gladdened the deep-
    drinking champions!

Rich was the house; wherever thou lookedst, still met
    thy gazings

Close-filled cellars, and crowded presses, and well vic-
    tualed store-rooms.

Many a jewel there, too, was hidden, the booty of conquest,

Gold carv'd o'er with runes, and silver artfully graven.

Three things yet, among all this wealth, most precious
    were valued.

First of the three, that sword which from father to son
    went an heir-loom;

Angervadil the brand was hight, and the brother of
    lightning.

Forg'd had it been in some eastern land (saith ancient
    tradition),

Harden'd in dwarf-fires red; and at first Bjorn Blue-tooth
    had borne it.

Bjorn, nathless,* both the sword and his life lost soon at
    one venture—

Southward, in Groning's Sound, when he fought 'gainst
    the powerful Vifil.

Vifil had but one son, hight Viking.   Now, old and
    decrepit,

Dwelt there at Woolen Acre a king with a fair blooming
    daughter.

* Nathless, nevertheless

Just thereupon, from the wood's deep shades, came a grim-
    looking giant,

Taller by far than other men, and all hairy and savage;

Fierce from th' old chief, then, he combat claims, or his
    daughter and kingdom.

None could accept his challenge, for steel was not in the
    country

Edg'd that it bit on his iron-hard skull; so they nam'd
    him Grim Iron-head!

Viking alone, who his fifteenth winter newly had finish'd,

Brav'd the wild foe — on his arm and Angervadil depend-
    ing;

Then, at one blow, he the foul fiend clave, and the fair
    one delivered.

Viking to Thorstein, his son, this falchion gave; and from
    Thorstein

Went it to Fridthjof his heir. When in wide hall drawn
    it glitter'd

Like quick lightning flash there through, or a sky-stream-
    ing northlight.

Hammer'd gold was the hilt, but the blade was cover'd
    with runics

Wonderful, all unknown in the North, but known at the
    sun's gates —

There, where our fathers dwelt, till th' asas led them
    up hither.

Dead-pale flickered those runes, when blest peace rul'd in
    the country;
But, should Hild* begin her sport, then burn'd every letter
Red as the comb of the fighting-cock; quick lost was that
    hero
Meeting in battle's night that blade high-flaming with
    runics.
Widely renowned was the sword, of swords most choice
    in the Northland!
Next most precious in price was an *arm-ring*, all over
    famous;
Forg'd by the halting Volund 'twas, th' old North-story's
    Vulcan.
Three full marks weigh'd the ring, and of pure gold Vo-
    lund had wrought it.
Heav'n was grav'd thereupon, with the twelve immortals'
    strong castles —
Signs of the changing months, but the skald had sun-
    houses nam'd them.
Alfheim there was beheld, Frey's castle; the sun 'tis who,
    new-born,
Heav'n's steep heights slow 'ginneth to climb, uprising at
    Yule time.
Sokvabek also was there; in its hall sat Odin with Saga,
Drinking his wine from a golden bowl; that bowl is
    wide ocean

    * One of the valkyries, goddess of war.

Tinted with gold from morn's red beams; but Saga, the
    spring, is

Trac'd on the green-blooming plains with flow'rets, 'stead
    of with rune-marks.

Balder was also there on his throne, hot midsummer's
    sun, which

Down from the firmament pours rich beamings, of *goodness* the token;—

For in all *good* is streaming light, but *evil* in darkness.

Alway to tread, tires the sun in her course; and good-
    ness is like her,—

Soon turning giddy at such far heights; with a sigh, both
    wearied,

Sink to the land of the shades, Hel's home; 'tis Balder
    on death pile.

There, too, saw one the peace-fort, Glitner, where Forset'
    th' appeaser,

Balance in hand grave sat, the assize- and autumn-
    judge faultless.

These fair signs, and many thereto (light's conflicts be-
    tok'ning

Far o'er the sky's arch'd vault, and in each man's breast
    when he museth),

Th' artist had carv'd on the ring, while a splendid, firm-
    clasping ruby

Crowned its embracing round—as the bright sun crown-
    eth her heaven.

Long this ring had an heir-loom been, for the race
    reach'd backward,

Though by the mother's side great Volund reckon'd its
    founder.

Yet was this jewel once carried off by Sote, the pirate,

Who, o'er the north seas, pillaging rov'd, but afterward
    vanished.

Fame gave out, at the last, that Sote had buried in *Bret-*
    land

Ship and rich goods and live self on the coast, in his
    wall'd-about barrow;

But no rest found he there, and his cairn was ceaselessly
    haunted.

Thorstein, also, that rumor had heard, and with Bele, his
    friend-chief,

Climb'd his good dragon-ship, salt billows clove and steer'd
    to the cairn-strand.

Wide as a temple's arch, or some palace, firmly imbedded

'Mong hard gravel and verdant turf, upheap'd was the
    grave-mound.

Light from its depths shone out; through a chink of the
    doorway in-gazing,

Saw those champions the viking-ship well pitched and
    well fastened —

Anchors and yards and masts still secure; but a figure
    all grizzly

High on the stern was sitting, a blue-flame mantle about
    him,

Dreadful and grim; fierce-scour'd he the blood-stain'd
    blade he had wielded,

Yet could not its stains scour away; all the gold he had
    plunder'd

Lay heap'd up and about; himself on his arm bore the
    bracelet.

"Now," whisper'd Bele, "we'll straight go down and
    fight with the goblin,

Two against one fire-sprite!" But half-wroth answer'd
    him Thorstein:

"One 'gainst one was the use of our fathers; alone will
    I fight him!"

Long was it now contended which of the two should
    encounter

First that perilous foe; till at last took Bele his steel-
    helm,

Shook two lots, and decided the quarrel. Glimmering
    star-light

Show'd his lot to brave Thorstein again. At one blow
    of his iron-lance

Locks and strong bolts gave way. If a champion ques-
    tioned him ever

What in that night-gloomy deep he'd seen, he silently
    shudder'd.

Chantings wild heard Bele first, most like to a spell-song;

Then came loud-clashing sounds, as of swords cross'd
    fiercely in conflict;

Lastly a horrible scream. Then was silence. Out tot-
    tered Thorstein,

Stagg'ring, pale and confused — for with death, demon-
    death, had he battled.

Th' arm-ring yet grasped he tight; " 'Tis dear-bought,"
    often observed he.

" Once, but once in my life, I've trembled —'twas when I
    took it ! "

Widely renowned was that gem, of gems most choice in
    the Northland.

Lastly: the swift-winged *Ellide* rank'd 'mong the family
    treasures.

Viking, 'twas said, as he homeward return'd from a far-
    stretching foray,

Sailing along his coasts one day, saw a man on a ship-
    wreck,

Who yet merrily swung up and down, as sporting with
    ocean.

Tall was the man, and nobly formed, and his features
    were open,

Glad, and yet changeable, just like the sea when it plays
    in the sunshine;
Blue was his mantle; of gold his belt, set about with red
    corals;
White like to wave-foam flow'd his beard, but his hair
    floated sea-green.
Viking right to the spot steers his snail, and rescues him
    helpless;
Home to his halls then led he him shiv'ring, and feasted
    him nobly.
Yet, when his host bade him sleep in peace, light-smiling
    he answer'd:
" Fair is the wind, and my ship, as thou saw'st, is not to
    be slighted;
Full this night some hundreds of miles hope I well to
    sail forward.
Thanks, nathless, for thine offer; 'tis well meant; would
    that I only
Had some keepsake to give ; but my wealth lies deep
    'mong the sea-waves.
Yet on the shore some present, perchance, thou'lt find in
    the morning!"
There by daybreak was Viking, when lo! like a sea-eagle
    darting
Fierce on his prey through the air, flew a dragon-ship
    right in the haven!

None on board could be seen, not ev'n could a steersman
    be notic'd,
Yet trac'd the rudder its winding path 'mong the cliffs
    and sunk shoal-rocks —
Just as some spirit had dwelt therein. As it near'd the
    smooth beach-sand,
Reev'd of itself was the sail, no mortal touching the
    canvas;
Down to the bottom, too, sank the hook'd anchor, ocean's
    sands biting.
Mute stood Viking and gazed; but then sang the fresh-
    sporting billows:
"Æger, the rescued, forgets not his debt. See! he gives
    thee yon dragon!"
Royal the present was; for th' oak-beams, gently inbending,
Join'd were not—as is wont in a ship—but had grown
    all together.
Dragon-shap'd it lay on the sea; full high o'er the waters
Rose its proud head,' while its wide throat flam'd, with
    red gold thickly cover'd;
Speckled with yellow and blue was the belly; but back
    toward the rudder
Curv'd its strong-knit tail in a ring, all scaly with silver;
Black were its wings, with edgings of gold; when each
    one was full-stretch'd,

Flew she with th' whistling storm for a wager; but the
    eagle came after!

Saw'st thou the vessel with arm'd men fill'd, thou straight-
    way hadst fancied

Some king's city was floating past, or some quick-swim-
    ming fortress.

Widely renown'd was this ship, of ships most choice in
    the Northland!

These, and yet more thereto, young Fridthjof heir'd from
    his father.

Scarce through the North was there found an inheritance
    richer or larger,

Kings' sons only excepted — for kings are still the most
    mighty.

Yet, though not a king's son, was his temper kingly by
    nature —

Friendly, and noble, and gentle; thus daily grew he more
    famous.

Champions twelve, too, had he — gray-haired, and princes
    in exploits,—

Comrades his father had lov'd, steel-breasted and scarr'd
    o'er the forehead.

Last on the champions' bench, equal-ag'd with Fridthjof,
    a stripling

Sat, like a rose among wither'd leaves; Bjorn called they
    the hero —

18

Glad as a child, but firm like a man, and yet wise as a
 graybeard;

Up with Fridthjof he'd grown; they had mingled blood
 with each other,

Foster-brothers in Northman wise; and they swore to
 continue

Steadfast in weal and woe, each other revenging in battle.

Now 'mong his champions and crowding guests who had
 come to the grave-feast,

Fridthjof, a sorrowful host (his eyes full of fast-falling
 tear-drops),

Drank, as his sires had before, "to his father's mem'ry;"
 and thoughtful

Lists to the song of the skalds in his praise — their loud
 thund'ring drapa.

Then to his father's seat, now his own, stepp'd he boldly,
 and sat him

Down 'mid its Odin and Frey; that is Thor's own place
 up in Valhal!

CANTO IV.

FRIDTHJOF'S COURTSHIP.

I.

RIGHT well peals the song in the chieftain's hall,
  And skalds the high deeds of his sires recall;
But that song cheereth
Not Fridthjof; he heeds not the skald nor heareth.

II.

And th' earth is once more clad in waving green,
O'er the seas dragons swimming again are seen;
But war's son wanders
Thro' deep woods, and sad on the pale moon ponders.

III.

Yet late was he happy — so happy, so glad —
For cheerful king Halfdan as guest he had,
And Helge glooming,
And with them their sister brought they, the blooming.

IV.

He sat by her side, gently pressing her hand —
A pressure at times felt he back, warm and bland;
And still, enchanted,
Saw features so dear, so noble, so vaunted!

17

v.

Of those joyous days spoke they long with delight,
When morning's fresh dews still on life glitter'd bright;
Ere childhood closes
On scenes, in high souls, still fresh like group'd roses,

VI.

She playful salutes him from dale and from park,
From the names which grew on the birch-tree's bark,
And thence where flourish
(On the green hill planted) th' oaks heroes nourish.

VII.

"Over-pleasant the palace now scarce could appear,
For Halfdan was childish and Helge severe:
Those two kingly heirs,
They listen to nothing but praises and pray'rs.

VIII.

"And friend found she none (here she blush'd like a rose),
With whom her sad heart could its plaints repose;
The king's halls compare
To Hilding's free valleys,— how stifling they were!

IX.

"And the doves they had tam'd and fed day by day
Had fled, frighten'd off by the hawk, far away;—
All are bereft me,
But one pair alone;— take one of those left me.

X.

"Home, doubtless, again the sweet bird will fly,—
Sure longs she, like others, her friend to be nigh;
Runes kindly tender
Bind fast 'neath her wing; none marketh the sender."

XI.

So sat they, close whisp'ring the whole day through,
Still whisp'ring as close when toward ev'ning it grew:
When spring's day dieth —
So, whisper'd 'mong green lines, its soft breath sigheth.

XII.

But now is she absent, and Fridthjof's light heart
Is absent with her; his young blood, at the smart,
Mounts quick to his cheeks,
And he burns, and sighs alway, and never speaks.

XIII.

His sorrow, his grievings, he wrote by the dove,
And glad sped she off with the letter of love;
Alas! she never
Came back. From her mate she would not sever.

XIV.

But Bjorn was not pleas'd with such trifling as this.
"What is there," cried he, "our young eagle, amiss?
So silent, so tamed;
Has its breast been pierc'd through, or its strong wing
     lamed?

XV.

"What wilt thou? For have we not more than we need
Of rich, yellow bacon, and brown-foaming mead?
And bards, too—many
Drawl rhymes night and day—if thou lackest any?

XVI.

"'Tis true thy good courser paws fierce in his stall;
And for prey, for his prey, screams the falcon's wild call.
But Fridthjof getteth
Up cloudward to hunt, and sad-pining fretteth.

XVII.

"Ellide, too, now has no sport on the sea;
Now ceaseless her cable she jerks to get free,—
Ellide! still thee;
Fridthjof, the peaceful, no war-sport will thee!

XVIII.

"Who dies in his bed also dies; ere 'tis past,
My good spear, like Odin's, shall carve me at last,—
That cannot fail us;
Hel, then, the blue-white, will welcome and hail us!"

XIX.

Then Fridthjof his dragon's tight moorings set free,
And the sails filled fast,—loud snorted the sea;
Right over the bay
To the king's sons steer'd he his course through the spray.

XX.

On Bele's cairn sitting the kings he saw;
Their people they heard and judg'd after law;
But Fridthjof speaks out
With voice that is heard hills and dales round about:

XXI.

"Fair Ing'borg, ye kings, right dear is to me!
I ask her now from you, my own bride to be;
For doubtless Bele
Our long-foreseen union had sanction'd freely.

XXII.

"He let us grow calmly in Hilding's grove,
Like young trees up-shooting together above;
And love's Freyja bound
Their tops with gold twine rich-encircling them around.

XXIII.

"No king was my sire, not a jarl ev'n, 'tis true;
Yet skald-songs his mem'ry and exploits renew.
The rune-stones will tell
On high-vaulted cairn what my race hath done well.

XXIV.

"With ease could I win me both empire and land,—
But rather I stay on my forefathers' strand,
While arms I can wield;
Both poverty's hut and king's palace I'll shield.

XXV.

"On Bele's round barrow we stand, each word
In the dark deeps beneath us he hears, and has heard;
With Fridthjof pleadeth
The old chief in his cairn; think! your answer thought
  needeth!"

XXVI.

Then Helge rose up, and right scornful begun:
"Our sister is not for a peasant's son;
Proud Northland chiefs shall
Dispute, but not thou, for the daughter of Valhal.

XXVII.

"Boast on, that the Northmen their hero thee style,—
With hand-strength win men, with words women beguile:
But blood Odin-sprung
I never can give to an arrogant tongue!

XXVIII.

"My kingdom requires not thy service, I can
Protect it myself. Wouldst thou yet be my man,
A place I proffer
'Mong those of my household,—such can I offer!"

XXIX.

"I'll scarcely be _thy_ man," was Fridthjof's reply;
"Like my father, a man for myself am I
From thy silver slide
Fly, Angervadil! not a breath mayst thou bide!"

XXX.

The falchion's blue steel in the sun bright glanc'd,
And redly the runes on that flame-blade danc'd.
" Thou, Angervadil,
Thou, at least," said Fridthjof, " art high-born and noble.

XXXI.

"And, but for the peace this barrow should crown,
On the spot I'd hew thee, swarthy-king, down!
But dear 'twill cost thee,
Hereafter, too near my good sword to trust thee!"

XXXII.

This said, at one blow clove his battle-brand keen
Grim Helge's gold war-shield, as 't hung on the green;
It's halves straight follow,
Clashing the cairn; that crash downward sounds hollow.

XXXIII.

" Well struck, my good blade! Lie thou there now, and
     dream
Of exploits more noble — till then hide the gleam
Of rune-marked slaughter:
Now homeward we'll sail o'er the dark-blue water."

19

CANTO V.

KING RING.

I.

KING RING, he push'd back his gold chair from the
board,
  And his champions rise,
And skalds, and would hear from the North's fam'd lord
His kingly word;—
  Gentle was he as Balder, as Mimer wise.

II.

Like the gods' own groves, heard his land no alarm,
  Peace-shadow'd reposes;
Profan'd by no arms its green-wood so calm,
And hedg'd from harm
  Fresh flourish'd the grass, their sweets shed the roses.

III.

All alone Justice sat, at once mild and severe,
  On his seat of dooming;
And peace paid willing its debt ev'ry year;
And far and near,
  Bright-wav'd in the sunshine, gold corn-crops were
    blooming.

IV.

The snails, too, came swimming, with breasts of black,
   And wings stretch'd whitely,
From a hundred coasts, and from each far track
Wealth brought they back
   Various and wondrous, as wealth summons lightly.

V.

And peace in his domains, and liberty, dwell
   United and glad,
And all lov'd their country's father well,
Though each would tell
   At the diet, unfetter'd, what thoughts he had.

VI.

Thus peaceful and blest he his Northern throne fills
   For winters thrice ten;
And none ever angry went home to his hills,—
And nightly thrills
   Odin's hall with his people's benison.

VII.

And king Ring, he push'd back his gold chair from the
     board,
   And glad uptread
All his chiefs, and would hear from the North's fam'd lord
His kingly word:—
   But deeply he sigh'd, and then spoke and said:

VIII.

"In Folkvang's bow'rs sits my queen, I know,
 On purple cov'ring;
But here o'er her dust verdant grasses grow,
And, by the flow
 Of the stream round her grave-mound, flow'r-sweets
  are hov'ring.

IX.

"No queen shall I find so good and so fair,
 My kingdom's glory;
Valhal's rewards 'mong the gods she will share;
But my country's pray'r
 And my babes for a mother implore me.

X.

"King Bele right oft came up to my hall
 With summer's breezes;
On the daughter he's left my choice doth fall,—
That lily tall
 And slender, whose cheek still with morn's blush pleases.

XI.

"'Tis true that she's young; and girlhood, I know,
 Sweet flow'rs most weareth;
While I'm in my sear-leaf, and winters strow
E'en now their snow
 On the thin scatter'd locks the king beareth.

XII.

"But can she an upright, true man love,
　　Nor his white hairs reckon?
And to those dear infants a mother prove
Whose own's above,
　　To his throne autumn then the spring will beckon.

XIII.

"Take gold from the vault-rooms, take gems for the bride,
　　From yon strong oak-presses;
And follow, ye minstrels, with harpings of pride,—
For festive tide,
　　And wooing-hour, Brage still blesses!"

XIV.

Then out went the youths with glad tumult away,
　　With gold and with pray'rs,
And next came the harpers, in long array,
With chantings gay,
　　And stood before Bele's royal heirs.

XV.

Days two, ay! days three, were in wassail spent,
　　The fourth not endeth
Ere to Helge they call, on quick answer bent;
Rose up and went—
　　For each longing glances now homeward sendeth.

XVI.

Both falchion and horse offers Helge the king
    I' the grove leaf-laden —
Vala and pale priest questioning
What best might bring
    Happy fates to his sister, that fair young maiden.

XVII.

But the lungs, and the priest, and the vala show
    That it may not be;
Then, scar'd by the sign, Helge bade them go,
With changeless no!
    For man must obey when the gods decree.

XVIII.

But waggish king Halfdan, he said with a smile,
    "Farewell to the feast;
King Greybeard himself should have ridden a mile;
Myself, the while,
    Would the good old man gladly have holp on his beast."

XIX.

Then wroth go th' envoys with Helge's reply,
    Nor forget the story
Of Halfdan's insult. Ring answers them, dry,
" We soon shall try
    King Greybeard's revenge for his glory."

XX.

His war-shield he struck, as it hung o'er his head
  On the high-stained lind;
Then swift o'er the billows dragons tread,
With combs blood-red,
  And helmets fierce nod in the rushing wind.

XXI.

And the message of war to king Helge flew,
  Who mutter'd grimly,
"Hard fight shall we have, for Ring's men are not few;
But shelter due
  My sister shall find where Balder stands dimly."

XXII.

All pale sits the loving-one there, full of woe,
  On the blest dais stilly;
She broiders in silk and in gold also,
And tears o'erflow
  Her white-heav'd bosom,—dews so drench the lily!

CANTO VI.

FRIDTHJOF AT CHESS.

I.

BJORN and Fridthjof, both contending,
O'er their splendid board were bending;
 Now on silver squares thick gather,
 Now on gold, the struggling foes.
Then came Hilding, gladly greeted,—
"Welcome!—the high-chair waits, be seated!
 Drain thy horn, kind foster-father,
 Let our doubtful contest close."

II.

"Bele's sons," quoth Hilding, "send me;
Arm'd with pray'rs, to thee I wend me.
 Evil tidings round them hover,
 All the land on thee relies."
Answered Fridthjof: "Bjorn, in danger
Stands thy king! beware the stranger;
 Yet a pawn can all recover —
 Pawns were made for sacrifice."

III.

"Fridthjof, anger not the kings so;
Strong, remember, eaglets' wings grow.

Forces Ring full well despises,
Conquer yet, opposed to thine."
"Bjorn, the foe my castle craveth!
But th' attack with ease it braveth;
    Grim and high the fierce wall rises,
    Bright the shield-tow'r shines within."

IV.

"Ing'borg wastes the day in weeping,
Sad, tho' in Balder's sacred keeping;
    Tempts not war for her release, and
    Mourn unheeded her blue een?" *
"Bjorn, thou in vain my queen pursuest,
She from childhood dearest, truest!
    She's my game's most darling piece, and
    Come what will, I'll save my queen!"

V.

"What! not e'en reply conceded?
Fridthjof, go I thus unheeded?
    Till that child's-play yonder endeth
    Must my suit unheard remain?"
Fridthjof rose, and as h' addresses
The old man, kind his hand he presses:
    "Father, nought my firm soul bendeth;
    Thou hast heard, yet hear again:

* Eyes.

VI.

"Yes! my words take back unvarnished,—
Deeply they've my honor tarnished;
 No strong ties to them unite me,
 Never will I be their man."
"Well, in thine own path thou goest;
I blame *not* the rage thou showest.
 All for the best guide Odin rightly."
 So old Hilding's answer ran.

CANTO VII.

FRIDTHJOF'S BLISS.

I.

LET Bele's sons at pleasure wander
  From dale to dale for sword and shield;
Mine get they not; with Balder yonder
  Is all my world, my battle-field.
Proud king's revenge,— the wide earth's sadness,—
  I there will not look back upon,
But only drink the gods' own gladness,
  With Ing'borg in sweet union.

II.

Long as day's purple beam abideth
  Which, warm, the sun on flow'ret show'rs,—
That rose-stain'd gauze-web like which hideth
  My Ing'borg's bosom, world of flow'rs,
Consum'd by longings fierce, undying,—
  So long I stray upon the strand,
And with my sharp sword write, deep-sighing,
  That loved one's name upon its sand.

III.

How ling'ring go the tedious moments!
  Thou Delling's son, why dronest thou?

Thou, sure, hast seen the groves and mountains,
　　The sounds and islands, long ere now?
In western halls dwells no fond maiden
　　Who, long since, waits thy dawn above,
And then, to thy young breast flies, laden
　　Still first, still last, with tales of love?

IV.

At length thy toilsome route is over,
　　Thou sinkest to thine ocean-bed;
And eve, the gods' glad sports to cover,
　　Draws round her curtains rosy-red.
Earth's streams love-whisper to each other,
　　Heav'n's breezes whisper love's caress;
Hail! welcome, Night, the gods' own mother,
　　With pearls upon thy bridal dress.

V.

Those high, cold stars, how stilly glide they,
　　Fond lover like, on silent toe!
Ellide, fly o'er frith and tide-way,—
　　Shoot on, blue billow, faster go!
The white gods' grove-land yonder bloometh,
　　To the good gods our course is bound;
And 'neath there Balder's temple gloometh,
　　Love's goddess shelter'd in its round.

VI.

How blest I now the shore am treading!
 I glad could kiss thee, earth! and you,
Small flow'rs, the crook'd path quaintly threading
 With white and red, I'd glad kiss too!
Thou moon, who thus thy light-floods streamest
 Round grove and temple, cairn and tomb,
How fair thou sittest there and dreamest,
 Like saga in a· marriage-room!

VII.

My feelings' voice, sweet brook, who taught thee,
 As with those flow'rs thou whisp'rest low?
And, Northland's nightingale, who brought ye,
 Stol'n from my breast, that plaintive woe?
See! fairies paint with ev'ning's blushes
 My Ing'borg's shape on sky-cloth blue;
But envious Freyja forward rushes,
 And far hence blows each beauteous hue.

VIII.

But fade and welcome, airy semblance!
 Here comes herself, than hope more fair,
And faithful as is youth's remembrance;
 She comes—and love rewards my pray'r!
Come, dearest! let these arms inclose thee!—
 Come to this heart, with love on fire;

Come to my breast, and there repose thee,
   My life's bright star, my soul's desire!

IX.

Like lily-stalk thy frame is slender,
   Yet like ripe rose-bud full and free;
As th' gods' high will thou'rt pure, yet tender,
   And warm as Freyja's thought to be!
My fair one, kiss me! Let my passion
   Light kindred flamings in thy soul;—
Ah! at that kiss the round earth's fashion
   Has gone, yon heav'n's fires cease to roll!

X.

Nay, love! no perils here attend us!
   Bjorn and his champions, all in arms,
Stand there below, and would defend us,
   If need were, 'gainst a world's alarms;
Myself, how gladly thy defender!—
   I'd fight as now I clasp thee here;
How bless'd, bright Valhal would I enter,
   If *thou* wert my valkyrie!

XI.

Thou whisp'rest "Balder,"—his wrath fearest!
   That gentle god all anger flies.
We worship here a lover, dearest!
   Our heart's love is his sacrifice.

That god whose brow beams sunshine splendor,
  Whose faith lasts through eternity,—
Was not his love to beauteous Nanna
  As pure, as warm as mine to thee?

XII.

His image see!—himself broods o'er it,—
  How mild, how kind his bright eyes move!
An off'ring bear I here before it,
  A warm heart full of purest love.
Come, kneel with me! No altar-incense
  To Balder's soul more grateful is
Than two hearts vowing in his presence
  A mutual faith as true as his!

XIII.

To that far heav'n my love belongeth,
  More than this earth,—receive it then;
In heav'n 'twas nurtured, and it longeth
  To reach its starry home again.
How bless'd were he already yonder!
  How bless'd who now with thee could die,—
And, conqu'ring, 'mong the gods could wander
  Embracing his pale maid on high!

XIV.

Then, when from silver gates out riding,
  Its champions rush'd to war's fierce glee,—

Still at thy friendly side abiding
　　Should I be found,—still gaze on thee!
Did Valhal's blushing maids round proffer
　　The mead-horns, rich with foam of gold,
I thee alone would pledge, thee offer,
　　In gentle whispers, love untold.

XV.

A leaf-deck'd bow'r I there would build us,
　　Near some bold headland's dark-blue bay;
The deep grove's verdant shades would shield us,—
　　That grove whose gold-fruit blooms for aye!
When Valhal's sun flam'd up again (and
　　How dear, how lord-like is its glow!)
Back to the gods returned we then, and
　　Yet long'd we home again to go!

XVI.

Yes, there I'd crown with stars far-glancing
　　Thy brow and locks of waving light;
In Vingolf's hall I'd lead thee dancing,
　　Till rose-red blush'd my lily white!
Then, from the mazy course I led thee
　　To love's and peace's blissful bow'r,
Where silver-bearded Brage 'd wed thee
　　With bride-songs new each eve's soft hour.

XVII.

How, through the grove, the quail is screaming;
    That song is from high Valhal's strand.
How, o'er the sound, the moon is gleaming;
    He shines from out the spirits' land.
That song, that light, both herald truthful
    A world of love from sorrow free;
Ah! fain I'd see that world so youthful,
    With thee, my Ingeborg, with thee!

XVIII.

Nay, weep not! Life as yet red streameth
    Through these full veins! Oh, weep no more!
The dreams that love and proud youth dreameth
    So soon from earth up heav'nward soar.
Should once half op'd those pretty arms be,
    Once hither turn'd those loving eyes,
Entranc'd no more, my maid quick charms me
    Back from the glories of the skies! . . . .

XIX.

"The lark; hush!" No! those light-trill'd numbers
    Some cooing dove's fond faith exprest:
In grassy tuft the lark still slumbers,
    Close by its mate, in soft warm nest.
They, happy they! can love united
    At dawning as at closing day;

20

Through heaven's wide space they soar delighted,
   Not freer the wings that cleave their way. . . . .

XX.

"See! that's the dawn there!" No! dim streaming
   Some beacon's flame illumes yon east.
We yet can speak our hearts' fond dreaming,
   Not yet dear lovely night hath ceas'd.
O'ersleep thee, golden star, I pray, nor
   Make haste from thy long sleep to wake;
For Fridthjof mayst thou sleep all day, or —
   If so thou wilt — till Ragnarok!

XXI.

In vain! fresh dawn-streaks heav'n discloses,
   Morn's wind e'en now blows keen and bleak,
Already bud those eastern roses,
   Fresh like to those on Ing'borg's cheek.
Hark! sweet that feather'd song-troop twitters,
   Unthinking, in the bright'ning sky;
Existence moves, the billow glitters,
   And far the shades and lover fly!

XXII.

There comes she now in all her glory!
   Pardon me, golden sun, my pray'r;
I feel, I know, a god's before me —
   But yet how brilliant, oh! how fair!

Oh, happy he, who trod unclouded
  And valiant as thou treadest now;
And proud and glad his weak life shrouded
  In light and vict'ry — like as thou!

XXIII.

Behold! before thee, god of splendor,
  The fairest stands in all the North.
Become, bright sun, her strong defender —
  Thine image she on this green earth.
Her soul is pure as thine own lustre:
  Her eye, like thine own heaven. is blue;
And round.her forehead ringlets cluster
  Dyed in thine own dark-golden hue! . . . .

XXIV.

Farewell, my dearest! We each other
  Some longer night again shall see.
Farewell! — yet one kiss! Ah! another
  On those red lips accord to me!
Sleep now; and all these scenes dream over;
  At midday wake, and faithful tell
The hours, like me: Regret thy lover,
  And burn as I. Farewell! Farewell!

CANTO VIII.

THE PARTING.

INGEBORG.

IT dawns already; and still is Fridthjof absent!
Yet yester-sun beheld the thing proclaim'd
On Bele's cairn; that spot was chosen well,
For there his daughter's fate should be determin'd!
How many fond entreaties hath it cost me,
How many tears (by Freyja all up-reckon'd!)
Hate's icy wall to melt round Fridthjof's heart,
And tempt the promise from that proud one's mouth,
Again to stretch his hand in reconcilement!
Severe, alas, is man! and for his glory
(For so he calls his pride) but little recketh
If, rudely stepping, he should trample down
A faithful heart or two, all bruis'd and broken,—
Yes! clinging to his breast, weak, fragile woman,
Some moss-plant likens, whose pale tints creep o'er
The hard, bare rock, and there unseen, unmark'd,
Her painful hold scarce keeps of granite cliff,
Nurtur'd—sad food! by night's slow falling tears!
　　My fate, then, yesterday was fixed for ever,
And o'er it ev'ning's sun hath set already.

But Fridthjof comes not! All those pale stars yonder
Are one by one expiring, and are gone:
And, with each single star that morning quenches,
A hope my breast had nurtur'd dies away.
But, ah! why hope I longer? Valhal's gods
Love me not now, for I have anger'd them.
The lofty Balder, in whose shade I shelter,
Is injur'd,— for a passion earthly, human,
Can ne'er be pure enough for gods to look on!
No! never dare this world's vain joys intrude
Beneath those arches, where the reverend
And high superior pow'rs have fix'd their dwelling.
And yet my fault is — what? In virgin love!
What is 't that tender, gentle god displeases?
As Urd's clear crystal wave is 't not all pure,
And innocent as Gefiun's morning-dreamings?
Through heav'n advancing, yonder high-born sun
Her pure eye turns not from two loving hearts;
And day's sad widow, starry night, with joy
Listens, 'mid all her mourning, to their oaths;
Ah! how can innocence beneath heav'n's vault
Be construed crime beneath these temple arches?
'Tis true I Fridthjof love! Yes! long as mem'ry
Can stretch her records have I lov'd but him;
The twin of my existence is this feeling,—
I know not its commencement, nor can once

Conceive th' idea that it hath not been so.
The rip'ning fruit about its kernel sitteth,
And round its substance grows its bowl of gold,
Maturing slowly in the summer's sun;
I so have grown around that kernel-feeling
While rip'ning up to woman, and my life
Is only th' outward shell of my affection.
Forgive me, Balder!—with a faithful heart
Thy halls I enter'd, and when thence I go
Still faithful is it! Yes, it follows me
When Bifrost's bridge I traverse, boldly treading
With all my love before the gods of Valhal.
Bright shields his mirrors, shall he there stand forth
An asa-son as they, and with dove-wings
Unfetter'd take his course to whence he came.
The blue eternal space Allfather's bosom
For ever shelters. Nay, why frownest thou?
Why darkens Balder's brow 'mid morn's fresh dawning?
In these my veins, as in thine own, red rushes
Old Odin's blood; what wilt thou then, my kinsman?
My love I cannot, will not, sacrifice,—
For know, god! that thy lofty heav'n 'tis worthy;
But all my being's bliss I well can offer,
I that can cast far from me, as a queen
Her royal robes throws by and doffs her state,—
Nathless a queen as ever! Yes, 'tis done!

Never, O lofty Valhal, need'st thou blush
To own thy cousin. I go to meet my fate
As to meet his the hero. There comes Fridthjof!
How wild, how pale his looks! 'Tis past, 'tis o'er.
My wrathful norn there comes as his attendant.
Be strong, my soul! . . . Tho' late, yet welcome, Fridthjof!
Our fate is fix'd; upon thy brow 'tis written,
And all may read it.

FRIDTHJOF.

Are not blood-red runes
Carv'd deep, too, there — loud-speaking insult, shame,
Contempt and exile?

INGEBORG.

Fridthjof, come, bethink thee!
What happen'd, tell me; for the worst, long since,
I darkly boded. I'm prepar'd for all.

FRIDTHJOF.

I sought the diet, gathered at the barrow,
Round whose smooth grassy sides, shield joining shield,
And sword in hand, our North's brave warriors stood,
In rings within each other, till they reach'd
The summit. But upon the judgment-stone,
Like some dark thunder-cloud, thy brother sat,—
That pale bloodman with looks of dusky gloom;
And near him Halfdan, that fair, full-grown child,

Was seen, all thoughtless, playing with his sword.
Then stepp'd I forth and spoke: " War stands and strikes
His glitt'ring shield within thy boundaries;
Thy realm, king Helge, is in jeopardy;
But give thy sister, and I'll lend mine arm
Thy guard in battle. It may stead thee well!
Come! let this grudge between us be forgotten,
Unwilling bear I such 'gainst Ing'borg's brother.
Be counsel'd, king! Be just, and save at once
Thy golden crown and thy fair sister's heart!
Here is my hand,— by Asa-Thor I swear
Never again 'tis stretch'd in reconcilement!"
Then rose the thing* tumultuous. Thousand swords
On thousand shields loud hammer'd deaf'ning plaudits;
Up heav'nward flew the weapon-clang, and heav'n
Drank, glad, free men's assent to right, to justice,—
"Yes! give him Ing'borg, that fair, slender lily,
The loveliest ever grew in these our vales.
What swordsman in our land is like to him?
Ay! give him Ing'borg!" Then my foster-father
Old Hilding, with his silv'ry beard, uprose
And spoke right wisely many a weighty word
And pithy proverb, biting falchion-like.
Nay, Halfdan even, from his kingly seat
Upstanding, ask'd, with words and looks, consent.
In vain, in vain! But wasted was each prayer—

* Thing—diet.

Like sunshine lavish'd on the naked rock,
No harvest tempting from its barren bosom.
Thus cold, thus hard, was Helge's gloomy brow,
Still like itself—a chilling "No!" to mercy.
"The peasant's son," so, scornful glancing, spoke he,
"Might Ing'borg claim, but thou, the temple-forcer,
Art scarce, methinks, a match for Valhal's child.
Say, Fridthjof, Balder's peace hast thou not broken,
Not seen my sister in his house, while Day
Concealed himself, abash'd, before your meeting?
Speak! yea or nay!" Then echoed from the ring
Of crowded warriors, "Say but nay, say nay!
Thy simple word we'll trust; we'll court for thee,—
Thou, Thorstein's son, art good as any king's.
Say nay, say nay! and thine is Ingeborg!"
"The happiness," I answered, "of my life
On one word hangs; but fear not therefore, Helge!
I would not lie to gain the joys of Valhal,
Much less this earth's delights. I've seen thy sister,
Have spoken with her in the temple's night,
But have not, therefore, broken Balder's peace!"
More none would hear. A murmur of deep horror
The diet traversed; they who nearest stood
Drew back, as I had with the plague been smitten.
And, when I round me gaz'd, pale superstition
Had lam'd each tongue, and white-limn'd ev'ry cheek
21

But late with cheerful hope so brightly blooming.
Then conquer'd Helge. With a voice as hoarse
And gloomy as dead vala's, when to Odin
She sang, in Vegtamsqvida, how destruction
Should whelm his asas and how Hel should triumph,
So hoarse he spoke: "By our great father's laws
To banishment or death I could condemn thee
For this thy crime; but mild as is that Balder
Whose shrine thou insultedst shall my judgment be.
Far westward lieth, garlanding broad ocean
An isle group govern'd by jarl Angantyr.
His gold the jarl paid yearly in the days
Of Bele's reign, but now keeps back his tribute.
Away, then, o'er the sea! Collect the money —
This penance fix I for thy hardihood!
'Tis said," he added, with mean scoundrel-scorn,
"That Angantyr's hard-handed, and sits brooding
Like Fafner, that famed dragon, o'er his gold.
But who can face our Sigurd, bane of Fafner?
Now, an thou wilt an exploit dare, more manly
Than witching timid girls in Balder's grove.
Till summer breathe again, we'll here await thee
With all thy fame, and with the gold in special;
Else, Fridthjof, art thou doom'd a branded coward,
And exil'd all thy days from this our land!"
His verdict thus he gave, and clos'd the diet.

INGEBORG.

And thy resolve?

FRIDTHJOF.

What! have I then a choice?
Is not my honor bound to this demand?
Yes! it shall be redeem'd, though Angantyr
'Neath Nastrand's floods his paltry gold hath hidden
To-day, e'en, voyage I.

INGEBORG.

And leave thy Ing'borg?

FRIDTHJOF.

Leave thee, ah no! Thou sharest all my wand'rings.

INGEBORG.

Alas, I cannot!

FRIDTHJOF.

But hear me!—then reply!
Thy brother, in his wisdom, hath forgotten
That Angantyr was once my father's friend
As well as Bele's. With good will, perhaps,
He'll yield what I would have; but should he not,
A sharp persuader, pow'rful advocate,
Hangs here, my left side's ornament and strength.
The gold so dearly lov'd I'll send to Helge,
And thus will free us both, at once, forever,
From that crown'd hypocrite's red off'ring-knife.

Ourselves, fair Ing'borg, will Ellide's sails
O'er unknown waves expand. She'll bound along
And bear us to some far-off, friendly strand,
A safe asylum for our outlaw'd love.
This North—what boots it me? What boots a people
That pale at ev'ry word their diar* speak?
They would, with daring hand, my heart-hopes dash,
The blooming flow'r-cup of my very being;
I swear by Freyja that it shall not be!
A wretched thrall is fasten'd to the sod
Where first he grew; but I will be a freeman,
Free as the mountain-breezes,—one handful
Of dust from Thorstein's grave, and one from Bele's,
Will yet find room on shipboard; that is all
We want or ask from this our foster-earth.
A sun far brighter shall we find, my dearest,
Than this which shines so pale on cliffs of snow;
A sky more beautiful than this will hail us,
Whose mild soft stars with heav'nly glance look down.
In warm-breath'd summer night, on many a pair
Of faithful lovers sate in laurel-groves.
My father, Thorstein, Viking's son, far wander'd
On sea-king exploits, and full oft beguil'd
Long winter-ev'nings by the blazing hearth
With tales of Greekland's† ocean, where fair islands

* Icel. *diar*, pl. gods or priests; here priests. The word occurs only
twice in the Old Norse literature. (American editors.)
† Greece.

Like green groves rise from out the laughing wave.
Of old a mighty race lived there, and gods
Still mightier dwelt in marble sanctuaries.
Now stand they desolate; wild luxuriant herbage
O'erspreads their lonely avenues, flow'rs shoot
From runes which speak of wise antiquity,
And rich-curled tendrils of the vineyard south
Slim columns circle with their green embrace.
But round these ruins, in unsown harvest-crops,
Gives th' untouch'd earth all man can want or wish;
While fresh leaves glow with clust'ring golden apples,
And bending boughs full purple grapes weigh down,
All tempting, rich and juicy as — thy lips!
There, Ing'borg, 'mid that sea's bright waves we'll 'stablish
A little North, more beautiful than this;
Those slender temple-arches will we fill
With faithful love, and entertain again
Forgotten gods with human happiness.
Should loose-sail'd bark float slowly past our isle
(For storms have there no home-land) in the blush
Of eve's soft light, while some glad mariner
Looks out from rose-dyed billows to the shore,
He then shall view, within the temple's threshold,
That other Freyja (in their speech methinks
She's Aphrodite hight), and, wond'ring, see
Her golden locks light-flutt'ring in the zephyr,

And eyes more bright than brightest southern skies!
As years roll by shall slow shoot up around her
A little temple-race of fairy creatures,
With cheeks where, 'mong the North's snow-drifts, the South
Would seem t' have planted ev'ry freshest rose!
Ah! Ing'borg, ah! how fair, how near, how tempting
Stands all earth's joy to two fond faithful hearts!
Yes! have they courage close to grasp her to them —
She willing follows and a Vingolf builds us
Already here, beneath the fleeting clouds.
Come, dearest, haste thee! Ev'ry word we utter
Is one more moment stolen from our bliss.
Come, all's prepar'd. Ellide spreads, impatient,
Dark eagle-wings for flight; and fresh'ning breezes
Point out the path, forever, from a strand
Where gloomy fears hold awful sway around. . . . .
But why delay?

INGEBORG.

I cannot follow thee.

FRIDTHJOF.

Not follow? Not——

INGEBORG.

Ah, Fridthjof, thou art happy!
Thou follow'st none, but art thyself the foremost,
Like thy good dragon-ship's high-lifted stem;
While at the rudder stands thy will, and steers

Thy course with steady hand o'er angry waves.

How otherwise, alas! it is with Ing'borg!

In other's hands my fate reposes, and

Their prey they slip not, bleed it as it will!

Self-sacrifice, and tears, and languishing,

And wasting grief — such the king's daughter's freedom!

FRIDTHJOF.

What hinders, then, thy freedom? Bele sits

Within his cairn!

INGEBORG.

My father's Helge, now;

He holds my father's place, and his consent

Decides my hand. No! Bele's daughter steals not

Her happiness, however near it be.

Ah! what were woman, should she burst those bonds

With which Allfather fastens to the strong

Her weak existence? Some pale water-lily

She likens, as on ev'ry light-moved wave

It rises; trembles, falls; and o'er its head

The seaman's keel its reckless way pursueth,

Nor marks that it cuts through her stalk so slender.

Such is that lily's destiny; but still,

Long as the sands beneath her deep root grasps,

The plant her value hath, and borrows dyes

From pale relation-stars above, itself

A star soft-floating on the billowy blue.

Ah! should she struggle loose, away she drives,

A wither'd leaf around the desert waters.

The night just gone — that night how fearful was it!

I waited thee expectant, and thou cam'st not;

And night's dark children — gloomy, black-hair'd thoughts,

In long procession pass'd before mine eye,

All watchful, burning, and without a tear;

Nay, Balder's self, the bloodless god, beheld me

With looks of threat'ning and an angry mien:

The night just gone, my fate I've well consider'd,

And firm resolv'd t' abide it. I remain

A duteous off'ring at my brother's altar.

And yet 'twas well I heard not, then, thy story

Of islands fabled in the gorgeous clouds,

Where evening's blush is spread unceasing over

A quiet flower-world, full of peace and love.

Who knows his own heart's weakness? Childhood's
        dreamings,

So long all silent, now once more rise up,

Low-whisp'ring in mine ear, with voice familiar

As 'twere a sister's, and as soft and tender

As some fond lover's when he courts his maid

I hear you not; I cannot, will not hear you,

Ye tempting voices, once so dearly lov'd.

What would the South with me, the Northland's daughter?

Too pale am I for all its rose-retreats;
Its burning sun would parch a soul as mine —
Too cold and hueless for its glowing rays.
Yes! full of longing would mine eye turn often
To yonder pole-star, ever steadfast standing
A heavenly sentinel o'er our fathers' graves.
My noble Fridthjof, born his land's defender,
Shall never flee inglorious from its shores;
His dear-bought fame shall never cast behind him
For aught so worthless as a young girl's love!
A life whose golden-threaded days the sun
Spins year from year the same, is beautiful;
But this eternal oneness woman's soul
Alone can please; to man, and most to thee,
Life's changeless calm is changeless weariness.
Then joys thy proud soul, when the tumbling tempest
On foaming courser sweeps o'er ocean's deeps,
That so, for life or death, on thin plank riding,
Thou mayst contend with danger for thine honor.
The beauteous wilderness thou paintest, would,
Too, many an unborn exploit slow entomb;
And, with thy shield, thy glad, free, dauntless spirit
Dark rust would gnaw. But it shall not be so!
Not I, at least, my Fridthjof's name will steal
From bard-harp'd songs; not I, at least, will quench
My hero's glory in its first red dawn.

Be wise, dear Fridthjof; heav'n's dread lofty norns
Command; let us give way; at least our honor
May still be sav'd from out our fortunes' shipwreck —
For ah! our life's chief bliss is gone forever!
We must, *must* part!

FRIDTHJOF.

    Nay! wherefore must we? Is't
For that a sleepless night untunes thy spirit?

INGEBORG.

'Tis that my worth and thine must both be rescued!

FRIDTHJOF.

On man's firm love rests woman's dearest value!

INGEBORG.

Not long he loves whom he esteems no more.

FRIDTHJOF.

Can his esteem, then, light caprices purchase?

INGEBORG.

Caprice! a noble one — the sense of duty!

FRIDTHJOF.

But yesterday our love was still most righteous.

INGEBORG.

Nor less to-day: the more would flight be crime.

FRIDTHJOF.

Necessity invites us ; come, no more!

INGEBORG.

Necessity is what is right and noble!

FRIDTHJOF.

The sun high riseth. Come! our time goes quickly.

INGEBORG.

Alas! 'tis gone already — gone forever!

FRIDTHJOF.

Once more, consider! was that word thy last?

INGEBORG.

All *well* have I considered — 'tis my last.

FRIDTHJOF.

Then, Helge's sister, fare thee well! adieu!

INGEBORG.

Oh, Fridthjof, Fridthjof, is it thus we part?
What! hast thou not *one* friendly look to give
Thy childhood's friend? Hast thou no hand to stretch
Toward her, unfortunate, who once was loved?
Think'st thou I rest on roses here, and motion
My whole life's bliss away, and coldly smile?
From this torn bosom can I rend a hope
Grown with my very being, and feel no pang?

Ah! wast not thou my heart's first morning-dream?
Whatever joy I knew, I called it Fridthjof;
And all that life holds great, or good, or noble,
Put on thy features to my youthful eye.
Dim not this glowing image, nor repay
Thus sternly woman's weakness, when she offers
Whatever on this earth *was* dearest to her,—
Whate'er in Valhal's halls will dearest prove.
Enough, O Fridthjof, has that off'ring cost me,
And well deserves one word of tender comfort.
I know thou lov'st me: I have known it long,
E'en since first 'gan to dawn my young existence;
And, year on year, where'er afar thou rovest,
Thy Ing'borg's mem'ry must, will, follow thee!
But loud-clash'd arms still ease the pangs of sorrow,—
Yes! far, far ocean's wild fierce tumult drives her;
Nor dares she, timid, sit on champion's bench
'Mong wine, and healths, and songs of victory.
But yet at times. whene'er in deadest night,
Thou must rest in their order days long fled,—
One pallid form will slow glide in among them;
Thou know'st it well, saluting thee from regions
Far off. but dear: 'tis that pale virgin's image
Whom holy Balder in his temple guards.
Thou mayst not. dearest! must not, turn away.
From that sad phantom's features. No! low whisper

Some friendly word in greeting! Night's faint winds
On faithful wings that word will carry me;
One comfort left, my last, mine only one!
My loss, alas! naught here can dissipate;
All, all around me is its guardian!
These high-arch'd temple-vaults speak thee alone,
And, bright with moonlight rays, the god's own image
Thy features takes, instead of threat'ning gloom.
Should yonder sea attract,— there swam thy keel,
Its path swift cutting to the longing Ing'borg;
Should yonder grove,— there many a tree uprises
Whose tender bark with Ing'borg's name was carv'd,—
That name, alas! the growing bark slow covers,
And this, tradition saith, betok'neth death!
Where last he saw thee, bright-eyed day, I ask,—
Where last, the night; but both are silent; nay,
The very sea, which carries thee, replies
With naught but sighs half-utter'd to the shore.
With ev'ning's blush I'll greet thee, when 'tis quench'd
In those thy billows; and heav'n's swiftest vessel,
The long-stretch'd cloud, shall never flit above me —
But freighted with the poor forsaken's grief!
Thus, seated in my maiden-bow'r, I'll hold me
The black-clad widow of my life's delights;
There in my web I'll broken lilies broider,
Till spring his cloth shall weave, embroidering

Its woof with fairer lilies on — my grave.

But touch I my sweet harp in songs lamenting

My grief in all its deep-ton'd bitterness,

Fast-flowing tears will then, as now ——

FRIDTHJOF.

Thou conqu'rest, Bele's daughter; weep no more!

Forgive mine anger; 'twas my sorrow only

Disguis'd one moment in the dress of wrath,

A dress it cannot wear beyond a moment.

My own good norn thou art, my Ing'borg; yes!

What noble is, a noble mind best teaches;

The wisdom of necessity can have

No advocate more eloquent than thou,

My beauteous vala, with thy rosy lips!

Yes! I will yield to dire necessity,—

Will part from thee, but never from my hope,

I take that with me o'er the western waters;

I take that with me to the gates of death!

Next spring, I trust, again shall see me here;

King Helge yet again shall meet his foe.

My promise then performed, his claim fulfill'd,

And that great crime aton'd I'm charg'd withal;

I'll ask thy hand,—nay, boldly will demand it

In open council, 'mid the glitt'ring steel,

And not from Helge, but the North's free people,

For they, king's daughter, can dispose of thee —

Let him deny who dares, and hears my reason.
Till then, farewell!   Forget me never; and,
In sweet remembrance of our youthful love,
This arm-ring take, a fair Volunder-work,
With all heav'n's wonders carv'd i' th' shining gold.
Ah! the best wonder is a faithful heart. . . . .
How prettily becomes it thy white arm —
A glow-worm twining round a lily-stem. . . . .
Farewell, my bride! my best belov'd, farewell!
A few short months, and — Oh! how diff'rent then! [*Goes.*]

INGEBORG.

How glad, how daring-all, how full of hope!
His good sword pointing to the norn's fair bosom,
"Thou shalt," saith he, "thou shalt give way."   Alas!
The stern norn, my poor Fridthjof, yields to no one;
Right on she goes, and laughs at Angervadil!
My gloomy brother, ah! how little know'st thou!
Never can thy frank hero-spirit fathom
His dark soul's depths, and all that envious hatred
Which burns and smoulders in his remorseless breast.
His sister's hand he'll never give thee.   Sooner
He'd give his crown, his life, to wild destruction,
And offer *me* t' old Odin, or t' old Ring,
That hoary chief whom now he battles sore.

        *   *   *   *   *
Where'er I look, no hope remains for me,

Yet glad I see thy heart still keep the stranger;
Myself alone shall know my grief, my danger;
But oh! may all good gods attend on thee!
On this, thine arm-ring, may I yet count over
Each sep'rate month of tedious, fretting pain;
One, two, four, six — then perhaps returns the rover,
But — ne'er to find his Ingeborg again!

CANTO IX.

INGEBORG'S LAMENT.

I.

SUMMER is past,
 Ocean's broad bosom's upheav'd by the blast;
Yet oh, how gladly out yonder
Far would I wander!

II.

Long did I view
Westward his sail on the wave as it flew;
Sail, ah, how bless'd! that abideth
Still where he rideth.

III.

Swell not so high,
Billow of blue; fast enough he sweeps by.
Guide him, ye stars! In his danger
Shine on the stranger.

IV.

When, in the spring,
Homeward he hastens, no Ing'borg will bring
Welcomes i' th' valley to meet him,
Hall-words to greet him.

22

V.

Deep under ground,
Pallid and cold for her love she is found!
Or, a sad victim, her brothers
Give her to others.

VI.

Mine shalt thou be,
Hawk he forgot; yes, I'll love as did he;
Ing'borg will feed thee, through endless
Skies hunting friendless.

VII.

Here, on his hand,
Work I thy form on the cloth's broad band:
Pinions of silver and glowing
Gold-talons sewing.

VIII.

Freyja one day
Falcon-wings took, and through space hied away;
Northward and southward she sought her
Dearly-loved Oder.

IX.

Ah! could I wear
Thine, they, alas! would not carry me there;
Wings like the gods', to the lonely,
Death giveth only.

X.

Pretty one! keep
Fix'd on my shoulder, and gaze on the deep;
Gaze we and long as we will, no
Keel cleaves the billow.

XI.

When I am dead,
Doubtless returns he; then mind what I said:
Fridthjof, whose tears will bewail me,
Hail me, ah! hail me!

CANTO X.

FRIDTHJOF AT SEA.

I.

B UT, wood * and afeard
Helge stood on the shore,
To the goblin so weird
Dark spells mutt'ring o'er.

See! heav'n's vault now clouds are treading;
Crashing thunders Ran's wastes sweep,
Fast her boiling waves are spreading,
Sparkling froth o'er all the deep.
See! i' th' sky red lightnings fasten
Here and there a bloody band;
Ocean's sea-birds, frighten'd, hasten,
Harshly screaming, to the strand,—

"Desp'rate weather, comrades!
Hark! the storm I hear a-
Far his pinions flapping,—
·But we grow not pale:
Sit in peace with Balder,

---

* Wood — an obsolete word, allied to the German *wuth*, and meaning mad, furious — See Webster's Dictionary, *sub voce.*

Think of me and long!—Oh,
Beauteous in thy sorrow,
Beauteous Ingeborg!"

II.

'Gainst Ellide came
    Of trolls a grim pair;
'Twas the wind-cold Ham,
    'Twas Hejd with snow-hair.

Then the storm unfetter'd wingeth
    Wild his course; in ocean's foam
Now he dips him, now up-swingeth,
    Whirling toward the god's own home:
Rides each horror-spirit, warning,
    High upon the topmost wave—
Up from out the white, vast, yawning,
    Bottomless, unfathom'd grave.

"Fairer was our voyage,
    Moonlight glitt'ring round us,
O'er the mirroring billows
    Hence to Balder's grove:
Warmer than 'tis here, my
, Ing'borg's heart was beating,—
    Whiter than the sea-foam
Swell'd her bosom then!"

III.

Now, Solund's Isles see
    'Mong white breakers stand;—
There all calm the waves be,
    There's your port, steer to land!
But the dauntless˙ viking fears not
    On his true-fast oak so soon;
Hard the helm he grasps, and hears not,
    But with joy, winds sport aboon.
Tighter still the sail he stretches,
    Faster still he cuts his way,—
Westward, west, due west, he fetches,
    Rush the billow as it may!

    " Fain one moment longer
    Fierce I'd fight the tempest;
    Storms and Norsemen flourish
    Well together here.
    For a gust to landward,
    Should her ocean-eagle,
    Fearful, feebly flutter—
    How would Ing'borg blush!"

IV.

But each wave's now a˙ hill,
    Down yet deeper they reel,
Blasts in cordage sing shrill,—
    Strains the grating keel:

Yet howe'er the surges wrestle,
  Whether for or 'gainst they rise,—
Still Ellide, god-built vessel,
  All their angry threats defies,
Like some star-shoot in the gloaming,
  Glad she bounds along, and leaps
Goat-like o'er rough mountains roaming,
  Now o'er heights and now o'er deeps!

    " Better felt soft kisses
    From my bride with Balder,
    Than, as here I stand, to
    Taste this up-thrown brine.
    Better 'twas t' encircle
    Ing'borg's waist so slender,
    Than, as here, tight-clasping
    This hard rudder bar!"

          v.

    But the snow-big cloud
      Icy knife-gusts pours;
    And on deck, shield, shroud,
      Clatter hailstone showers;
And from stem to stern on board her,
  Naught thou canst for night descry,
Dark 'tis there, as in that chamber
  Where the dead imprisoned lie.

Down 'mid whirlpool-horror dashes
　　Th' implacable bedevil'd wave;
While gray-white, as strown with ashes,
　　Gapes one endless, soundless grave.

　　　"Ran our beds of blue is
　　　Spreading 'mong the billows,
　　　But for me is waiting
　　　Thy bed, Ingeborg!
　　　Yes! stout-hearted fellows
　　　Lift thy oars, Ellide,
　　　Gods thy good keel builded,—
　　　Yet awhile we'll swim!"

　　　　　　VI.

　　O'er the starboard broke
　　　　Now a mountain-sea,
　　And with whelming stroke
　　　　Swept her deck all free.

Fridthjof then his armlet taking
　　(Three marks weigh'd it, and was old
Bele's gift, nor morn's awaking
　　Sun outshone its fine-wrought gold),
Quick the dwarf-carv'd ring in pieces
　　Hews relentless with his sword,
And, the fragments sharing, misses
　　None of all his line on board.

"Gold, on sweetheart ramblings,
Pow'rful is and pleasant;
Who goes empty-handed
Down to sea-blue Ran,
Cold her kisses strike, and
Fleeting her embrace is —
But we, ocean's bride be-
Trothe with purest gold!"

VII.

Threat'ning still his worst,
   Roars the storm again;
Quick the sheet is burst,
   Snaps the yard in twain.

'Gainst th' half-buried ship, commotion-
   Toss'd high waves to boarding go;
And howe'er they bale, is ocean
   Not so soon bal'd out, we know!
Not e'en Fridthjof now doubts longer
   That he carries death on board;
Yet than storm or billow stronger,
   Higher sounds his lordly word:

"Hither Bjorn! the rudder
Grasp with *bear-paw** strongly;
Valhal's pow'rs sure send not
Weather such as this;

* A pun on the name Bjorn, which means *bear*.
23

Witchcraft's workings! Helge,
Coward-scoundrel, doubtless
Conjured has these billows,—
I will up and see!"

VIII.

Like marten he flew
    Up the bending mast;
And there, fast-clinging, threw
    Many a glance o'er the waste.
Look! as isle that loose-torn drifteth,
    Stops that whale Ellide's way;
Sea-fiends two the monster lifteth
    High on's back, through boiling spray;
Hejd* is wrapp'd in snowy cov'ring,
    Fashion'd like the white-furr'd bear,—
Ham,* 'mid whistling winds, grim, hov'ring,
    Storm-bird like assaults the air.

"Now, Ellide! show us
Whether, as 'tis boasted,
Hero-mood thy iron-fast
Round oak-bosom holds!
Listen! art thou truly
Æger's god-sprung daughter,
Up with copper-keel, and
Gore that spell-charm'd whale!"

* Hejd and Ham are the names of the two witches.

IX.

And Ellide hears
    Her young lord's behest,—
With one bound-gulf clears
    To the troll-whale's breast.

From the wound a stream out-gushes,
    Up toward heav'n, of smoking blood;
And, gashed through, the beast down-rushes,
    Roaring, to the deepest mud;
Then, at once, the hero slingeth
    Two sharp spears; one the ice-bear's hide
Pierceth, the other deadly springeth
    Through yon pitch-black eagle's side.

    " Bravely struck, Ellide!
    Not so soon will Helge's
    Dragon-ship leap upward
    Out from bloody mud;
    Hejd nor Ham much longer
    The up-toss'd sea will keep, for
    Bitter 'tis to bite the
    Hard blue-shining steel."

X.

And the storm — it had fled
    At once from the sea;
Only ground-swells led
    To the isle on their lea.

And at once the sun fresh treadeth,
  Monarch-like, in hall of blue;
Joy o'er ship and wave he spreadeth,
  Hill and dale creates anew.
Sunset's beamings crown with gold the
  Craggy rock and grove-dark plain;
All with glad surprise behold the
  Shores of Efjesund again.

  "Ing'borg's prayers — pale maidens
  Up to Valhal rising —
  Lily-white, on heav'n's own
  Gold-floors bent the knee?
  Tears in light-blue eyes, and
  Sighs from swan-down bosoms,
  Th' asas' stern hearts melted,—
  Thank, then, thank the gods!"

XI.

But Ellide rose
  Sore jarred by the whale,
And water-logg'd goes,
  All awear'd by her sail.

Yet more wearied than their dragon,
  Totter Fridthjof's gallant men;
Though each leans upon his weapon,
  Scarcely upright stand they then.

Bjorn on powerful shoulder dareth
  Four to carry to the land;
Fridthjof, all alone, eight beareth —
  Sets them so round th' upblaz'd brand.

    "Nay, ye white-faced, shame not!
    Waves are mighty vikings;
    Hard's th' unequal struggle —
    Ocean's maids our foes.
    See! there comes the mead-horn,
    Wand'ring on bright gold-foot;
    Shipmates, cold limbs warm, and —
    Here's to Ingeborg!"

CANTO XI.

FRIDTHJOF AT THE COURT OF ANGANTYR.

I.

NOW say we, ocean quitting,
　　How Angantyr was then
Within his fir-hall sitting
　　At wassail with his men.
Right glad he was, and bended
　　His eye blue waves upon,
Where evening's sun descended
　　All like a golden swan.

II.

Outside the window chances
　　Old Halvar watch to be;
Right earnest were his glances—
　　The mead, too, guarded he:
One custom miss'd he never—
　　To scan the bottom o'er,
And then, in silence, ever
　　The horn thrust in for more.

III.

Now far i' th' hall, loud rattling,
　　His empty horn he threw,

And cried: "'Gainst storm-waves battling
    A ship at hand I view;
On board half-dead they tarry,
    Now come they to the land,
And two tall giants carry
    The pale ones to the strand."

IV.

The jarl's keen gazings wander
    Where bright waves mirroring flow:
"Ellide's sail is yonder,
    And Fridthjof's there, I trow;
His gait and brow discover
    Again old Thorstein's son,—
Search all the Northland over,
    Ye'll ne'er find such a one!"

V.

Then berserk Atle springeth,
    Fierce-grinning, from his place
(Blood-stain'd, his black beard flingeth
    Brute grimness o'er his face),
And screams, "I'll prove the saying
    That Fridthjof, all his days,
Unnerves the sword from slaying,
    Nor e'er for quarter prays."

VI.

And up with him all eager
    His twelve dread champions spring;
Impatient th' air they dagger
    And sword and bill-axe swing.
Then coastward storm'd they, heated,
    To where the dragon lay,
And Fridthjof, careless seated,
    Full stoutly talk'd away.

VII.

"Right well I now could kill thee,"
    With shouts 'gan Atle cry;
"Thou yet mayst either will thee
    To battle here or fly:
But if for peace thou prayest,
    Though champion hard and bold,
Through me the jarl thou mayest
    In friendly guise behold!"

VIII.

Said Fridthjof: "With my voyage
    I'm spent, 'tis true,—yet may
Our falchions prove our courage
    Ere peace from thee I pray!"
Then steel full soon did lighten
    In sun-brown champion hand,

And quick its flame-runes brighten
On Fridthjof's sharp-tongu'd brand.

IX.

Fast now are sword-thrusts given,
And death-blows hail around;
At once fly both shields, riven
In halves, upon the ground.
Their fight's uncensurable,
They firm their circle tread,
But keen bit Angervadil
And straight broke Atle's blade.

X.

"My sword," said Fridthjof, "never
'Gainst swordless man I wave;
But an thou wilt, however,
A diff'rent sport we'll have."
Then storm they, nothing yielded,
Two autumn billows like!
And oft, with steel round shielded,
Their jarring breasts fierce strike.

XI.

All like two bears they wrestle
On hills of snow, and draw
And strain, each like an eagle
On the angry sea at war.

The root-fast rock resisted
   Full hardly them between,
And green iron-oaks down twisted
   With lesser pulls have been.

XII.

From each broad brow sweat rushes,
   Their bosoms coldly heave,
And stones and mounds and bushes
   Dints hundredfold receive.
With awe its close abide the
   Men steel-clad on the strand;
That wrestling-match was widely
   Renown'd in Northern land.

XIII.

At last to th' earth down-reeling
   Has Fridthjof fell'd his foe,
And 'gainst his bosom kneeling,
   Fierce words succeed the blow;
"If but my sword I brandish'd,
   O swarthy berserk-beard,
Its point ere now, base vanquish'd,
   Had through thy back appear'd!"

XIV.

"Let not that hindrance 'larm thee,"
   Grim Atle proudly cried;

"Go! with thy rune-blade arm thee,—
   I'll lie as I have lain.
We both at last must wander
   Bright Valhal's halls to view;
To-day can I go yonder,
   To-morrow haply you."

XV.

And long pause Fridthjof made not,
   That play he finish will;
He Angervadil stay'd not,
   But Atle yet lay still.
Whereat, his heart relenting,
   He quick held in his brand,
And checked his wrath, presenting
   The fallen foe his hand.

XVI.

Now Halvar warn'd right loudly,
   And raised his wand of white:
"This fray ye sport so proudly
   Here causeth no delight.
High-smoking long have gold and
   Fair silver dishes stood;
The savory meats grow cold, and
   My thirst doth me no good."

XVII.

Appeas'd, each now advances
 Within the jarl's hall door,
And much meets Fridthjof's glances
 He ne'er had seen before.
The bare walls from the weather
 No rough-plan'd planks protect,
But precious rich-gilt leather,
 With fruits and flowers bedeck'd.

XVIII.

There midst the floor ascended
 No blazing hearth-fire's light,
But 'gainst the wall was bended
 The marble chimney bright.
No smoke the dark roof tarnished,
 No soot the beams o'ercast;
Glass panes the windows garnished,
 And locks the door held fast.

XIX.

There many a candle brightened
 From silver arms; no torch
With crackling blaze enlighten'd
 The champions' rude debauch.
Whole-roast, rich odors flinging,
 A stag the board adorns,

Its gold-hoof raised for springing,
   And leaf'd its grove-like horns.

XX.

Behind each chief, a virgin
   Stands up, with lily dye,
Just like some star emerging
   From out a stormy sky;
Each step brown locks discloses,
   Clear sparkle eyes of blue,
And, like to rune-sprung roses,
   Small lips bud forth to view.

XXI.

But high, right kingly seeming,
   Sat th' jarl in silver chair,
His helm with sun-rays streaming,
   His mail with gold wrought fair;
And glist'ning stars o'erpowdered
   His mantle rich and fine,
Its purple edging border'd
   With spotless ermeline.

XXII.

Steps three he took to meet him,
   To his guest his hand stretch'd free,
Then friendly thus did greet him:
   "Come, seat thee next to me!

Full many a horn I've emptied
　　With Thorstein, my good fier!*
His son, the wide-commended,
　　Shall sit his host as near!"

XXIII.

The goblet then he crowneth
　　With Sik'ley's† richest wine;
Its flame-sparks nothing drowneth,
　　It foams like ocean's brine.
" My old friend's son, I send thee
　　A welcome here again;
I drink — ' to Thorstein's mem'ry,'
　　Myself and all my men!"

XXIV.

A bard from Morven's‡ mountains
　　Now sweeps the harp along,
From Gælic music-fountains
　　Springs sad his hero-song;
But in Norselandic chanteth
　　Another, ancient-wise,—
He Thorstein's exploits vaunteth,
　　And takes the skaldic prize.

* Fier — man, especially a young doughty man (cp. Anglo-Sax. *fir*, gen.
fires, the chief of living beings, man; *fira bearn*, children of men, etc.)
† Sikeley (Sikel Isle) — the Icelandic name of Sicily.
‡ Morven — the north of Scotland.

XXV.

Now the jarl to ask delighted
  Of northern kinsmen dear,
And Fridthjof all recited
  In words well weigh'd and clear;
Nor truth's just measure broke he,
  Impartial was his doom;
Like queenly Saga spoke he
  In mem'ry's holy room.

XXVI.

When next he all repeated
  On th' ocean's deeps he'd seen,
And how 'mid waves defeated
  The king's grim imps had been;
Then joy the champions proudly,
  Then Angantyr smiles too,
And shouts, reëcho'd loudly,
  His brave adventures drew.

XXVII.

But when his tale he changes
  To Ing'borg, his belov'd,
How tender-sad she ranges,
  Her grief how noble prov'd,—
Then many a damsel sighing,
  With cheeks on fire, doth stand;

How fain she'd press, replying,
　　That true-love knight's bold hand!

XXVIII.

At last, the young chief 'ginneth
　　His errand to speak about,
And th' jarl's kind ear he winneth,
　　Who patient hears him out:
"I tribute-bound was never,
　　My people too is free;
We'll 'Bele' drink, but ever
　　His friends, not subjects, be.

XXIX.

"His sons I know not; would they
　　Draw taxes from my land,
As all brave princes should, they·
　　Can ask them sword in hand;
When here, my falchion reckons,
　　Thy father yet was dear."
Then with his hand he beckons
　　To his daughter sitting near.

XXX.

Then up that flow'r-shoot tender
　　Sprang quick from gold-back'd chair,
Her waist was all so slender,
　　Her breasts so round and fair.

That little rogue, young Astrild,
  Her dimpled cheeks disclose,
Like butterfly, wind-carried
  To some just-op'ning rose.

XXXI.

To her virgin bower she speedeth,
  And green-work'd purse she brings,
Where many a wild thing treadeth
  In woodland wanderings;
And o'er the sea, sail whit'ning.
  Do silver moonbeams shine;
Its locks are rubies bright'ning,
  Its tassels golden twine.

XXXII.

Her gentle sire has taken
  The purse she thus doth hold,
And fills to th' brim, down-shaken,
  With far-off-minted gold:
"My welcome's gift I bear thee,
  Be it used as best it may;
But now shall Fridthjof swear me
  All winter here to stay.

XXXIII.

"Mood vanquishes all over,
  But now the storm-winds reign.

24

And Hejd and Ham recover,
    I fear, their strength again;
Ellide springs not always
    So luckful as before;
Though one we've miss'd, the billows
    Right many whales ride o'er."

XXXIV.

Thus quaff'd they there and jested
    Till morn relit her torch,
But that gold wine-cup zested
    A feast, no wild debauch;
At last a brimming bumper
    They drain " to Angantyr,"
And Fridthjof thus the winter
    Pass'd out with right good cheer.

CANTO XII.

FRIDTHJOF'S RETURN.

BUT spring breathes soft in yon heav'n of blue,
    And earth's green verdure again is new;
His host then Fridthjof thanketh; in motion
Once more out over the plains of ocean,
On sun-bright pathway his coal-black swan
Her silv'ry furrow with joy ploughs on,
For western breezes, spring's music bringing,
Like nightingales in the sails are singing;
And Æger's daughters, in blue veils dight,
The helm leap round, and urge on its flight.
Ah! pleasant 'tis, when, from far-off sailing,
Thy prow thou turn'st to thy homeland!—hailing
The coast where smoke from thy own hearths curl'd,
And mem'ry guards her fair childhood world.
The fresh-stream'd fountain thy play-place washes,
While barrows green hold thy father's ashes;
And, full of longing, thy faithful maid
With seaward gaze on the cliff is staid.
Days six he sails; on the seventh's dawning
A dark-blue stripe he discerns, which morning
At heav'n's far border shows slowly rise
Till rocks, isles, "land," quick salute his eyes.

His land it is from the deep that springeth,
Its shades they are which the green wood flingeth,
Its foaming torrents he hears war there,
As breast of marble the rock lays bare.
He hails the headland, the strait he haileth,
And close to Balder's retreat he saileth,
Wherein, last summer, so many a night
With Ing'borg seated he dream'd delight.
"Why comes she not? Has she no fond presage
How near I swing on the dark-blue sea-surge?
But haply, abandoning Balder's walls,
She sorrowful sits in her regal halls,
Her harp soft striking, or bright gold weaveth."
The temple's pinnacles sudden leaveth
His falcon then, and from heav'n hath sped
To Fridthjof's shoulder, as oft he'd fled;
His white wing ceaseless he flaps above him,
And, faithful, thence no allurements move him;
With fire-bright talon he ceaseless scrapes,
Nor rest he gives nor repose he takes.
To Fridthjof's ear then his crook'd bill wended,
As though some message to give 'twas bended,
Perhaps from Ing'borg, his dear-lov'd bride,—
But broken sounds — what can they betide?

Ellide, rustling, the cape now passes,
Glad, bounding hind-like o'er verdant grasses;

For well-known waves 'gainst the keel have gone;
But Fridthjof, joyful, her prow upon,
His eyes oft rubs, and his hand upholdeth
Above his brow, and the shore beholdeth.
But rub he or look as he may, no more
His Framness home shall he e'er explore.
The nak'd chimney is grimly tow'ring,
Like champion-skel'ton in grave-mound low'ring;
Where court-halls stood is a fire-clear'd land,
And ashes whirl round the ravag'd strand.
Then Fridthjof quick from the ship advances,
O'er burnt demesnes casting angry glances,
His father's grounds and his childhood's walks;—
But rough-hair'd Bran up to meet him stalks,
His faithful dog that for him bold wrestled
Full oft with bears in the forest nestled;
How glad his gambols, how glad his leaps,
How high to his master he springing keeps!
His milk-white courser (with mane gold-blended,
And hind-like legs and a neck swan-bended),
Which Fridthjof once had so often rode,
With lofty bounds from the dale, too, trode,
And turns his neck, neighing glad, and lingers,
And bread will have from his master's fingers.
Poor Fridthjof, poorer by far than they,
Has naught for his fav'rites, howe'er they pray.

As sad and houseless he stands, round-viewing
For land he'd heir'd, the burnt woodland ruin,
See! aged Hilding advances there,
His foster-father, with silver hair.
"At this black show can I scarcely wonder,—
When th' eagle's flown they his dwelling plunder,
A kingly exploit for peace I see;
Oath Helge took right well keepeth he,—
The gods to worship, mankind abhorring.
His 'Progress'* call we an arson warring,—
Not grief, but anger it works, I swear.
But Ing'borg's—tell me, I pray thee—where?"
"Dark words I bring," said this yeoman hoary:
"Not glad, I ween, wilt thou find my story.
Thou scarce hadst sail'd when king Ring drew nigh,
Shields five 'gainst one could I well descry.
At dises'-dale, by the stream they battled,
And blood-red foaming its waters rattled.
King Halfdan jested and laugh'd away,
Nathless he struck like a man that day;
The kingly stripling my target shielded,
His skill's first trial such pleasure yielded.
But short enough did their war sport last,
For—Helge fled, and then all was past !

* Progress—Swed. Eriksgata (æ-riks-gata, all-realms-circuit), the regular
"Progress" or royal tour of the newly-elected sovereign to receive homage
and confirmation from the several things (diets) of his different provinces.

But the asa-kinsman in all haste lighted
Thy halls so fair, as he 'scap'd affrighted.
Now two hard terms for the brothers stand;
To Ring they yield shall their sister's hand
(For atonement could but by her be tender'd),
Or—land and crown must be both surrender'd:
And peaceful heralds right frequent ride,—
But now king Ring hath ta'en home his bride!"

   "Oh, woman, woman!" cried Fridthjof, madly,
"When thought with Loke first shelter'd gladly,
A lie it was! and he sent it then
In woman's shape to the world of men!
Yes! a blue-eyed lie, who with false tears ruleth,
Enchanteth always, and alway fooleth;
A rose-cheek'd lie, with rich-swelling breast,
And in spring-ice virtue and wind-faith drest.
With guileful heart she, deceitful, glances,
And perjury still on her fresh lips dances!
And yet how dear to my soul was she—
How dear was then, ah! yet is, to me!
In all my sports, far as mem'ry reaches,
My mate was Ing'borg! remembrance teaches
That of each high exploit my proud youth dream'd,
Herself as prize still most precious seem'd.
Like two fair trees, by one root united,
Has Thor one stem with his lightnings blighted,

Straight withers the other; is one all green,
With verdure crown'd is its spouse-trunk seen;
So our grief and gladness were thus one only!
Not us'd is Fridthjof to think him lonely;
Now *is* he lonely. Thou lofty Var!
Where pencil-bearing thou journeyest far,
And oaths on tablets of gold inscribest,
Let be those fool'ries! Thou dreams describest,
Thy tablets marking all full of lies;
On faithful gold, what a pity 'tis
Of Balder's Nanna some tale fame telleth!
On human brow now no truth more dwelleth,
In human bosom all faith is spent,
Since Ing'borg's voice has to guile been lent;
That voice like zephyr o'er flow'r-meads creeping,
Like Brage's music his harp-strings sweeping!
Ah! ne'er mine ear shall those harp-tones drink;
Of that false bride ne'er again I'll think.
The dancing storm-wave shall be my pillow,
Thou blood shalt drink, thou wide ocean billow!
Where sword-blades scatter the barrows' seed.
O'er hill. o'er dale shall my footsteps speed!
All crown'd, perchance, I may meet a stranger,
I'd know if then I shall spare from danger!
Some youth, perchance, I may meet, all calm,
And full of love 'mid the shields' alarm,—

Some fool on honor and truth depending,—
From pity I'll hew!—his poor life quick-ending:
I'll save from shame; he shall glorious die—
Not guil'd, betray'd, nor despis'd—as I!"

    "How still boils over," now Hilding pleaded,
"Youth's hot fierce blood; and yet, son, how needed
To cool its fervors are years of snow.
That noble maiden not wrong thou so!
My foster-daughter impeach not! Better
The norns impeach then; for who can fetter
Their angry fates, which on this our world
Heav'n's thunder-land hither down hath hurl'd?
Her sorrows nobly to none proclaiming,
E'en legend-Vidar in silence shaming,
Her grief was still,—as in south-wood side
Some turtle-dove's, when her mate hath died.
Her heart, nathless, she to me disclosed,
And endless pangs in its depths reposed.
The water-bird, when death-pierced her breast,
To th' bottom dives, with one comfort blest—
That burning day will not see her bruises,
Lies so below, and her life-blood loses.
Thus shrank her pain to the realms of night,
None knew but I all her griefs aright!
'For Bele's realm they've an off'ring bound me,
And winter's verdure is hung around me,

25

While fragrant snow-flow'rs bloom round my hair;
I'm a peace-maid now;—sure the victim's fair!
Ah! death were easy! but death pain stilleth;
Atonement only scorn'd Balder willeth,
A lingering death, no repose it meets,
Its heart still flutters, its pulse still beats!
But the weak one's struggles reveal thou never,
None pity shall, though I grieve for ever;
King Bele's daughter her woes will bide.
Yet Fridthjof hail from his once hop'd bride!'
The wedding day came at last (its token
I'd willing see from my rune-staff broken).
To the temple glided a long-drawn train
Of white-rob'd virgins and sword-clad men;
A gloomy minstrel before them wended.
O'er black-hued palfrey the pale bride bended,
Like that pale spirit which sits up o'er
The dusky cloud when the thunders roar!
My lily tall, from her saddle bearing,
I led then forth through the temple, faring
To th' altar-circle where, priests among,
Lofn's vows she took with unfalt'ring tongue.
To th' White God, too, she long pray'rs presented;
And all, save only the bride, lamented.
Then first the ring on her tap'ring arm
Grim Helge mark'd, and straight snatch'd the charm;

Now Balder weareth the glittering trifle
My rage I then could no longer stifle,
My good sword quick from its scabbard forth
I drew — then little was Helge worth;
But Ing'borg whispered, "Let be! a brother
Could this have spar'd — I had borne all other;
Yet much we suffer before we die —
Allfather 'tween us will doom on high!"

"Allfather dooms!" mutter'd Fridthjof, glooming;
" But I, too, may for awhile be dooming.
'Tis Balder's midsummer holy feast,
And crown'd i' th' temple will stand his priest;
That arson-king, who his sister blooming
Has sold. I'll, too, for awhile be dooming!"

CANTO XIII.

BALDER'S PYRE.

I.

MIDNIGHT'S sun, all blood-red bright,
  Far-off hills o'erbended;
It was not day, it was not night,
  Between them 'twas suspended.

II.

Balder's pyre, of the sun a mark,
  Holy hearth red staineth;
Yet, soon dies its last faint spark,
  Darkly then Hoder reigneth.

III.

Ancient priests around the temple-wall
  Stood, and the pile-brands shifted;
Silver-bearded and pale, they all
  Flint-knives in hard hands lifted.

IV.

Helge, crown'd, standeth them beside,
  Help 'mid the circle proff'ring.
Hark! then clatter, at midnight's tide,
  Arms in the grove of off'ring.

V.

" Bjorn, the door hold close, man — so!
　　Pris'ners they'll all obey me;
Out or in whoe'er would go,
　　Cleave his skull, I pray thee! "

VI.

Pale waxeth Helge, — that voice too well
　　Knows he, and what presaging.
Forth trod Fridthjof, and dark words fell
　　Storm-like in autumn raging.

VII.

" Here's the tribute, prince, thy breath
　　Order'd from western waters;
Take it, then for life or death
　　Fight we at Balder's altars!

VIII.

" Back shield-covered, my bosom bare,
　　Nought shall unfair be reckon'd.
First, as king, strike thou! * Beware,
　　Mind, for I strike the second.

IX.

" Yonder door! — nay, gaze, fool, here!
　　Caught in his hole the fox is;
Think of Framness, and Ing'borg dear,
　　Fam'd that for golden locks is! "

* The challenged party had a right to strike first.— See " The Saga of
Thorstein, Viking's Son," ch. IV, p. 10.

x.

So his hero-accents rang;
    Th' purse from his belt then freely
Drew he, and careless enough it flang
    Right at the son of Bele.

xi.

Blood from his mouth gush'd out straightway,
    Streaming blackly splendent;
There by his altar swooning lay
    Th' asas' high descendant.

xii.

"What! thine own gold bear'st not?—shame!
    Shame! coward-king vile-shrinking;
Angervadil none e'er shall blame
    Blood so base for drinking!

xiii.

"Silence! priests with off'ring-knife,
    Chiefs, yon moon lights dimly!
Noise might cost each wretched life;
    Back!—for my blade thirsts grimly.

xiv.

"Rageful thine eye, white Balder, shines;
    Yet, why so anger-swollen?
Yon fair ring thine arm round-twines,—
    Pardon me, but 'tis stolen!

XV.

"Not sure for thee Volund, smith kept
    Graving that jewel's wonders!
Violence stole, and the virgin wept.
    Down with all scoundrel plunders!"

XVI.

Brave he pull'd; but fast grown seem'd
    Th' arm and the ring so curious;
When loos'd at last, where th' altar gleam'd
    Brightest, the god leapt furious.

XVII.

Hark, that crash! Gnawing gold-tooth'd flame
    Rafter and roof o'er quivers;
Bjorn turns pale as he stands, and shame!
    Fridthjof feels that he shivers.

XVIII.

"Bjorn, release them! Unbar the door,
    Guarding is now all over:
Th' temple blazes; pour water, pour
    All the sea thereover!"

XIX.

Now from temple and grove and strand,
    Chain-like, they clasp each other;
Billows, wandering from hand to hand,
    Hissing the fires would smother.

XX.

Rain-god like sits Fridthjof there,
 High o'er beams and waters,
All-directing with lordly air,
 Calm 'mong the hot fire-slaughters.

XXI.

Vain! Fire conquers; rolling past,
 Smoke-clouds whirl, and smelted
Gold on red-hot sands falls fast,—
 Silver plates are melted.

XXII.

All, all 's lost! From half-burn'd hall
 Th' fire-red cock up-swingeth,— *
Sits on the roof, and, with shrilly call
 Flutt'ring, his free course wingeth.

XXIII.

Morning's winds from the north rush by,
 Heav'nward the fire-wave surges;
Balder's grove is summer dry,
 Greedy the fierce blaze gorges.

XXIV.

Raging, from branch to branch it flew,
 Still round the goal ne'er closing;
Ah! how fearful that wild light grew,
 Balder's pyre, how imposing!

* See "Norse Mythology," p. 421.

XXV.

Hark! how it snaps i' th' gaping root;
    See! from the top sparks shower;
'Gainst Muspel's sons, the red, what boot
    Man's art, man's arm, man's power?

XXVI.

Fire-seas tumble in Balder's grove;
    Shoreless the billows wander;
Sun-beams rise, but frith and cove
    Mirror hell's flame-lights yonder!

XXVII.

T' ashes soon is the temple burn'd,
    T' ashes the grove so blooming:
Fridthjof, grief-full, away has turn'd,
    Day o'er his hot tears glooming!

CANTO XIV.

FRIDTHJOF GOETH INTO BANISHMENT.

H IS ship's deck slight
    I' th' summer-night,
Bore th' hero grieving.
Like waves high heaving,
Now rage, now woe,
Thro' his bosom flow.
Smoke still ascended,
The fire not ended.

"Thou temple smoke
Fly up! invoke
From Valhal's tower
God Balder's power;
Send th' white god's wrath
To blight my path!
Fly up! and chatter
Till the arches clatter.
Say, temple-round
Burnt thus to th' ground;
Thus down fell sudden
Thine image wooden,
Like all wood lay

And burn'd away!
The grove, too, mention,—
Secure since falchion
Had thigh-girt been,
Now waste; not e'en
Was the honor gotten
To sink, time-rotten.
This — more thereto
Which all may view
To Balder carry;
Nor fail nor tarry,
Mist-courier! High
To th' mist-god fly!

    " Each skald, sure, raises
Mild Helge's praises
Who thus has bann'd
From yond' my land;
From him bans never!
Well! naught can sever
From that blue realm
Where billows whelm.
Thou mayst not rest thee,
Thou still must haste thee,
Ellide, out
Th' wide world about.

Yes! rock on! roaming
Mid froth salt-foaming,
My dragon good!
Nor drop of blood
Will hurt, thou knowest,
Where'er thou goest.
When storms hoarse cry,
My house thou'rt by;
For Balder's brother,
He burn'd mine other.
Yes! thou'rt my North,
My foster-earth!
From that down yonder
I now must wander.
Yes! thou'rt my bride!
Black weeds thy pride;
For ah! how dare one
Trust her, that fair one?

"Thou free broad sea!
Unknown to thee
Are despot's glances
And tyrant's fancies.
Where freemen swing
Is he thy king,
Who never shivers
Howe'er high quivers,

With rage oppress'd,
Thy froth-white breast!
Thy plains, blue-spreading,
Glad chiefs are treading;
Like ploughs thereon
Their keels drive on;
And blood-rain patters
In shade th' oak scatters,
But steel-bright there
The corn-seeds glare!
Those plains so hoary
Bear crops of glory,
Rich crops of gold!
Thou billow bold,
Befriend me! Never
I'll from thee sever!
My father's mound
Dull stands, fast-bound,
And self-same surges
Chant changeless dirges;
But blue shall mine
Through foam-flow'rs shine,
'Mid tempests swimming,
And storms thick dimming,
And draw yet mo*
Down, down, below.

* Mo — more.

My life-home given,
Thou shalt, far driven,
My barrow be—
Thou free, broad sea!"

Thus fierce he grieveth,
And sorrowing leaveth
His prow so true
The reeds it knew,
All gently gliding
'Mong rocks still biding,
To watch i' th' North
The shallow firth.
But vengeance wakens!
With twice five dragons
Swam Helge round
And closed the sound.
Then each loud crieth:
"Now Helge dieth
This one fight o'er—
Then thrives no more,
The bright moon under,
That Valhal's wonder:
Above he'll rise
T' his home, the skies:
That blood immortal,
Seeks Odin's portal."

The word scarce said,
With unseen tread
Some pow'r fast clingeth
T' each keel that swingeth;
And see! they slow
Are drawn below
To Ran's host dying;
E'en Helge trying
From half-drown'd prore
Scarce swims ashore.

But glad Bjorn proudly
Shouts, laughing loudly.—
"Thou asa-blood,
That trick was good!
Unseen, unfearful,
I scuttled cheerful
The ships last night;
The thought was bright!
What Ran infoldeth
I hope she holdeth,
As heretofore;
Yet pity sore,
They went to th' bottom,
Their chief forgotten!"

In angry mood
King Helge stood,

Scarce death-deliver'd;
His drawn bow quiver'd,
Steel-cast and round,
'Gainst rocky ground;
Himself not knew it,
How hard he drew it,
Till th' steel bow sprang
With snapping clang.

But Fridthjof weigheth
His lance, and sayeth:
" Held back, this free
Death-eagle see!
If out he dashes
He mortal gashes
That tyrant-thing,
A coward king
Who needless shrinketh;
My lance ne'er drinketh
A craven's blood.
Ay! 'tis too good
For such achievements!
'Mong rune-stone grievements
It carv'd may stand,
But ne'er shall brand
That scoundrel-framing
Which thy name's shaming!

Thy manhood's bloom
Finds shipwreck's doom,
And 'scaping hither
On shore, will wither.
Rust steel may break,
Not thou,—I'll take
A mark far higher
Than base peace-buyer;
Take care how near
Thine own appear!"

To an oar cut down, he
Then grasps a pine tree,
(That mast pine fell
In Gudbrand's dell,)
Its mate then heaveth,
And th' ocean cleaveth.
Strong pulls he takes,—
As reed-shaft breaks,
As cold-blade snappeth,
Each oar quick cracketh.

Day's orb now shin'd
Hill-tops behind;
Fresh breezes bounded
From shore, and sounded
Each wave to dance

In morning's glance.
Where the high surge leapeth
Ellide sweepeth,
Glad stretch'd her wings,—
But Fridthjof sings:

I.

"Heimskringla's forehead,
  Thou lofty North!
Away I'm hurried
  From this thine earth;
My race from thee goes,
  I boasting tell;
Now, nurse of heroes,
  Farewell! Farewell!

II.

"Farewell, high gleaming,
  Thou Valhal's throne,
Night's eye, bright beaming
  Midsummer's sun!
Sky! where, as in hero's
  Soul, pure depths dwell,
And thronging star rows,—
  Farewell! Farewell!

III.

"Farewell, ye mountains,
  Seats glory for;
Ye tablet fountains
  For mighty Thor!
Ye lakes and high lands
  I knew so well,
Ye rocks and islands,
  Farewell! Farewell!

IV.

"Farewell, cairns dreaming
  By wave of blue,
Where, snow-white gleaming,
  Limes flow'r-dust strew.
But Saga spieth
  And doometh well
I' th' earth what lieth;—
  Farewell! Farewell!

V.

"Farewell, ye bowers,
  Fresh houses green,
Where youth pluck'd flow'rs
  By murm'ring stream;
Ye friends of childhood,
  Who meant me well,

Ye're yet remember'd;—
  Farewell! Farewell!

VI.

"My love insulted,
  My palace brent,
My honor tarnish'd,
  In exile sent,—
From land, in sadness,
  T' the sea w' appeal,—
But life's young gladness—
  Farewell! Farewell!"

CANTO XV.

THE VIKING-CODE.

I.

FAR and wide, like the falcon that hunts through
    the sky, flew he now o'er the desolate sea;
And his vikinga-code, for his champions on board, wrote
    he well;—wilt thou hear what it be?

II.

"On thy ship pitch no tent; in no house shalt thou sleep;
    in the hall who our friends ever knew?
On his shield sleeps the viking, his sword in his hand,
    and for tent has yon heaven the blue.

III.

"With a short-shafted hammer fights conquering Thor,
    Frey's own sword but an ell long is made,—
That's enough. Hast thou courage, strike close to thy
    foe: not too short for thee then is thy blade.

IV.

"When the storm roars on high, up aloft with the sail;
    ah! how pleasant's the sea in its wrath!
Let it blow, let it blow! He's a coward that furls;
    rather founder than furl in thy path.

v.

"On the shore, not on board, mayst thou toy with a maid;
　　Freyja's self would prove false to thy love;
For the dimple deceives on her cheek, and her tresses
　　would net-like entrap thee above.

VI.

"Wine is Valfather's drink; a carouse thou mayst have,
　　.but yet steady and upright appear;
He who staggers on shore may stand up, but will soon
　　down to sleep-giving Ran stagger here.

VII.

"Sails the merchant-ship forth, thou his bark mayst
　　protect, if due tribute his weak hand has told;
On thy wave art thou king; he's a slave to his pelf,
　　and thy steel is as good as his gold!

VIII.

"With the dice and the lot shall the booty be shar'd,
　　and complain not however it goes;
But the sea-king himself throws no dice on the deck,
　　only glory he seeks from his foes.

IX.

"Heaves a viking in sight, then come boarding and
　　strife, and hot work is it under the shield;
But from us art thou banish'd, forget not the doom
　　if a step or a foot thou shalt yield!

X.

" 'Tis enough shouldst thou conquer! Who prays thee for
    peace has no sword and cannot be thy foe:
Pray'r is Valhal's own child — hear the pale virgin's voice;
    yes! a scoundrel is he who says no!

XI.

" Viking-gains are deep wounds, and right well they
    adorn if they stand on the brow or the breast.
Let them bleed, twice twelve hours first must circle
    ere bind them who vikinga-comrade would rest!"

XII.

Thus his laws carv'd he out, and fresh exploits each day
    and fresh fame to strange coast-lands he brought;
And his like found he none on the blue-rolling sea, and
    his champions right willing they fought.

XIII.

But himself sat all darkly, with rudder in hand, and
    look'd down on the slow-rocking spray: —
" Deep thou art! Peace perchance in those depths still
    may bloom, but above here all peace dies away.

XIV.

" Is the White God enrag'd, let him take his good sword.—
    I will fall should it so be decreed:
But he sits in yon sky, gloomy thoughts sending down,—
    ne'er my soul from their sadness is freed."

XV.

Yet when battle is near, like the fresh eagle flying,
    his spirit fierce soars with delight;
Loudly thunders his voice, and with clear brow he stands,
    like the light'ner still foremost in fight.

XVI.

Thus from vict'ry to vict'ry he ceaselessly swam, on
    that wide foaming grave all secure;
And fresh islands he saw, and fresh bays in the South,
    till fair winds on to Greekland allure.

XVII.

When its groves he beheld in the green tide reflected,
    its temples in ruin bent low,
Freyja knows what he thought, and the skald, and if e'er
    thou hast known how to love, thou wilt know!

XVIII.

"Here our dwelling had been! Here's the isle, here's the
    land; of this temple my sire oft would tell;
Hither 'twas, hither 'twas I invited my maid; — ah! she
    cruel the North lov'd too well!

XIX.

"'Mong these happy green vales dwells not peace? and
    remembrance, ah! haunts she not columns so fair?
Like the whisp'rings of lovers soft murmur those springs,
    and with bridal-songs birds fill the air.

XX.

"Where is Ingeborg now? Is so soon all forgot—for a
chief wither'd, gray-hair'd, and old?
I, I cannot forget! Gladly gave I my life yet once more
that dear form to behold!

XXI.

"And the years have gone by since my own land I saw,
kingly hall of fair Saga the queen!
Rise there yet so majestic those mountains to heav'n,
keeps my forefather's dale its bright green.

XXII.

"On the cairn where my father lies buried, a lime-tree I
planted,—ah! blooms it there now!
Who its tender shoot guards? Give thy moisture, O
earth! and thy dews, O thou heaven, give thou!

XXIII.

"Yet why linger I here, on the wave of the stranger?—
is tribute, is blood, then, my goal?
I have glory sufficient, and beggarly gold, and its brightness deep scorneth my soul.

XXIV.

"There's the flag on the mast, to the Northland it points,
and the North holds the country I love;
Back to northward I'll steer, and will follow the course
of the breezes fresh-blowing above."

CANTO XVI.

BJORN AND FRIDTHJOF.

FRIDTHJOF.

BJORN! I'm awearied of surge and of sea!
  Billows, at best, are tumultuous urchins;
   Northland's firm, fast-rooted, dear belov'd mountains
Wondrously tempt me, afar though they be.

  Happy whom never his land has outdriven,
None ever chas'd from his father's green grave!
  Ah! too long, yes too long, have I striven,
Peaceless and sad, on this ocean's wild wave!

BJORN.

Ocean is good, blame it not; for out yonder
  Freedom and gladness abide on its breast;
  Nothing know I of weak womanish rest,
Onward I love with the billows to wander.

  When I am old, on the blossoming earth
I, too, will grow soil-fast as the grass is;
  Goblet and battle shall now be my mirth;
  Now I'll enjoy each young hour as it passes!

FRIDTHJOF.

Yet, by hard ice we are hunted on land;
  See! round our keel the big waves lie all lifeless.

Winter I waste not, the long and the strifeless,
Here 'mong the rocks of a desolate strand.

Yule shall again in the Northland delight me,
Guesting with Ring and the bride that he stole.

Yes! I'll again view those locks streaming brightly;
Tones still so lov'd shall yet speak to my soul!

BJORN.

Good! hint no longer. Revenge is our duty!

Ring shall acknowledge a viking's dire.

Sudden at midnight his palace we'll fire;
First burn the old warrior, then ravish the beauty.

Haply it chances, in vikinga-wise,
Isle-duel worthy the chieftain thou deemest;

Or, thou mayst challenge to host-fight on ice;
Say! I'm prepar'd for whatever thou schemest!

FRIDTHJOF.

Arson, oh name not,—and think not of war:

Peaceful I go. The good king has not wrong'd me;

She, too, is guiltless. Yes! gods avenge strongly —
I their insulter—the crime they abhor.

Little on earth may I hope. There remaineth
Now but to part from the bride I hold dear.

Part, ah! for aye. When soft spring again reigneth,
Then, if not sooner, I haste to thee here.

BJORN.

Fridthjof, I cannot excuse, man, thy madness.

What! for a woman lament so sore!

Women, good lack! the whole earth swarm o'er;

Thousands, one gone, will soon banish thy sadness.

Quick, if thou wilt, where the south sun glows;

Cargoes I'll bring of such wares, more than others,

Gentle as lambs and as red as the rose,

Then draw me lots, or divide them like brothers.

FRIDTHJOF.

Bjorn, thou art open and glad, like as Frey;

Boldness in fight, skill in counsel, thou showest;

Odin and Thor both together thou knowest;

Freyja, the heav'nly, thou dost not obey.

Speak we not now of the power each god keepeth;

Rouse not, enrage not, the eternal again;

Sooner or later, the sparkle that sleepeth

Wakes in the bosom of gods and of men.

BJORN.

Go not alone. Seldom way-laid returneth.

FRIDTHJOF.

Well am I followed: My sword's at my side.

BJORN.

Hagbart, forget not, of hanging died.

FRIDTHJOF.

He who is taken, his hanging well earneth.

BJORN.

Fall'st thou, war-brother, I'll 'venge thee well;
Blood-eagle lines on thy foe shall be flowing.

FRIDTHJOF.

Bjorn, 'tis not needed. The cock's loud crowing
Hears he no longer than I. Farewell!

CANTO XVII.

FRIDTHJOF COMETH TO KING RING.

I.

KING RING, on high-seat resting, at Yule drank
    mead so bright,—
His queen was sat beside him, all rosy-red and white;
Like spring and autumn seemed they, each other near,
    to be;
The fresh spring Ing'borg liken'd—the chilly autumn he.

II.

Unknown, an ancient wand'rer now treadeth in the hall,
From head to foot all darkly his thick fur-garments fall;
A staff he feebly holdeth, and bent they see him go,—
That old man yet was taller than all the rest, I trow.

III.

He sat him on the bench there, right down behind the door;
For that the poor man's station is now, and was before;
The courtiers eye each other, and basely him deride,
And many a finger pointeth to that grim bear's rough hide.

IV.

Then like two vivid lightnings, the stranger's eyes fierce
    flash,
While one hand graspeth quickly a lordling-youth too rash;

Right warily the courtier he twirleth round about,
Then silent grew the others — as we had done, no doubt.

V.

"What noise is that down yonder? Who breaks our
    kingly peace?
Come up to me, old fellow! your words to me address!
Your name, your will, whence come ye?" Thus the angry
    king demands
Of the aged man, half hidden by the corner where he
    stands.

VI.

"Right much, O king, thou askest, yet answer'd shalt
    thou be;
My name I give not, that sure can matter none but me.
In Penitence I'm foster'd; and Want was all I heir'd,
The wolf from came I hither, for last his bed I shar'd.

VII.

"In former days I, joyous, the dragon's back bestrode;
With wings so strong, he gladly and safe o'er ocean rode:
Now lies he lam'd and frozen, full close along the land,
Myself, too, am grown old and burn salt upon the strand.

VIII.

"I came to see thy wisdom, through all the country known,
And was not made for th' insults thy people here have
    shown;

By the breast a fool I lifted, and round about did swing,
Yet stood he up uninjur'd,—forgive me that, O king!"

IX.

"Not ill," the monarch crieth, "thou joinest words and
    wit,
And the ag'd one ought to honor; come, at my board
    here sit.
But your disguise let fall now, and like thyself appear;
Disguis'd thrives gladness never, and I'll have gladness
    here!"

X.

From off the guest's high head then the hairy bear-
    hide fell,
And, 'stead of him so ancient, a stripling all see well;
His lofty temples shading, bright ringlets flow'd unbound,
Like some gold wave encircling his full broad shoulders
    round.

XI.

And proud he stood before them in velvet mantle blue,
With hand-broad silver girdle where beasts green woods
    range through;
With cunning skill had th' artist emboss'd them out
    to-day,
And round the hero's middle each other hunted they.

XII.

His armlet, red gold trinket, to his arm right splendid
    clung;
Like standing heav'n-snatch'd lightning, his shining war-
    sword hung;
His hero-glance slow wander'd all calm o'er guest, and ha';
He stood there fair as Balder, and tall as Asa-Thor.

XIII.

The astonish'd queen's pale cheeks how fast-changing
    rose-tints dye!
So purple northlights, quiv'ring, on snow-hid meadows lie.
Like two white water-lilies on storm-wave wild that rest,
Each moment rising, falling,—so heaves her trembling
    breast!

XIV.

Then loud blew signal-trumpets; death-still became all
    there;
For now was the hour of promise, and Frey's boar in
    they bear.
His grim mouth holds an apple, his shoulders garlands
    grac'd,
And down on silver charger four bended knees he plac'd.

XV.

And quick king Ring he riseth, with gray locks thinly
    crown'd,

Then, first the boar's brow touching, his vow thus speaks
    around:

"I swear to conquer Fridthjof, stout champion though
    he be,

So help me Frey and Odin, and Thor more strong than
    he!"

XVI.

With mocking laugh, undaunted, the stranger-chief up-
    rose,

While, flash-like, hero-rage o'er his scornful face quick
    goes;

The sword upon the table he dash'd with fearful clang,

And up from the oaken benches each warrior sudden
    sprang.

XVII.

"And hear thou, good sir monarch, for I'll too make my
    vow,—

Young Fridthjof is my kinsman, I've known him up till
    now.

I swear to shelter Fridthjof, though all the world with-
    stood,

So help my fav'ring norn me, and this my falchion good!"

XVIII.

With smiles the king him answer'd: "Full bold thy
    accents fall,

Yet words were never fetter'd in northern kingly hall.
Queen, fill for him that horn there with wine thou
    prizest best;
Till spring returns, the stranger, I hope, will be our
    guest."

XIX.

The horn which stood before her the queen then rais'd
    with care,—
From the urns' forehead broke,—'twas a jewel rich and
    rare;
Its feet were shining silver, with many a ring of gold,
While wondrous runes adorn'd it, and curious shape of old.

XX.

The goblet to the hero she reach'd, with downcast eyne,
But much her hand it trembled and spill'd the sparkling
    wine;
As ev'ning's purple blushes on snowy lilies stand,
So burn'd those drops all darkly on Ing'borg's fair, white
    hand.

XXI.

Straight from the noble ladye glad took the guest that
    horn,.
Not two men could have drain'd it, as men are now
    y-born;

But easily, and willing the gentle queen to please,
The mighty stranger drain it in but one draught she
    sees.

XXII.

The skald, too, his harp awak'ning, as by Ring's board
    he sate,
A heart-sprung legend chanted of northern lover's fate;
Of Hagbart and fair Signe he sang with voice so deep,
That steel clad bosoms melted—each stern eye long'd to
    weep.

XXIII.

Then harp'd he Valhal's glories, rewards th' einherjes
    gain'd,
And eke their fathers' exploits, by land and sea obtain'd;
His sword then grasp'd each warrior, enkindled ev'ry
    look,
And ceaseless round th' assembly its course the full
    horn took.

XXIV.

So, deeply in that king's-house they drank all through
    the night,
A Yule carouse each champion enjoy'd with such delight!
And then to sleep loud haste they, so glad, and free from
    care:
But aged Ring he slumbered by Ing'borg's side the fair!

CANTO XVIII.

THE SLEDGE EXCURSION.

I.

KING RING to a banquet sets out with his queen,
    So clear sweeps the mirror-like lake's frozen sheen.

II.

"Keep back!" said the stranger, "that icy path shun;
'Twill give way; cold and deep for a bath its waves run."

III.

"Not so soon," answers Ring, "can a king be drown'd,
Let the coward who fears it the lake go round!"

IV.

Fierce frowns the tall champion, dark threats in his eyes,
And quick on his feet steel skate-shoes he ties.

V.

Then away darts the courser, away in his might;
He, flame snorting, gallops—so wild his delight!

VI.

"On! speed thee!" cries Ring; "on, my swift-of-foot good!
Let us see if thou springest from Sleipner's high blood!"

VII.

Like the storm in its wrath they dash o'er the lake;
Ring heeds not the cry of his queen, "It will break!"

VIII.

Nor idleth the steel-footed warrior; his speed
Outstrips, when he wills it, yon fast-flying steed.

IX.

And many a rune, too, on the ice he engraves;
Fair Ing'borg drives o'er her own name on the waves.

X.

Thus forward they rush on the glassy-smooth path,
But beneath them false Ran her an ambush hath:

XI.

In her silvery roof a deep fissure she reft,
And the royal sledge lies in the opening cleft.

XII.

Then pale, pale as death, waxes Ring's lovely bride,
But, a whirlwind no swifter, the guest's at her side!

XIII.

With iron heel boring, he the ice firmly treads;
So, the charger's mane grasping, his hands deep imbeds;

XIV.

And then without effort he pulls, at one spring,
On the ice, as before, sledge, charger and Ring.

XV.

"Full sooth," cries Ring quickly, "my praise hast thou
    won;
Not better could strong-handed Fridthjof have done!"

XVI.

So back they return to the palace once more;
The stranger will there the long winter pass o'er.

CANTO XIX.

FRIDTHJOF'S TEMPTATION.

I.

SPRING is come; birds sweetly warble, smiles the
    sun, the woods are green,—

And, unchained, the murm'ring streamlets dancing sea-
    ward down are seen.

Glowing red as Freyja's cheeks, young op'ning rosebuds
    freshly part,

And to life's glad joys, to hope and courage, wakes man's
    heaven-touched heart.

II.

The aged king to hunt will go,—the queen, too, shall
    attend the sport,

And in motley groups, assemblies gay deck'd, thronging,
    all the court.

Bows are clattering, quivers rattle, fiery coursers paw
    the ground,—

And th' impatient hooded falcon screams upon his prey
    to bound.

III.

See! there comes the hunt's proud mistress,—Fridthjof!
    ah! nor look, nor heed!

Star-like on a spring-cloud resting, so she sits her milk-
    white steed.
Half a Freyja, half a Rota, both eclips'd if she were by,—
From her rich, light, purple bonnet, plumes blue-tinted
    wave on high.

IV.

Look not on those eyes' bright azure! look not on those
    locks of gold!
Ah! beware that waist — 'tis tapering; nor such round,
    full breasts behold!
Gaze not at the rose and lily on her changing cheek
    that meet!
List not to that voice so clear, like spring's soft music
    sighing sweet!

V.

Now the long-stretched line is ready. Hark, away! O'er
    hill and dale
Horns sound shrilly, and straight up to Odin's hall the
    glad hawks sail,—
Quick to lair and covert fly the screaming game from
    such affray;
But with outstretch'd spear the fair valkyrie gallops on
    her prey.
28

VI.

Old and feeble, Ring can now the lengthen'd chase no
     longer keep;
Fridthjof only, dark-brow'd, silent, near him rides as
     forth they sweep;
Sad, sore, gloomy thoughts are rising thickly in his
     troubled breast,—
And go where he will, still croak they, mutt'ring cease-
     less words unblest.

VII.

"Why, alas! free ocean left I?—to my danger rashly
     blind;
Grief fares hardly on the billows, scatter'd by the
     fresh'ning wind.
Droops the troubled viking,—danger soon to tread the
     war-dance charms;
And away his black dreams vanish, dazzled by the glance
     of arms.

VIII.

"Here how chang'd all is! unutterable longings whirl
     their wings
Flutt'ring round my burning forehead. Trance-like are
     my wanderings;
Balder's sanctuary never *can* forgotten be,—nor yet
The oath she sware,—not she, no! no! the cruel gods
     have broken it.

IX.

"Yes! the race of man they hate; its joys they view with
    wrathful look.

Fiends! to plant in winter's bosom rosebud mine they
    grimly took;

Winter! he the rose's guardian!—what! his heart to feel
    its price!

No! bud, leaf and stalk his cold breath slow enfrosts
    with glitt'ring ice!"

X.

Thus lamented he. And now they came where, threat'ning
    rocks among,

Birch and elm high o'er a valley darkly-cluster'd shadows
    flung.

"See this pleasant dell, how cool!" the king, his charger
    leaving, said;

"Come! I'm wearied,—here I'll slumber; yon green bank
    shall be my bed."

XI.

"Rest not here, O king! the ground too hard and cold
    a couch would be;

Heavy sleep would follow; rise, regain thy halls, led back
    by me."

"Sleep," said Ring, "like the other gods, when least
    expected, comes; my guest

Surely will not grudge his host one balmy hour's unbroken rest."

XII.

Fridthjof now his rich-wrought mantle, loosing, on the
green turf laid,
And upon his knees secure, his head the white-haired
monarch staid.
Heroes so, on war-shield pillowed — hushed the battle's
wild alarm,—
Peaceful slumber; so rests the infant, cradled on its
mother's arm.

XIII.

Calm he sleeps.   But hark! a bird, all coal-black, sings
from yonder bough:
"Haste thee, Fridthjof, slay the dotard! end at once
your quarrel *now!*
Take his queen; she's thine; her sacred kiss of plighted
troth she gave.
Here no human eye can see thee; silent is the dark,
deep grave."

XIV.

Fridthjof listens.   Hark! a snow-white bird then sings
from yonder bough:
"Though no human eye should see thee, Odin's eye
would see it.   How!

Wouldst thou, scoundrel, murder sleep? Shall helpless
    age thy bright sword stain?
Know, whate'er thou winnest, hero-fame at least thou
    wilt not gain."

XV.

Thus contending, sang the birds: but Fridthjof seized his
    falchion good,
And with horror threw it from him, far into the gloom-
    ful wood;
Down to Nastrand flies the coal-black tempter; but, light
    wings his stay,
Like a harp-tone warbling, hieth the other sunward quick
    away.

XVI.

Straight awakes then the aged sleeper. "Sweet, indeed,
    my rest hath been;
Well they slumber in the shade whom warrior guards
    with war-blade keen.
But where *is* thy war-blade, stranger? lightning's brother's
    left thy side;
Who has parted friends that never from each other should
    divide?"

XVII.

"Little boots it," answered Fridthjof; "ne'er the North
    I brandless knew;

Sharp, O king, the sword's tongue is. Yes! words of
    peace it speaks but few.

Imps of darkness haunt the steel,—hell-spirits sprung
    from Niflheim;

Sleep itself they spare not,—and e'en silver locks but
    anger ·them!"

XVIII.

"Youth! I slept not! only would I thus thy hero-soul
    first try,

Fools may th' untried man or sword all fondly trust; so
    will not I!

Thou art Fridthjof! I have known thee since thou first
    my halls didst find;

Ring, though old, has long perceiv'd his clever guest's
    most secret mind.

XIX.

"Wherefore to my palace creptst thou!—nameless and in
    close disguise?

Wherefore, but to make an aged chieftain's bride thy
    stolen prize!

Never, Fridthjof, 'mid glad guests her station honor
    nameless took;

Sun-bright is her shield,—her open face would spurn
    dissembled look.

XX.

"Fame a Fridthjof's exploits rumored, terror both to gods
and men;

Desp'rate, careless which, that viking shields would cleave
or temple bren!

Soon, methought, this chief will march with upborne
shield against my land;

Soon he came,—but hid in tatters, and a beggar's staff
in hand!

XXI.

"Why those down-cast glances? I, too, have been young;
I've felt that truth—

Life is but a life-long contest, and its berserk's-course is
youth;

Youth, 'mid shields round-pressing fierce, shall strive till
passion's rage expire;

I have prov'd and pardon'd,—I have pitied and forgot
mine ire.

XXII.

"Listen! Old I wax, and feeble, soon shall in my cairn
recline;

Then my kingdom take, young warrior; take my queen
too, she is thine!

Be till then my son, and share my hall's free welcome
as before!

Swordless champion shall protect me; so our ancient feud
    is o'er."

XXIII.

"Thief-like," answered Fridthjof grimly, "came I not
    within thy hall;

Had I wish'd to seize thy queen, say, who could stand
    me,—who appall?

Ah! I fain would see my bride once more, but once
    her charms would view;

And, weak madman-like, my love's half-slumb'ring flame
    I wak'd anew!

XXIV.

"Ring, I go! Its guest thy court too long already shel-
    ter'd hath;

Gods implacable upon my head devote pour all their
    wrath.

Balder with the bright-hued tresses, he whose love each
    mortal shares,

Me alone fierce hates—of all mankind rejects alone my
    pray'rs!

XXV.

"Yes, his fane I laid in ashes! Varg i Véum* am I hight!

Sounds my name, loud shrieks the child, and festive
    boards joy flies affright.

* See Vocabulary.

Yes, her long-lost son my country has rejected and
opprest.

Outlaw'd in my home-land am I;—outlaw'd, peaceless in
my breast!

XXVI.

"On the fresh green earth no longer, peace vain-seeking,
will I live;

'Neath my foot the ground burns hotly, and the tree no
shade will give.

Ingeborg, my own, I've lost; his spoil the white-hair'd
king retains;

Set, extinguish'd is my life's bright sun, and round me
darkness reigns.

XXVII.

"Hence, then, to my ocean will I. Out my dragon-ship!
Hurrah!

Glad one, bathe again thy pitch-black bosom in the salt
waves afar;

Flap thy wings in storm-clouds bravely; hissing, cut the
high-dash'd foam;

Fly where'er a guide-star kindles, far as conquer'd billows
roam.

XXVIII.

"Rattling tempests, horrid rolling-deep-voic'd thunders,
will I hear;

29

Fridthjof's soul is then most calm when most the crashing
    din is near.

Hark, old chief! — shields clang — darts hiss — out on mid-
    ocean roars the fray;

Joyful shall I fall — to hear the gods, appeas'd, my pardon
    say!"

CANTO XX.

KING RING'S DEATH.

I.

SKIN-FAXE, streaming
  Mane-gold-fire, raises
Spring's sun from ocean, more fair than before;
  Morn's ray, bright beaming,
  Twice lovely blazes,
And plays in the hall. Hark! who taps on the door?

II.

  Buried in sorrow,
  Fridthjof advanceth.
Pale sits the king; fair Ingeborg's breast
  Heaves like the billow.
  Faint-trembling, chanteth
The stranger "farewell" to the halls of his rest.

III.

  "My wing'd steed out yonder
  Waves bathe so gay, now;
My sea-horse is longing to dash from the strand;
  Far must he wander,
  Th' guest must away now,—
Away from the friend that he loves, and his land.

IV.

"Ing'borg, the unbroken
Ring I restore thee;
Mem'ries all sacred within it remain;
Give not the token.
Pardons I o'er thee
Speak—for on earth thou ne'er seest me again.

V.

"Never again the
Fire's light-curl'd daughters
See I from th' north rise. Man is a slave;
Norns three they reign; the
Wild waste of waters,
There is my fatherland, there is my grave!

VI.

"Nor on the strand go,
Ring, with thy consort,
Least when pale stars gleam bright o'er the bay;
For 'mid the sand, O
Chief, may be uptoss'd
Th' outlaw'd young viking's bones, bleach'd in the spray."

VII.

Saith Ring: "How it wearies,
List'ning to livelong
Plainings from men, as from girls when they cry.

Loud in mine ear is
Long since my death-song
Echoing. What then? Who are born — they must die.

VIII.

"Strengths none deliver;
Tears ne'er atone; no
Strugglings avail, from the norns' firm decree.
Ring is the giver;
Ing'borg's thy own; so
My son's firm defense in my realm shalt thou be.

IX.

"Friends oft have spoken,
Seated in halls here;
Well have I lov'd golden peace all around.
Yet have I broken
Shields in the valley,
Shields on the sea, — nor grew pale at the sound.

X.

"Bleeding now, Geirs-odd
Quick will I carve me;
North-kings it fits not to die in their bed.
Little this final
Exploit will cost me;
Living, we're scarce more at ease than the dead."

XI.

To Odin then true-fast

Carves he fair runics,—

Death-runes cut deep on his arm and his breast.

Sparkling the contrast!

See! how those streams mix,—

Silver hairs purpling on bosom at rest!

XII.

"Wine bring so mellow;

Hail to thy mem'ry!

Hail to thy glory, thou North blooming bright!

Harvests' deep yellow,

Minds thinking clearly,

The achievements of peace, were on earth my delight!

XIII.

"Oft sought I, fruitless,

Peace where, 'mid slaughter,

Wild chieftains dwelt; but she'd flown far away.

Now stands the bloodless

Tomb's gentle daughter,

Fav'rite of heav'n, and awaits me to-day.

XIV.

"Gods, all, I hail ye!

Valhal's great sons a'!

Earth disappears; to the asas' high feast

Gjallarhorn bids me;
Bless'dness, like a
Gold helmet, circles their up-coming guest."

XV.

With one hand then clasp'd he
Ing'borg, his dear one;
The other to his son and the viking he bends;
So, closing gently
His eyes to the clear sun,
Sighing, the king's soul to Allfather ascends.

CANTO XXI.

RING'S DIRGE.

I.

TH' hero-sprung sov'reign
　　Sits in his barrow,
Battle-blade by him,
Buckler on arm;—
Chafing, his courser
Close to his side neighs,
Pawing with gold-hoof
The earth-girded grave.

II.

Royally Ring now
Rides over Bifrost;
Rocks with the burden
The arch-bended bridge.
Wide-ope spring Valhal's
Vast-vaulted portals,
Th' asas his hands, glad
Hurry to grasp.

III.

Far on a foray
Fights puissant Thor, but

Welcomes with wine-cup
Allfather's wink.
Frey round the chieftain's
Crown plaiteth corn-ears,
Frigg binds bright-hued
Blue-flow'rs among.

IV.

White-bearded bard, ag'd
Brage, his gold-harp
Sweeps — and yet softer
Stealeth the lay;
Lull'd by the lyre-tones
Vanadis listens,
Bent o'er the board her
Bosom of snows.

V.

Swords, 'mid cleft helmets
Savagely sing, and
Fierce-boiling billows
Blood-red still run.
Arm-strength, which good gods
Give to the warrior,
Brutal as berserk
Bites on the shield.

VI.

Hail, then, to Valhal
Heav'n-honor'd prince, whose
Shield his sav'd country
Shelter'd with peace!
Type of tried strength, soft
Temper'd by love, like
Incense rich-rising,
Reach'dst thou the sky!

VII.

Words wise and chosen
Valfather whispers,
Seated by Saga,
Sokvabek's maid;—
So clang the chieftain's
Silver-clear tones, like
Mimer's fount flowing
Freshly and deep.

VIII.

Furious feudmen
Forset' appeases,
Doomer where Urd's bright
Welling waves flow;—
So on the doom-stone,
Dreadful but dear, wise

Ring hasten'd, heroes'
Hands to disarm.

IX.

Generous gifts, too,
Gave he rich, scatt'ring
Round him dwarf-day-shine,*
Dragon-bed bright;
Glad from his princely
Palm went the present;
Light from his lips flew
Love, pity, hope!

X.

Welcome, then, wise one!
Valhal's-heir, welcome!
Long shall the Northland
Laud thy lov'd name!
Brage, the mead-horn
Holding, hails courteous,—
Ring, norn's peace-pledge,
Prince from the North

* Gold. The dwarfs lived in the rocks, where they had no sunlight.

CANTO XXII.

THE ELECTION TO THE KINGDOM.

I.

TO thing, away o'er dale and hill
    The fire-cross speeds;
King Ring is dead,—his throne to fill
    A diet needs.

II.

To his wall-hung sword each yeoman flies,
    Its steel is blue,—
And quick its edge his finger tries,
    It bites right true.

III.

On shine, so steel-blue, joyful gaze
    His laughing boys;
The blade's too big for one to raise,
    It *two* employs.

IV.

From spot and stain his daughter frees
    The helm with care;
But how she blushes, when she sees
    Her image there!

V.

His shield's round fence, a sun in blood,
    Last guards his mail.
Hail iron-limbed freeman! warrior good!
    Hail, yeoman, hail!

VI.

Thy country's honor, glory, all,
    Thee gone, would cease;
In battle still thy brave land's wall,
    Its voice in peace!

VII.

Thus gather they, with clang of shields
    And arms' hoarse sound,
In open thing,— for heav'n's blue field
    Sole roof them around.

VIII.

But, standing on the thing-stone there,
    See Fridthjof hold
(A child as yet) the king's young heir,
    With locks of gold.

IX.

"Too young's that prince," loud murmur then
    The assembled throng;
"Nor judge he'll be among his men,
    Nor war-chief strong."

X.

But Fridthjof on his shield lifts high
　　The son of Ring;—
"Northmen! nor yet your land's hopes die,—
　　See here your king!

XI.

"See here old Odin's awful race
　　In image bright;
The shield he treads with youthful grace,—
　　So fish swims light.

XII.

"I swear his kingdom to protect
　　With sword and spear;
Till, with his father's gold-wreath deck'd,
　　I crown him here!

XIII.

"Forsete, Balder's high-born son,
　　Hath heard mine oath;
Strike dead, Forset', if e'er I'm won
　　To break my troth!"

XIV.

But thron'd king-like, the lad sat proud
　　On shield-floor high;
So the eaglet glad, from rock-hung cloud,
　　The sun will eye!

XV.

At length this place his young blood found
 Too dull to keep;
And, with one spring, he gains the ground,—
 A royal leap!

XVI.

Then rose loud shouts from all the thing,—
 "We, Northmen free,
Elect thee — shield-borne youth! like Ring,
 Thy father, be!

XVII.

"'Neath Fridthjof's guardian counsels live,—
 Thy realm his care;
Jarl Fridthjof, as thy bride we give
 His mother fair!"

XVIII.

"To-day," the frowning chief replied,
 "A king we choose,—
Not marry; when I take my bride,
 None for me woos.

XIX.

"To Balder's sacred grove I go;
 The norns, I dread,
I swore should there be met,—and know
 They wait my tread.

XX.

" Yes, all my fortunes, all my love,
    I them will tell;
Time's spreading tree beneath, above,
    Those shield-maids dwell.

XXI.

" Balder's, the light-hair'd pale god's wrath
    Still 'gainst me burns;
None else my heart's young spouse ta'en hath,
    None else returns."

XXII.

His brow slight kissing, Ring's fair child
    Salutes he low;
Then, silent, o'er the heath-plain wild
    He vanish'd slow.

CANTO XXIII.

FRIDTHJOF ON HIS FATHER'S BARROW.

I.

"HOW lovely smiles the sun, how friendly dances
    From branch to branch her mildly-soften'd beam!
In ev'ning's dews Allfather's look bright glances,
    As in his ocean-deeps, with pure clear gleam!
How red the dye that o'er yon hill advances,
    On Balder's altar-stone all blood its stream!
Soon sleeps the buried land on night's black pillow,
Soon she, yon golden shield, sinks 'neath the billow.

II.

"But first, on those dear spots I'll gaze and ponder,
    My childhood's friends, where charm'd so oft I've stood.
The self-same flow'rs still scent the eve, and yonder
    The self-same birds' soft music fills the woods;
And round that rock the tumbling waves still wander,—
    O happy he who ne'er has plough'd their flood!
To fame and name and exploits false waves wake thee.
But far, ah! far from home-land's vales they take thee!

III.

"Stream! well I know thee: oft, my heart by sadness
    Unblighted yet, I brav'd thy waters clear.
30

Dale! well I know thee; there we swore, weak madness!
  An endless faith—such faith we find not here!
Ye birches, too! whose bark in love's young gladness
  I carv'd with many a rune, unchang'd appear,—
With silv'ry stems, and leaf-crowns graceful bended
All, all's the same, 'tis my fond dream that's ended!

IV.

"Is all the same? Ah! here no Framness towers,
  No Balder's temple gems the sacred strand.
Yes! fair they were, my childhood's vales and bowers,
  Now waste and spoil'd by sword and flaming brand;
Man's vengeance, and the wrath of Valhal's powers
  Dark warnings speak from this black fire-brent land,—
Hence, pilgrim! here no pious step abideth,
For Balder's grove wild forest-creatures hideth!

V.

" Through all our life a tempter prowls malignant,
  The cruel Nidhug from the world below.
He hates that asa-light, whose rays benignant
  On th' hero's brow and glitt'ring sword bright glow.
Each scoundrel-deed which passion's rage indignant
  Prompts, he commits, curs'd tax to realms of woe:
And when successful, when the temple blazes,
His coal-black hands the fiend loud-clapping raises!

VI.

"Far-shining Valhal! is *no* atonement granted?
    Mild blue-eyed Balder, wilt thou take no fine?
Blood-fines take we when kinsmen fall; th' undaunted
    High gods themselves are sooth'd when altars shine.
O thou, of all the gods for love most vaunted,
    Some off'ring ask,—whate'er thou wilt is thine.
Could Fridthjof dream the flames would upward muster?
Give back, then, hero-god, my shield's stain'd lustre.

VII.

"Remove thy burden; 'tis too heavy for me!
    Extinguish in my soul these specters drear.
Repentance sues. The crime one moment saw me
    Dare, let a glorious life atone. Though here
The light'ner stood, I swear he would not awe me!
    The pale-blue Hel herself I would not fear!
At thee, whose looks the moon's white beams resemble,
And thy revenge, O gentle god, I tremble!

VIII.

"Here stands my father's cairn. Sleeps he here under?
    Ah! thither rode whence returneth none!
Yon starry tent his home, the shield's loud thunder
    Now hears he glad, or mead-draughts has begun.
From heav'n's fields look, thou asa-guest, nor wonder—
    Thy son invokes thee, Thorstein, Viking's son!

Nor runes I have, nor spells, nor wizard-token,—
But say how Asa-Balder's rage is broken." . . . .

IX.

"Has, then, the grave no tongue? From out his barrow
    Spake strong-arm'd Angantyr for sword of steel;
But what was Tirfing's price, though like swift arrow
    It struck, to what I ask? No sword reveal,
An isle-fight such will give,—but wounds that harrow
    The soul, Oh teach me, Asgard-chief, to heal!
My uncertain gaze direct; Oh lead my guesses!
Sore, Balder's wrath a noble mind distresses.

X.

"Thou speak'st not, father! Hark! in tones soft-blended
    The billow murmurs; let its words be thine!
The storm-wind rises, on his wings suspended,
    Oh whisper ere he go, some hint divine
Like golden rings the sunset clouds are bended.
    Let one of them thy thought's bright herald shine!
No word!—no sign!—thy son's distresses heed'st thou,
Dear father? Ah! poor death! What pity need'st
    thou?" . . . .

XI.

The sun is quench'd, and ev'ning's breeze is trolling
    To the earth's tir'd race its cloud-sprung lullaby;
And ev'ning's blush drives up, her chariot rolling,
    With rose-red wheels along the dark'ning sky;

Like some fair Valhal-vision, men consoling,
   She flies blue-tinted hills and valleys by.
Then sudden, o'er the western waters pendent,
An image comes, with gold and flames resplendent.

XII.

An air-born phantom call we such heav'n-wonder,
   (In Valhal sounds its name more fair, I ween;)
O'er Balder's groves it hovers, night's clouds under,
   Like gold-crown resting on a bed of green.
Above, below,—its rich hues Valhal's plunder,—
   It glows with pomp ne'er 'fore by mortal seen.
At last, to a temple settling, firm 'tis grounded,—
Where Balder's stood, another temple's founded.

XIII.

Of Breidablik an image, o'er the rifted
   And cavern'd cliff high walls like silver shone.
The steel-cut pillars deep-blue tints quick shifted,
   One splendid jewel was its altar-stone;
Light hung the dome, as though by sprites uplifted,
   And clear and pure as winter's starry zone;
And high therein, rich sky-blue dresses wearing,
Sat Valhal's deities, bright gold-crowns bearing.

XIV.

And see! the norns are in the porch assembled,
   On rune-carv'd shields supported gallantly;

Three rose-buds in one urn the group resembled,—
    All solemn sweetness, charming dignity.
And Urd all silent, points where th' ruins trembled,
    But Skuld doth show the new fane's majesty,
And scarce had Fridthjof, glad and wond'ring, banish'd
His troublous dread—when straight the pageant vanish'd!

xv.

"Enough, ye maidens, Time's pure spring attending!
    Thy sign it was, O hero-father good!
The ruin'd temple shall again, o'erbending
    The steep as erst, stand beauteous where it stood.
How sweet—with peaceful exploits thus contending—
    To atone the impetuous rage of youth's hot blood!
Once more the fierce-rejected hopeful liveth;
Appeas'd and mild—the White God now forgiveth!

xvi.

"Hail, welcome stars! up yonder wand'ring nightly;
    Your silent courses glad I see once more!
Hail, northern-lights! up yonder flaming brightly;
    Red temple-fires ye were for me before!
Green flourish, cairn!—and, from the wave trill'd lightly
    Again, thou wondrous song, soft music pour!—
Here on my shield I'll sleep, and dreaming wonder
How man's appeas'd, and gods forget their thunder!"

CANTO XXIV.

THE RECONCILIATION.

I.

FINISH'D great Balder's temple stood;
    Round it no palisade of wood
Ran now as erst;
A railing stronger, fairer than the first,
And all of hammer'd iron — each bar
Gold-tipp'd and regular —
Walls Balder's sacred house. Like some long line
Of steel-clad champions, whose bright war-spears shine
And golden helms afar — so stood
This glitt'ring guard within the holy wood.

II.

Of granite blocks enormous, join'd with curious care
And daring art, the massy pile was built, and there
    (A giant-work intended
    To last till time was ended)
It rose like Upsal's temple, where the North
Saw Valhal's halls fair imag'd here on earth.

III.

Proud stood it there on mountain steep, its lofty brow
Reflected calmly on the sea's bright-flowing wave;

But round about, some girdle like of beauteous flow'rs,

Went Balder's dale, with all its groves' soft murmur'd
    sighs,

And all its birds' sweet-twitter'd songs,—the home of
    peace!

IV.

High was the bronze-cast portal, and two rows   .

   Of circling columns on their shoulders strong

The dome's arch'd round bore up; and fair as shows

    A gold shield bright

    All vaulted light,—

So fair, so light, above the fane that dome it hong.

V.

Farthest within, the god's high altar rested,

   Hewn all of one sole block

   From northern marble rock;

And round thereon its scroll the serpent twisted,

   With solemn rune

   Each fold thick strewn,

Whose words, from Hávamál and vala taken,

Deep thoughts in ev'ry human bosom waken;

   While in the wall above

A niche was seen, with stars of gold

On dark-blue ground; and there, behold!

All mild and gentle as the silver moon

Sitting heav'n's blue aboon,

The silver image stands of Balder, god of love!

VI.

So seemed the sanctuary. Forth in pairs now tread
Twelve temple virgins; vests of silver thread
Adorn each slender form, and roses red
O'er ev'ry cheek soft graces shed, and spread
O'er ev'ry innocent heart a fragrant, fair rose-bed,
Before the White God's image; and around
The late-bless'd altar dancing, light they bound
As spring-winds leap where rippling fount-waves sound,
As woodland elves that skip along the ground,
Skimming the high-grown grass

Which morning's dew

Still hangs with sparkling gems of ev'ry hue;—
Ah! how those jewels tremble as the fairies pass.

VII.

And, while the dance went round, a holy song they sung
Of Balder—that mild god—and how he was belov'd
By ev'ry creature, till he fell by Hoder's dart,
And earth and ocean wide, and heav'n itself, sore wept!
How pure, how tender that song it pealeth!

Sure never sprang

Such tuneful clang

31

From mortal breast!   No! heav'n revealeth
Some tone from Breidablik, from out the god's own hall,
All soft as lonely maiden's thoughts on him she loves,
What time the quail calls deeply 'mid the peace of night;
The North's tall birches bath'd i' th' moon's pale-quiv'ring
    sheen.

VIII.

And Fridthjof, leaning on his sword, whose glance
Shines far around, stood lost as in a trance,
And charm'd, and silent, gaz'd upon the dance.
Thereat his childhood's mem'ries how they throng
Before his raptur'd eye!   A jocund train, and long,
    And innocent, and glad, and true,
    With eyes like heav'n's own blue,
And heads rich-circled by bright-golden tresses;
His former youth-friend, each with some sweet sign
    addresses.
    Then all his viking life,
    With scenes of murd'rous strife
    And bold adventure rife,
Like some dark, bloody shadow sinketh
Fast down to night.   Ah! glad he drinketh
Forgetfulness' sweet cup, and thinketh,
"Repose at last those sea-king exploits have;
I stand a flow'r-crown'd bauta-stone upon their grave."

IX.

High and still higher mounts the sweet-ton'd lay,
And upward as its warbled harm'nies roll,

    The hero's soul

    Wings glad its flight

    To Valaskjalf the bright,

From earth's low valleys far, far, far away!

    As from the mountain's breast,

    In ice-mail drest,

Its winter-cuirass melts and falls

    When back again

    To gods and men

Spring's sun life's joy recalls;

So human vengeance vanishes,

So human hate he banishes;

And, as he stands in silent ecstasy,

His hero-bosom swells with peace's sun-lit sea.

X.

Yes! 'twas as if he felt the heart of nature beat
Responsive to his own; as if, deep-mov'd, he'd press
In brotherly embrace Heimskringla's orb, and peace
Straight make with all creation — while the god looks on.
Then up the temple trod great Balder's priest supreme,
Not young and fair, the White God like, but tall of mien,
With heav'nly mildness on his noble features stamp'd,

And grac'd with silver beard that down to his girdle
    flow'd.
Unwonted rev'rence Fridthjof's haughty soul now felt,
And the eagle-pinions on his helm he bended deep
As the age-crown'd seer advanc'd, who words of peace
    thus spoke:

XI.

" Son Fridthjof, welcome!—yes, I've long expected
That thou shouldst come,— for force, 'tis true, still wanders
Round land and sea afar, wild berserk like,
That pale with rage the shield's hard border biteth;
But yet at last it home returns again,
Outwearied and all calm.   The strong-armed Thor
Full oft against giant Jotunheim did wend,
But spite his belt celestial, spite his gauntlets,
Utgard-Loke still his throne retains;
Evil, itself a force, to force yields never!

XII.

" Goodness, not join'd with strength, must child's-play be:
On Æger's bosom so the sun shines prettily;
But fickle as the flood the graspless splendor see,
As sink or rise the billows — thus, all changeably,
The fairy brightness flitteth, moving endlessly,
And force, from goodness sever'd, surely dies;
Self-eating, self-consum'd, as sword that lies

In some damp cairn—black rust corrodes the prize!
Yes! life's debauch fierce strength's mad riot is!
But ah! oblivion's heron flutters still
O'er goblet-brim that traitorous sweet draughts fill,
And deep's the waken'd drunkard's shame for deeds of ill!

XIII.

"From th' earth all strength proceeds, from Ymer's body;
The wild tumultuous waters are its veins,
Its ev'ry sinew is of smithied brass;
But still 'tis empty all, and bare, and barren,—
Till heav'n's bright goodness rise,
Till fruitful sun-beams stream from laughing skies;
Then blooms the grass, then purple flow'rs their broid'ry
    weave,
Then rounds the gold fruit, fresh crowns the forest leave,
And men and animals from mother earth new life receive.

XIV.

"Thus 'tis with all Ask's children. In the scale
Of ev'ry human life Allfather placeth
Two weights, each other balancing when right
The beam is pois'd; and earthly strength we call
The one, while th' other hight is heav'nly goodness.
Strong is great Thor, no doubt, when Megingarder
He braces tightly o'er his rock-firm loins
And strikes his best; and Odin too, I trow,

Is wise enough, by Urd's bright silver wave
Sitting and gazing downward, while his eagles,
Swift messengers, come flying from afar
And tell to th' asas' sire this round world's tidings;—
But, son! they both grew pale, the vivid brightness
Of both their crowns half faded, when white Balder,
The gentle deity, the banding gem
In Valhal's wreath divine all sudden fell!
Then on Time's wide-stretched tree its leaf-crown's glory
Fast wither'd, while grim Nidhug bit triumphant
Its deep-torn roots! Then old Night's prison'd forces
Broke loose at once, while Midgard's serpent dash'd
With venom'd tail the far-empoison'd skies,
And Fenris howl'd and roar'd, and Surt's old fire blade
From Muspelheim blaz'd bright. Wherever, since,
Thy vision gazes, still through all creation
The rocking battle goes! The gold-comb'd cock
The gods in Valhal loudly crow'd to arms;
The blood-red cock as shrilly summons all
On earth and down beneath it.

XV.

" Ah! peace till then
Sat thron'd in Valhal,—sat enthron'd 'mong men,—
In human bosom, and in each god's breast
Breath'd heav'nly rest!

XVI.

"But here what happens hath already happen'd
On a still grander scale above us. Man's
But Valhal imag'd faintly,—heav'n's soft light
Reflected dim in Saga's rune-grav'd shield.

XVII.

"Each heart its Balder hath. Hast thou forgot, my son,
Those days ere life's dark struggles had begun,—
When all existence was so glad, so fresh, so one
As is the woodland songster's dream
When summer eve's warm breezes gently stream
Lulling each drowsy flow'ret's head,
Rocking that songster's own soft leaf-green bed?
Ah! then, thou asa-born,—thou moving image fair
Of glorious Valhal!—still in thy spirit pure
Did Balder's life endure!
To th' child the god lives ever, and whene'er
A new-born infant sees the day,
Hel, that goddess grim, restores her prey.

XVIII.

"But in each human soul we find
That night's dark Hoder, Balder's brother blind,
Is born and waxeth strong as he;
For blind is ev'ry evil born, as bear-cubs be.

Night is the cloak of evil; but all good
Hath ever clad in shining garments stood.
The busy Loke, tempter from of old,
Still forward treads incessant, and doth hold
The blind one's murder-hand, whose quick-launch'd spear,
Pierceth young Balder's breast, that sun of Valhal's sphere!

XIX.

"Then waketh hate; for prey springs violence quick
And hungry roameth, hill and valley round,
The sword's grim wolf, while dragons wildly swim
O'er redly-flowing billows; for pale Virtue
Sits hopeless, strengthless, shadow-like, with Hel,
All dead amongst the dead, and Balder's house,
Once tow'r'd so high, now lies a black'ning ruin.

XX.

"The lofty asas' life thus images
The lower course of man's existence;—both
Are great Allfather's thoughts, and alter never.
What hath been, as what shall be, knoweth well
The mystic vala's chant; that chant the sweet-ton'd,
Soft, cradle-lullaby of infant time
Its death-dirge also pealeth. Yes! the records
Of wide Heimskringla echo vala's song,
And man therein his own sad story readeth.

XXI.

"The vala asks thee,—mark, my son, her words,—
Grasp ye the sense, or no?

XXII.

" Thou wilt be reconcil'd. But reconcilement's — what?
Nay, youth undaunted, meet my gaze and turn not pale!
Th' atoner wanders round our earth, and death he's hight.
All time is, in itself, a troubled streamlet
From vast eternity; all earthly life
From great Allfather's throne hath fall'n, atonement
Restores us thither back, all cleans'd and pure.
Yes, th' asas ev'n have fall'n; and Ragnarok
Is their great day of reconcilement. Ah!
A bloody day 'twill be, on Vigrid's boundless,
Wild, death-strewn plain — for there shall th' asas perish!
But unaveng'd they fall not; no! all evil
Dies there an endless death, while goodness riseth
From that great world-fire, purified at last,
To a life far higher, better, nobler than the past.

XXIII.

"Yes! tho' from heav'n's proud brow the garland drops
Of faded stars, and earth sinks in the deep,
Fairer and newly-born her flow'r-crown'd head
Again shall rise above the crystal flood,
And younger stars shall hold, with purer lustre,
Their silent course above the new creation.

XXIV.

"But Balder then, where verdant hills fresh rise, shall rule
The new-born asas, and the pure-made race of men;
And those fair golden runic-tablets lost, alas!
In time's young dawning—Valhal's children, reconcil'd,
'Mong Ida-valley's fragrant grass shall find once more.
Thus is the death of fallen goodness only
Its reconcilement, its fierce furnace proof,—
Another birth to a far other life,
Which backward flies whence first it emanated,
And innocently playeth, infant-like
On parent-knee upborne. Ah! after all,
The best, the happiest, noblest, of existence
Beyond the tomb we find,—that green-deck'd portal
Of Gimle's paradise. Yes! low, and with but ill
Deep-stained is what we meet beneath heav'n's star-lit hill.

XXV.

"Yet ev'n this life atonement hath,—its lowly path
Dim antetype of that still higher,—the last day's fire!
        Imperfect and yet sweet it is!
        Like minstrel harmonies
When deep-skilled skald with ready finger sweeps
        The waking harp,
And broken chords doth strike, and keeps
        Now low, now sharp,

Tuning the quiv'ring strings
With dream-like fragment echoings,
Till, high upborne at last on music's wings,
With full tones richly peal'd, entranced he sings
Of exploits and of heroes brave;
Awaking from their grave
The mighty forms of old,—
While, charmed, his beaming eyes behold
All Valhal's glories, all great Odin's pillar'd gold!

XXVI.

"Earth is heav'n's shadow—human life the porch
And outer court of Balder's heav'nly temple.
The vulgar offer blood—they bring proud steeds,
With gold and purple deck'd, before the altar,—
It is a symbol, rightly read, that blood
Is the red dawn of every day of grace.

XXVII.

"But still the token
Can ne'er the substance be;
What thou thyself hast broken
None but thyself atones for thee!
The dead are reconcil'd in great Allfather's
Bosom celestial; but the sole atonement
Of him who lives, is in his own deep breast.
There is one off'ring which the gods prefer

To thousand hecatombs,—the sacrifice
Of that wild hate and burning, fierce revenge
Harbor'd in thine own bosom. Canst thou not
Their thirsty sabres charm to peace again—
Ah! canst thou not forgive—what wilt thou, youth,
In Balder's mansion here? What meant thou, say,
With this arch'd temple, built to peaceful powers?
No pil'd-up stones atone!
Such off'rings Balder will have none.
No! with mild,. merciful, pure peace alone ·
Atonement lives.
In heav'n, on earth, 'tis only peace that pardon gives.
First with thyself and with thy foe united be,—
Thou then art reconcil'd with yon pale deity.

XXVIII.

" In lands far south, 'tis said,
Is some new Balder worshiped,—
He, the pure virgin's son from heav'n who sped,
Sent by the Allfather's self to explain the dim
And yet unfathom'd runes which crowd the rim
Bord'ring the shield of darkness, that dread shield
Worn by the norns. And never would this Balder wield
Our earth's dark blood-stain'd arms. No! still in his
    glad field
Was peace his battle cry, his bright sword, love,

And o'er his silver helmet sat the dove
Of brooding innocence. His pious days
In sweet instruction pass'd, or pray'r or praise;
And when he died, his dying voice forgave,—
And now, 'neath far-off palms, still stands his shining
    grave.

This doctrine, say they, spreads o'er ev'ry land,
Melting hard hearts and joining hand in hand,
And on this earth, now reconcil'd again,
Upraising gentle peace's wide domain.
Not yet, alas!
Hath human lip to mine ag'd ear explain'd aright
This creed; but still, when better moments o'er me pass,
My dim gaze darkly sees afar its streaming light.
Ah! where is human heart that hath not, like as mine,
Presag'd its truths divine?
But this I know:—One day, with dove-white wings
She comes, and gently floats along, and sings
O'er all the hilly North. But *then* no North
Will send, as now, its savage warriors forth:—
No! while new chieftains reign, shall flourish other men;
And deep in hero-cairns, forgotten then,
Our bones will lie,
While Northland's oaks above us deeply sigh.
Ye happier race, ye sons who then shall drink
That new light's lustre foaming o'er the brink

Of truth's bright-beaming goblet,—hail, all hail!

Yes! words would fail

To speak how bless'd ye'll be,

If far from off your heav'n those shadows flee

Which have so gloomily,

As yet, hung thickly stretch'd on high,

Hiding like some damp veil life's sunny sky!

But still, ye sons, despise not us, your father's line.

Ah! with what eager gaze our eyne

Have ceaseless sought to drink those rays divine

Shining from life's and light's bright sun!

Know! he hath many envoys, but the Allfather's one!

XXIX.

"Thou hatest Bele's sons!—but wherefore hate them?

Forsooth, because that to a yeoman's child

They would not give their sister,—she, descended

From Seming's blood, th' illustrious Odin's offspring!

Yes, sprung from Valhal's throne is Bele's race,—

Bright genealogy, just source of pride!

But birth is chance, is fortune, thou observest,

And cannot be a merit. Know, my son,

That man still boasts of fortune, not of merit.

Say! is't not gen'rous gods who were the givers,

Should any noble quality adorn us?

With haughty pride thou art thyself inflam'd

At all thy hero exploits, all thy fierce-nerv'd
Resistless strength; but didst thou give thyself
This force? Was't not great Asa-Thor who strung
Firm as gnarl'd oak thy tough and sinewy arm?
Say, is't not god-sprung courage that so gladly,
So loudly throbs within that shield-hung fortress,
Thy fast arch'd breast? And that clear flaming glance
Leaping from out thine eye,—say, is't not lightning
From heav'n that playeth there? The lofty norns
E'en at thy cradle sang the princely legend
Of all thy life's adventures. Ah! from these
Thou hast no greater merit than have king Bele's
Two boasting sons that 'twas a king begat them!
Condemn not, judge not others' pride! then none
Will judge thine own. King Helge is no more!"
"King Helge, he,"—said Fridthjof,—"when, where, how?"

xxx.

"Thyself knowest well that whilst thou here hast builded
This temple to the god, king Helge march'd
On painful foray 'mong the heathen Fins,
Scaling each mountain wall. In Finland's borders,
Rais'd on a barren, time-worn peak, there stood
An ancient temple consecrate to Jumala;
Abandon'd and fast-shut for many ages
This desolate fane had been, its ev'ry rite
Long since forgotten; but, above the portal,

An old and monstrous idol of the god
Stood, frail-supported, trembling to its fall;
This temple none dar'd enter, scarce approach;
For down from sire to son an eld tradition
Went dimly warning, that whoever first
The temple visited should Jumala view!
This Helge heard, and in his blind fierce rage
The pathless wilds trod 'gainst this deity
So hated from of old, all bent on razing
The temple's heathen walls. But when he'd march'd
Up where the ruin threaten'd, lo! all fast
The massy moss-grown door was clos'd; and, cover'd
With thick brown rust, the key still sat within it;
Grim Helge then, the door-posts gripping hard,
With rude, uncivil strain the mould'ring pillars
Fierce shook, and straightway with tremendous crash
The sculptur'd image fell, burying beneath it
Valhal's impious son; and so dread Jumala
His eyes behold. A messenger in haste,
These tidings brought ere yet last night was ended.

XXXI.

"Now, only Halfdan sits on Bele's chair,—
Thy hand, brave Fridthjof, offer him. Revenge
And passion sacrifice to heav'n's high gods;
This Balder's shrine demandeth. I demand, too,

As Balder's highest priest, in token meet
That peace's gentle chief thou hast not mocked
With vain professions and an empty homage.
Decide, my son!—shall Balder's peace be broken?
If so, in vain thou 'st built this fane, the token
Of mild forgiveness, and in vain ag'd priest hath spoken!"

XXXII.

Over the copper threshold Halfdan now,
With pallid brow
And fearful, fitful glance, advanceth slow
Tow'rds yonder tow'ring, ever-dreaded foe,
And, silent, at a distance stands.
Then Fridthjof, with quick hands,
The corselet hater, Angervadil, from his thigh
Unbuckleth, and his bright shield's golden round
Leaning 'gainst th' altar, thus draws nigh;
While his cow'd enemy
He thus accosts, with pleasant dignity:
"Most noble in this strife will he be found
Who first his right hand good
Offers in pledge of peaceful brotherhood!"
Then Halfdan, deeply blushing, doffs with haste
His iron-gauntlet and, with hearty grasp embrac'd.
Each long, long sever'd hand
Its friend-foe hails, steadfast as mountain bases stand!

XXXIII.

That ag'd and awful priest then glad removeth
The curse that rested on the varg i véum,
Fridthjof the outlaw; and as the last deep accents
Of reconcilement and of blessing sounded,
Lo! Ing'borg sudden enters, rich adorn'd
With bridal ornaments, and all enrob'd
In gorgeous ermine, ånd by bright-ey'd maidens
Slow follow'd, as on heav'n's broad canopy
Attending star-trains guard the regent moon!
But the young bride's fair eyes —
Those two blue skies —
Fill quick with tears,
And to her brother's heart she trembling sinketh;
He, with his sister's fears
Deep-mov'd, her hand all tenderly in Fridthjof's linketh,
His burden soft transferring to that hero's breast, —
Its long-tried, faith fit place for Ing'borg's rest;
Then to her heart's first, best beloved, her childhood's
     friend,
In nuptial band
She gives her lily hand,
As before pard'ning Balder's altar both low bend!

NOTES.

IN its present form Tegnér's "Fridthjof's Saga" was first published in the year 1825; but already before that the last nine cantos had been given to the public in a Swedish magazine called "Idun." The cantos XVI-XIX inclusive were published in 1820, and the cantos XX-XXIV in 1822. In 1871 twenty large editions of this celebrated poem had been, called for in Sweden alone. Nearly as many editions have appeared in Norway and Denmark; and in Icelandic there is now a splendid version by Matthías Jochumsson. England boasts eighteen different translations. Thirteen translations had appeared in Germany in 1863, when the ninth edition of Mohnike's version appeared. The poem has been reproduced in all European languages, even in Russian, Polish and modern Greek. H. W. Longfellow and Bayard Taylor are the only American authors who hitherto have published "Fridthjof's Saga" in whole or in part. The former has written an elaborate review with copious translations, the latter has edited Rev. William Lewery Blackley's translation with an introduction. The present (the appendix of this volume) is thus, as the reader will observe, the second American edition of the *whole* poem, but the writer of this (Anderson) has recently had the pleasure of reading in manuscript a complete American translation. It is the result of several years' patient and pains-taking labor of Mr. and Mrs. Thos. A. E. Holcomb. It is the *nineteenth* English but the *first* American *translation*, and it certainly will hold its own among any of its English predecessors. We have not the manuscript at hand, but the easy, graceful and musical flow of its metres has been ringing in our ear since Mr. Holcomb had the goodness to pay us a visit and read it to us. One feature of the Holcomb version is of special interest,— every canto is rendered in the same metre as the Swedish original, and the feminine rhymes are everywhere preserved. Moreover the *alliteration* in canto XXI of the original is reproduced,— a task that most of the other *English* translators have shrunk from in dismay.* In short, the Holcomb translation is in every way so excellent that it cannot fail to be received with generous favor, and we are glad that it is soon to be published.

In reference to Norse-mythological names, we refer the reader, once for all, to the Vocabulary and Index of Anderson's NORSE MYTHOLOGY, in which complete information concerning the Teutonic gods and their abodes will be found.

* George Stephens has alliteration.— See poem.

CANTO I.*

Stanza 16. Dryden in "Alexander's Feast" has the same thought:

> Happy, happy, happy pair!
> *None* but the brave,
> None *but* the brave,
> None but the *brave* deserves the fair.

Stanza 17. Reading the old sagas is to this day one of the highest pleasures of the Icelander. It is with this he passes the long winter evenings. This is the amusement of the company when many have assembled together. The master of the house first begins the reading, and the others continue it when he is tired. Some of them know sagas by heart, others use printed copies, or, for want of these, fair manuscripts — not seldom written by the peasant himself.—STRINHOLM.

Stanza 18. Light hair was common in the North; black, more rare; bright yellow, a beauty in either sex. Gold or silk colored hair, light-yellow tresses, bright-gold locks, etc., almost always belong in the sagas to the description of beauty. The olden Celts also admired light hair, and the "yellow haired laddie," and "lassie wi' the lint-white locks," continue favorites with their descendants to the present day.

Stanzas 24 and 25. The inhabitants of the old North were as remarkable as the modern Norsemen for their skill and ingenuity in all kinds of handiwork. The women excelled in embroidery, whereof we find many graphic descriptions in their old writings.— See *Elder Edda,* "Gudrun's Grief," str. 14, 15, 16. In the "Volsung Saga" we read: "Great delight had they in needle-work, and greatly was Gudrun's sorrow eased thereby."

Stanza 57. The free-born yields not; for still
    His arm wins worlds where'er it will.

Witness the Norse adventures, exploits and conquests in every part of Europe, and even in Africa and Asia, from the beginning to the end of those viking expeditions whereby Iceland, Greenland and Vineland (America) were discovered, England *twice* subdued, and the whole of Europe remodeled.

CANTO II.

The gnomes put in the mouths of the old men in this canto Tegnér has taken mostly from "Hávamál" of the *Elder Edda.* This poem, of which Tegnér has employed only about a dozen strophes, contains one hundred and thirty-eight stanzas, and constitutes a literary monument of the old Teutonic mind, so sublime, so full of wisdom, in short so remarkable, that it deserves to be immortalized in every language on earth. A literal translation of it may be found in Anderson's NORSE MYTHOLOGY, pp. 130-155.

Stanza 57. Norse kings and warriors are often mentioned in the sagas as choosing their burial-place by bays and arms of the sea; as if even when dead they could not be parted from their favorite elements. The latter half of this stanza has a striking parallel in "Ynglinga Saga," ch. 36,

* As stated in our preface, the most of these notes are taken from the work of George Stephens.

where we read: "So Yngvar the king fell and his host fled away. There rests he in his cairn, right along by the salt wave's side." Thus Thjodolf:

And the East Sea
For Sweden's king
Ocean's song
To ·gladden him chanted.

CANTO III.

"Not five hundred men (though ten twelves went to the hundred)," etc. The duodecimal computation is still common in Britain as well as in Scandinavia. The *long* or *great* hundred, or thousand. etc., are well known in most trades. The old Norsemen always employed great hundreds (120) in counting men.

"Vifil," "Angervadil." "Ellide," etc. The reader will observe that much of this canto is taken from "The Saga of Thorstein, Viking's Son."

"Sun's Gates." Mythology, etymology and history unite in pointing to western Asia as the ancient home of the worshipers of Odin.

"The twelve immortals." These are Odin, Thor, Balder, Tyr, Brage, Heimdal, Hoder, Vidar, Vale, Uller, Forsete, Loke.

"Autumn-judge." The old Norsemen held their judicial *thing* (diet, assize) in the autumn.

"And live self." Burial while living is not without example in the sagas. In the saga of Hakon the Good we read of several persons who caused themselves, while yet living, to be placed within their grave-hows together with much goods.

CANTO IV.

Stanza 20. It was very common in old times to hold public meetings on the hows of celebrated kings and warriors. Owing to the gradual elevation of the ground, all present could easily see the presiding officer or chief speaker. Gustavus Vasa addressed the Dalecarlians from Frey's How (called also Thing Hill) near Upsala.

Stanza 25. The Norsemen firmly believed in the dead life of the buried hero.

CANTO VI.

Stanza 2—"Get a pawn." The Swedish word for "pawn" is "bonde," and in this stanza has a double meaning, referring to the pawn on the chess-board and to the expression of the taunting Helge in canto IV: "Our sister is not for a peasant's son." "Bonde" means both pawn and peasant. The old sagas are full of puns and enigmas.

CANTO XIII.

Stanza 2—"Balder's pyre." This expression is used here in three different meanings. and refers: (1) To Balder's funeral pile in the mythology.; (2) to the emblematic fire upon the hearth: (3) to the burning temple and grove, in which the image of Balder was consumed as on a funeral pile.

CANTO XX.

Stanza 14. Compare with this stanza the last stanza of Ragnar Lodbrok's
"Death-Song":

> Cease my strain! I hear a voice
> From realms where martial souls rejoice;
> I hear the maids of slaughter call,
> Who bid me hence to Odin's hall.
> High-seated in their blest abodes
> I soon shall quaff the drink of gods.
> The hours of life have glided by,
> I fall, but smiling shall I die.

CANTO XXIV.

Stanza 5 —"The serpent twisted." It should be observed that the knots wont
to be engraven on runic monuments to denote an indissoluble bond of
fidelity and affection were commonly serpent-formed; and when such knots
occur, the first care of the runic decipherer is to find the head of the serpent, for here begins the reading of the inscription.

Stanza 11 —"Belt." Thor's belt was Megingjarder (belt of strength); and
whenever he girded himself with it, his strength was redoubled.

Stanza 12 —"Oblivion's heron." This expression refers to the following passage in "Hávamál":

> Oblivion's heron 'tis called
> That over potations hovers;
> He steals the minds of men.
> With this bird's pinions
> I was fettered
> In Gunlad's * dwelling.

Stanza 14 —"Gold-combed cock," etc. Such are the signs which, according to
the vala in "Völuspá" of the *Elder Edda*, shall usher in the Twilight of
the Gods (Ragnarok)· the day terrible alike to gods and to men. Thus the
Elder Edda:

> Among the gods crowed
> The gold-combed cock,
> He who wakes in Valhal
> The hosts of heroes;
> Beneath the earth
> Crows another,
> The root-red cock
> In the halls of Hel.†

Stanza 21 —"Grasp ye the sense, or no?" This is an imitation of the vala's
repeated question in the latter part of "Völuspá." She ends many stanzas
by saying. "Know ye now more or not?"

* Gunlad was the keeper of the poetic mead.— See NORSE MYTHOLOGY,
pp. 249-250.

† NORSE MYTHOLOGY, p. 420.

VOCABULARY.

Æger. The god of the sea.

Æger's daughters. The waves.

Alfheim. The palace of Frey.

Allfather (the Great Spirit). He that lives through all generations, and whom we dare not name; the Creator of the sun, the Ruler of all things; the Lofty one, the Ancient, the Revealer of mysteries, the Manifold, the great almighty God, whom all nations have sought in their mythological systems. He is the father of gods and men; nay, he is the *Indescribable*.

Angantyr. Jarl of the Orkneys. — See "The Saga of Thorstein, Viking's Son," ch. 24.

Angervadil (the wader through sorrow). Fridthjof's sword.

Asas. The Norse deities, whose chief was Odin.

Asgard. The celestial abode of the gods.

Ask. The first man created by the gods.

Astrild. The goddess of love. She is not mentioned in the Norse mythology, but appears in the poems of the later Norse skalds. The name is from the Teutonic root *ast*, love, and is connected with *Easter* (Germ. *Oster*), the feast of Venus among the Britons and Germans.

Balder. Odin's and Frigg's son. The god of innocence, piety, and light. He was often called the white god.

Balders-hage. Balder's meads. A sanctuary in Sogn in Norway, consecrated to Balder.

Bele. Son of Skate.—See "The Saga of Thorstein, Viking's Son," ch. 17.

Berserk. Etymology contested. It undoubtedly comes from *berr* (Germ. *bär*; Eng. bear, *ursus*) and *serkr* (cp. *sark*, Scot. for *shirt*). Hence bear-coats; and we also have men called wolf-coats. Berserks were wild warriors, or champions, in the heathen age.

Berserks-gang. Berserk's-course. The fit of fury which seized the berserk when dangerously excited by his martial frenzy.

Bifrost. The trembling bridge. The bridge betwixt heaven and earth, guarded against the giants by Heimdal. The rainbow.

Bjorn Blue-tooth.— See "The Saga of Thorstein, Viking's Son," ch. 3.

Blood-eagle. To carve the blood-eagle is an expression in the sagas referring to a cruel punishment given to detested enemies or the most wretched villains. It consisted in cutting the figure of an eagle on the back of the sufferer, parting the ribs from the back-bone and drawing the lungs from out the opening.

BRAGE. The god of poetry and song.

BRAN. Fridthjof's dog. His name seems to have been suggested to Tegnér by a passage in "Ossian" (Temora 8).

BREIDABLIK. Balder's dwelling. The broad-shining splendor, where nothing impure is found.

BRETLAND. The land of the Britons.

CHESS. The game of chess has been known in the North from the earliest times, and is mentioned again and again in the sagas. The Icelanders are to this day excellent chess-players.

DAY. The son of Night and Delling (day-break).

DELLING. One of the asas, the last husband of the giantess Night. Delling's son is Day.

DISES. Goddesses.

DISES' HALL. Pantheon.

DWARFS. The Cyclopes (Gr Κίκλωπες) in miniature. Pigmies hideous in form and malevolent in disposition, but excelling in mechanical skill. They made Draupner, Skidbladner, Gungner, etc. They dwelt in rocks and caverns, and had quickened as maggots in the body of the slaughtered Ymer.

DWERGMÁL. Dwarf-language, echo.

EARTH (Jord). Daughter of Night, spouse of Odin, mother of Thor, sister of Day, etc.

EAST SEA. The Baltic.

EPJE SOUND. At the Orkneys.

EINHERJES. The happy heroes in Valhal.

ELLIDE. Fridthjof's ship.

FAFNER. The famous dragon, who sat brooding over the enormous wealth procured for the death of Otter.— See NORSE MYTHOLOGY, p. 375.

FENRIS. One of the three monster-offspring of Loke and Angerboda. The giant wolf who devours Odin in Ragnarok.

FOLKVANG. Freyja's hall.

FORSETE. The son of Balder and Nanna; God of justice.

FRAMNESS. A promontory in Sogn, Norway, where Fridthjof's estate was situated.

FREY. Njord's son; the god of harvest.

FREYJA. Njord's daughter, Oder's wife; goddess of love.

FRIDTHJOF. The thief or spoiler of peace.

FRIGG. Odin's wife.

FYLKE originally meant a district capable of supporting an armed force of fifty warriors, and having its own independent chief.

GANDVIK (Serpent-bay). The White Sea, so called from its tortuosity.

GEFJUN. The goddess of virgin-purity.

GERD. Frey's wife.

GIMLE. The home of the righteous after Ragnarok.

GJALLARHORN. Heimdal's trumpet. Its sound was heard through all the worlds.

GLITNER. Forsete's dwelling.

GRONING SOUND (Gronsound). The sound betwixt the Danish Isles, Zealand, Moen and Falster.

HAGBART. One of the heroes in the Norse sagas. He was betrothed to the princess Signe, but enmity arose between her father, king Sigar, and him. Sigar took Hagbart prisoner and hanged him. Signe would not survive her lover, but set fire to her bower and perished in the flames. Hagbart and Signe in the North answers to *Romeo and Juliet* or *Abelard and Heloise* in the South and West.

HALFDAN. Son of Bele.

HÁVAMÁL (Song of the High one). One of the poems of the *Elder Edda*. A collection of maxims given by Odin.

HEIMDAL. The god of the rainbow, the warder of the gods.

HEIMSKRINGLA. The earth's circle; the world.

HEL. Goddess of death; daughter of Loke and Angerboda.

HELGE. Son of Bele.

HERSER. Captain-general, a dignity inferior to that of jarl.

HILD. One of the valkyries; goddess of war.

HILDING. The foster-father of Fridthjof and Ingeborg.

HODER. The god of darkness and winter. Balder's blind brother and by Loke's instigation Balder's murderer.

HOLM-GANG. A duel, so called because it was generally fought on a holm (rock-island).

IDAVELLIR. Ida-vales. Ida's plains; the place where the gods assemble.

IDUN. Brage's wife; the goddess of youth.

INGEBORG. Daughter of Bele.

IRON-HEAD. Kol's and Trona's third child hight Harek Iron-head.

JADAR. The present Jæderen in Stavanger Amt, Norway.

JARL. Earl.

JOTUNHEIM. The home of the giants.

JUMALA (the Supreme). From time immemorial the Finnish term for the Great God. To him no tokens were attributed and no distinguishing qualities. He *was* the Only, the Highest, he who himself invisible governed all. In Bjarmeland was set up his image, by itself; the lower deities had nothing such. Northward on a cape by Vin-å (the river Dvina) stood this Jumala idol, within a spot consecrated thereto and surrounded by a lofty paling. Rich and sacred it was and became a kind of national sanctuary for the Finnish tribes. It is worthy of remark that the name Jumiel occurs in the list of angelic princes given in the apocryphal book ascribed to Enoch. The Finnish name of God is still Jumala.

LOFN. Goddess of marriage.

LOKE. The god of evil; the instigator of Balder's death.

MEGINGJARDER. Thor's belt of strength.

MIDGARD-SERPENT. Loke's and Angerboda's offspring; brother of Hel and the Fenris-wolf. With his immense tail he encircles the whole earth.

MIMER. Owner of the fountain of wisdom at that root of Ygdrasil which extends to Ginungagap (chaos).

MORVEN. The north of Scotland.

MUSPELHEIM. Surt's realm; world of fire, south of Ginungagap.

MUSPEL's SONS. The flames (cp. the daughters of Æger).

NANNA. Wife of Balder.

NASTRAND (Corpse-strand). The abode of the wicked after death.

NIDHUG. A dragon forever gnawing at that root of Ygdrasil that goes to Niflheim.

NIFLHEIM. The nebulous world; the reign of cold and darkness north of Ginungagap.

NORN. There are three chief norns: Urd, Verdande, and Skuld — Past, Present, Future. They are the Fates, or Parcæ.

ODIN. The chief among the Teutonic gods.

ODIN's BIRDS. Hugin (reason) and Munin (memory).

ORKNEYS. The Orkneys belonged for a long time to Norway, and were a favorite resort for vikings.

RAGNAROK. The Twilight of the Gods; the end of the world; the last day.

RAN. Æger's wife; goddess of the sea.

RING-RIC. The realm of Ring, on the western border of Christiania-fjord.

ROTA. One of the valkyries.

RUNE. One of the characters of the Old Norse alphabet. The runic alphabet has sixteen letters. F, U, þ, O, R, K, are the first six runes; hence the runic alphabet (a, β) is called Futhorc. Professor George Stephens is the most distinguished runic scholar living.

RUNE-STAFF. Calendar-stave carved with runic signs. It may be used instead of a common almanac.

RUNE-STONE. A grave-stone carved with runes.

SAGA. The goddess of history; the Clio of the North. She sits at Sokvabek relating to Odin the fortunes of gods and men.

SEMING. One of Odin's sons. The historical Odin had three sons: Skjold, whom he made king of Denmark; Yngve, whom he made king of Sweden; and Seming, whom he made king of Norway. — See NORSE MYTHOLOGY, p. 232-236.

SIKELEY. Sicily. The Norsemen knew this country well. They conquered it in the eleventh century, and Roger united it to Naples by the name of the two Sicilies.

SKINFAXE. Sheen-fax (shining mane). The horse of Day. Night rides ahead with her steed Rimfaxe, who every morn bedews the earth with the foam of his bridle.

SKULD. The norn of the future.

SLEIPNER. Odin's eight-footed steed. Pegasos.

SOKN-SOUND. Between the islands Sokken and Bro, to the south of Bukken-fjord near Stavanger in Norway.

Sokvabek. The dwelling of Saga.

Solund Isle. At the outlet of Sogn-fjord in Norway lies a group of islands bearing this name.

Sote. A celebrated Norse freebooter.

Streitaland. The residence of king Ring.

Surt. The god of fire; the ruler of Muspelheim.

Syrstrand. The residence of king Bele and his family. It lies opposite Framness in Sogn-fjord.

Thor. The god of strength and thunder; the son of Odin and Earth; the slayer of giants.

Thorstein. Viking's son. The eldest son of Viking; the father of Fridthjof the Bold.

Thrudvang. Thor's realm.

Thing (originally meaning talk, conference). The public meeting, die assize, parliament, or wittenagemot of the Norsemen.

Tirfing. A sword fabricated by two skillful dwarfs as a ransom for their lives. It was bright as a sunbeam; its hilt and guard were of gold; it defied rust and fracture; would cleave iron or stone as easily as a garment; and whether in single or banded combat, conferred victory on the arm which wielded it; but it should also prove fatal to its original possessor and be the instrument of three heinous crimes. The prophesy was fulfilled.

Upland. A district in Norway comprehending the present amts of Christian and Hedemark, together with the Upper Romer-ric.

Upsala. A city and university seat north of Stockholm in Sweden, where there was in olden times a famous temple where the followers of Odin worshiped.

Urd. The norn of the past.

Urd's Fountain. The fountain of time. It was situated at that root of Ygdrasil that extends to Asgard.

Utgard. The capital of Jotunheim.

Vala. Prophetess. Her prophetic song is " Völuspá," the first poem in the *Elder Edda*. She corresponds to the southern sibyl.

Valaskjalf. Vale's citadel and Odin's throne.

Vale. Son of Odin and Rind.

Valfather. Father of the slain. One of Odin's names.

Valhal. The hall of the slain. The heavenly dwelling of the gods and the einherjes.

Valkyries. Choosers of the slain. Maids who on the field of battle elect those who are worthy of going to Valhal.

Vanadis. The vāna, *i.e.* fair goddess, or the goddess of the vans (deities of the water). A surname of Freyja.

Var. The goddess of oaths.

Varg i véum. Wolf in the sanctuary. Temple-defamer.

Vegtamskvida. The lay of the wayfarer; one of the songs of the *Elder Edda*, giving an account of Odin's visit to the realm of Hel to obtain from the vala information about Balder's fate.

VIDAR. The god of silence; one of the sons of Odin; next after Thor the strongest of the gods.

VIFIL.— See "The Saga of Thorstein, Viking's Son," ch. 1.

VIGRID. The battle-field of the gods at Ragnarok; a plain stretching an hundred miles each way.

VIKING.— See "The Saga of Thorstein, Viking's Son," ch. 3, 4.

VINGOLF. The floor of friends; the hall of the goddesses in Valhal.

VOLUND. A Finnish smith celebrated in the sagas for his great skill in his trade. He lived a long time at the court of the grim king Nidud in Norway. He finally freed himself from imprisonment and took vengeance on his oppressor. He is a mythical person and corresponds to Vulcan.

WHITE GOD. A surname of Balder.

WOOLEN ACRE. Formerly a fylke-kingdom in the present province of Vestmanland, Sweden.

YGDRASIL (Ygg's, i.e. Odin's bearer). A sacred tree so called because Odin once hung in its branches. It is the world-tree. The tree of Time.

YMER. The giant out of whose body the world was shapen.

PUBLISHED BY S. C. GRIGGS & CO., CHICAGO.

THE PILOT AND HIS WIFE.—By JONAS LIE. Translated from the Norse by MRS. OLE BULL. 12mo, Cloth. $1.50.

"The book abounds in a rare poetic force."—*The Nation.*

"Lie is a novelist of very marked genius."—*North American Review.*

"It opens to English readers new and vivid fields of romance."—*Hartford Post.*

"It fascinates the attention and moves the feelings with a strange power, and when the book is finished it is easy to realize that we have been under the spell of a master."—*Appleton's Journal.*

"In manner, plot and treatment, it is so totally different from all other writings as to excite the liveliest interest. * * Lie is a writer of marked peculiarities and rare genius. His dramatic powers are intense, but his presentations of the passions and inspirations, the workings of heart, and the struggles of soul, are more vivid and striking still. * * The beauty and poetry of the novel is found in the literary workmanship which gives us the character of 'Elizabeth.' It is essentially an orig·inal character, and a pure and noble conception."—*Sacramento Daily Union.*

"It is a remarkably attractive book. * * Some of the characters are exquisitely drawn, notably those of the pilot and his wife Elizabeth. The latter is a delightful creature. The reader cannot but be struck by the intense power with which the author manages the pathetic incidents of his story, and with the naturalness that pervades the whole. The artistic workmanship will strike every person of thought and culture, while the vivid descriptions in the more exciting portions will fully absorb the attention of those who read only for amusement. There is a freshness and originality in the book, an out-door flavor and breeziness, that cannot fail to win for it a high degree of favor."—*Boston Gazette.*

PETERSON'S NORWEGIAN-DANISH GRAMMAR AND READER.—With a Vocabulary, designed for American Students of the Norwegian-Danish Language. By REV. C. I. P. PETERSON, Professor of Scandinavian Literature. 12mo, Cloth. $1.25.

"I may say that I have myself read through the Norwegian-Danish Grammar of Peterson, and when I affirm that I find myself able to translate the reading exercises with great readiness, it may be inferred how well the book is adapted to forward one in a knowledge of this interesting but neglected language."—*A. Winchell, LL.D. Professor in Vanderbilt University, late Chancellor of the University of Syracuse.*

"I rejoice to see the door opened to American Students to the treasures of Norwegian letters, and in so attractive a manner as in Mr. Peterson's work. No more useful direction for philological study opens to English scholars now than the research into Anglo-Saxon and Norse Northern tongues. This work will be surely a valuable help in this direction."—*Prof. Frank Sewell, President of Urbana University.*

PRE-HISTORIC RACES OF THE UNITED STATES.

By J. W. FOSTER, LL.D., Author of "The Physical Geography of the Mississippi Valley," etc. 415 pages, crown 8vo, with a large number of illustrations.

Price, cloth--- $3 50
Half calf binding, gilt top------------------------------ 6 00
Full calf, gilt edges------------------------------------- 7 50

" One of the best and clearest accounts we have seen of those grand monuments of a forgotten race."—*London Saturday Review.*

" The reader will find it more fascinating than his last favorite novel."— *Eclectic Magazine, N. Y.*

" The book is literally crowded with astonishing and valuable facts."— *Boston Post.*

" It is an elegant volume and a valuable contribution to the subject. * * * Contains just the kind of information in clear, compressed and intelligible form, which is adapted to the mass of readers."—*Appleton's Popular Science Monthly.*

" The book is typographically perfect, and with its admirable illustrations and convenient index is really elegant and a sort of luxury to possess and read. * * Dr. Foster's style reminds us of Tyndall and Proctor, at their best. * * He goes over the ground, inch by inch, and accumulates information of surprising interest and importance, bearing on this subject, which he gives in his crowded but most instructive and entertaining chapters in a thoroughly scientific but equally popular way. We have marked whole pages of his book for quotation, and finally from sheer necessity have been compelled to put the whole volume in quotation marks, as one of the few books that are indispensable to the student, and scarcely less important for the intelligent reader to have at hand for reference."—*Golden Age, New York.*

A MANUAL OF GESTURE.—With over 100 Figures,

embracing a complete system of Notation, with the Principles of Interpretation and Selections for Practice. By Prof. A. M. BACON.

Price ---$1 75

" Prof. Bacon has given us a work that, in thoroughness and practical value, deserves to rank among the most remarkable books of the season. There has in fact, been no work on the subject yet offered to the public which approaches it for exhaustiveness and completeness of detail. * * It is of the utmost value, not merely to students, but to lawyers, clergymen, teachers, and public speakers, and its importance as an assistant in the formation of a correct and appropriate style of action can hardly be over-estimated."—*The Philadelphia Inquirer.*

" Prof. Bacon's Manual seems expressly arranged for the help of those who study alone and have undertaken self-instruction in the art of persuasive delivery. The work in the hands of our ministry, well studied, would have the effect of emphasizing the living words of the Gospel all over the land, and making them two-edged with meaning."—*The Chicago Pulpit.*

GETTING ON IN THE WORLD; or, Hints on Success in Life.—

By Wm. Mathews, LL.D., Professor of English Literature, etc., in the University of Chicago. Beautifully printed and handsomely bound.

Price, 1 vol., 12mo., Cloth.........$2 | Half calf binding, gilt top.......$3 50
The same, gilt edges .... 2 50 | Full calf, gilt edges............... 5 00

Contents: — *Success and Failure — Good and Bad Luck — Choice of a Profession — Physical Culture — Concentration — Self-Reliance — Originality in Aims and Methods — Attention to Details — Practical Talent — Decision — Manner — Business Habits — Self-Advertising — The Will and the Way — Reserved Power — Economy of Time — Money, its Use and Abuse — Mercantile Failures — Over-Work and Under-Rest — True and False Success.*

" A book in the highest degree attractive, * * and which will be sure to *pay in dollars and cents* many times over the cost of the work, and the time devoted to its perusal."—*Lockport Journal, New York.*

" It is sound, morally and mentally. It gives no one-sided view of life; it does not pander to the lower nature ; but it is high-toned, correctly toned throughout. * * There is an earnestness and even eloquence in this volume which makes the author appear to speak to us from the living page. It reads like a speech. There is an electric fire about every sentence."—*Episcopal Register, Philadelphia.*

" There is no danger of speaking in too high terms of praise of this volume. As a work of art it is a gem. As a counselor it speaks the wisdom of the ages. As a teacher it illustrates the true philosophy of life by the experience of eminent men of every class and calling. It warns by the story of signal failures, and encourages by the record of triumphs that seemed impossible. It is a book of facts and not of theories. The men who have succeeded in life are laid under tribute, and made to divulge the secret of their success. They give vastly more than ' hints ;' they make a revelation. They show that success lies not in luck, but in pluck. Instruction and inspiration are the chief features of the work which Prof. Mathews has done in this volume."—*Christian Era, Boston.*

THE GREAT CONVERSERS, and Other Essays.—

By Wm. Mathews, LL.D., author of " Getting On in the World."
1 volume, 12mo., 306 pages, with Map, price...................$1 75

" As fascinating as anything in fiction."—*Concord Monitor.*

" These pages are crammed with interesting facts about literary men and literary work."—*New York Evening Mail.*

" They are written in that charming and graceful style, which is so attractive in this author's writings, and the reader is continually reminded by their ease and grace of the elegant compositions of Goldsmith and Irving."—*Boston Transcript.*

" Twenty essays, all treating lively and agreeable themes, and in the easy, polished and sparkling style that has made the author famous as an essayist. * * The most striking characteristic of Prof. Mathews' writing is its wonderful wealth of illustration. * * One will make the acquaintance of more authors in the course of a single one of his essays than are probably to be met with in the same limited space anywhere else in the whole realm of our literature."—*The Chicago Tribune.*

THE WORLD ON WHEELS, and Other Sketches.—

By BENJ. F. TAYLOR. Illustrated. 1 vol., 12mo. Price, $1.50.

"Full of humor and sharp as a Damascus blade."—*Presbyterian, Phil a.*

"The pen-pictures of B. F. Taylor are among the most brilliant and eccentric productions of the day. They are like the music of Gottschalk played by Gottschalk himself; or like sky-rockets that burst in the zenith, and fall in showers of fiery rain. They are word-wonders, reminding us of necromancy, with the dazzle and bewilderment of their rapid succession."—*Chicago Tribune.*

"Reader, do you want to laugh? Do you want to cry? Do you want to climb the Jacob's ladder of imagination, and dwell among the clouds of fancy for a little while at least? Do you? Then get B. F. Taylor's World on Wheels, read it, and experience sensations you never felt before! * * It is a book of 'word pictures,' a string of pearls, the very poesy of thought."—*The Christian, St. Louis.*

"Another of Benj. F. Taylor's wonderful word painting books. * * In purity of style and originality of conception, Taylor has no superiors in this country. The book before us is a gem in every way. It is quaint, poetical, melodious, unique, rare as rare flowers are rare. He has an exquisite faculty of illustration that is unsurpassed in the whole range of American literature."—*St. Louis Dispatch.*

OLD-TIME PICTURES and SHEAVES of RHYME.

By BENJ. F. TAYLOR. Red line edition, small quarto, silk cloth, with eight fine full page illustrations.

Price..$2 00
The same, full gilt edges and gilt side.......................... 2 50

JOHN G. WHITTIER *writes :*—"It gives me pleasure to see the poems of B. F. Taylor issued by your house in a form worthy of their merit. Such pieces as the '*Old Village Choir,*' '*The Skylark,*' '*The Vane on the Spire,*' and '*June,*' deserve their good setting. * * I do not know of anyone who so well reproduces the home scenes of long ago. There is a quiet humor that pleases me."

"Unless it be Whittier, we know of no American poet so sweet, tender and gentle in his lyrics as B. F. Taylor. No writer of to-day sings the praises of rural life and scenery as eloquently, and we do not wonder that many of his poems have become classic. The holiday volume of his happy verses, OLD TIME PICTURES AND SHEAVES OF RHYME is a very eloquent and daintily bound volume, and comes from that growing and reliable publishing house of the West, S. C. Griggs & Company, of Chicago. Taking up this handsomely printed book, we hasten to linger on the delightful imagery and graceful diction of its pages, glowing as they are with pure and tender thoughts, and the earnest, indescribable music of sunny fields and rural joys. * * No one can read it but will be the better for so doing."— *The Albany Morning Express.*

PICTURES OF LIFE IN CAMP AND FIELD—By Benj.

F. Taylor, Author of "The World on Wheels," "Songs of Yesterday," etc.

12mo, cloth..$1.50

"The descriptions are singularly brilliant."—*New York Sunday Times.*

"The book will greatly interest large classes of readers."—*Boston Gazette.*

"A volume that embalms such stories of the nation's sorest hour of trial, cannot lack for thrilled and tearful readers."—*Chicago Tribune.*

"The war annals of ancient or modern times, from Cæsar's campaigns to the Franco-Prussian war, will furnish material no more beautifully wrought up than this, by the word-artist of the Great Rebellion."—*New England Journal of Education.*

"Every letter is replete with pathos ; every description is a power, and most of the anecdotes touching in the extreme. It is almost impossible to say which of these letters is best, but taken as a whole, they have formed a book that will live.—*Chicago Times.*

"The beauty of diction, amazing life-likeness, stirring action and rich coloring of these word-pictures of camp and field, have had a deservedly popular reception. . . . The art of the writer of these letters is marvelous. . . Their correctness as to facts is seldom to be questioned, and the beauty of the descriptions never."—*Syracuse Journal.*

PATMOS ; or, The Kingdom and the Patience.—By

J. A. Smith, D.D., Editor of the Standard. Square 16mo, cloth, $1.25.

"It merits universal circulation."—*Christian Standard, Philadelphia.*

"A book for the improvement of the heart."—*Christian Guardian, Toronto.*

"Admirably calculated to challenge the Christian reader to utmost doing and enduring for the sake of the Master."—*Watchman and Reflector, Boston.*

"No one can read the nine chapters which the volume contains, without receiving a new inspiration to faithful service in the cause of Christ."—*Zion's Advocate.*

"To earnest seekers for higher spiritual attainments the author has rendered a service at once great and beautiful. Originality of thought, beauty and purity of expression and graphic delineation, are among its marked features."—*National Baptist, Philadelphia.*

THE TRINITY.—By Rev. F. H. Burris. With an introduction by

Joseph Haven, D.D., LL. D. 12mo, cloth, $1.50.

"One of the most unique, sincere and thorough discussions of the subject of the Trinity, which we have ever seen . . . we commend its perusal to all our brethren."—*American Wesleyan, N. Y.*

"A thoughtful and very interesting book. . . . Much that he says is forcible and inciting to renewed thought."—*Christian Union, N. Y.*

ROBERT'S RULES OF ORDER, For Deliberative Assemblies.—

By Major H. M. Robert, Corps of Engineers, U. S. A. Pocket size, cloth, 75 cents.

This book is far superior to any other parliamentary manual in the English language. It gives in the simplest form possible all the various rules or points of law or order that can arise in the deliberations of any lodge, grange, debating club, literary society, convention, or other organized body, and every rule is complete in itself, and as easily found as a word in a dictionary. Its crowning excellence is a "Table of Rules relating to Motions," on two opposite pages which contains the answers to more than two hundred questions on parliamentary law, which will be of the greatest value to every member of an assembly.

"It should be studied by all who wish to become familiar with the correct usages of public meetings."—*E. O. Haven, D. D., Chancellor of Syracuse University.*

"It seems much better adapted to the use of societies and assemblies than either Jefferson's Manual or Cushing's."—*J. M. Gregory, LL. D., late President of the Illinois Industrial University.*

"I shall be very glad to see your Manual brought into general use, as I am sure it must be, when its great merit and utility become generally known.—*Hon. T. M. Cooley, LL. D , author of ' Cooley's Blackstone,' " etc.*

"After carefully examining it and comparing it with several other books having the same object in view, I am free to say that it is, by far, the best of all. The ' Table of Rules ' is worth the cost of the work."—*Thomas Bowman, D. D., Bishop of Baltimore M. E. Conference.*

"This capital little manual will be found exceedingly useful by all who are concerned in the organization or management of societies of various kinds. . . . If we mistake not, the book will displace all its predecessors, as an authority on parliamentary usages."—*New York World.*

"I admire the plan of your work, and the simplicity and fidelity with which you have executed it. It is one of the best compendiums of Parliamentary Law that I have seen, and exceedingly valuable, not only for the matter usually embraced in such a book, but for its tables and incidental matter, which serve greatly to adapt it to common use."—*Dr. D. C. Eddy, Speaker of the Massachusetts House of Representatives.*

MISHAPS OF MR. EZEKIEL PELTER.—Illustrated.

12mo, cloth...$1.50.

"So ludicrous are the vicissitudes of the much-abused Ezekiel, and so much of human nature and every-day life intermingle, that it will be read with a hearty zest for its *morals*, while the humor is irresistible. If you want to laugh at something new, a regular side-plitter, get this book."—*The Evangelist, St. Louis.*

"We have read Ezekiel. We have laughed and cried over its pages. It grows in interest to the last sentence. The story is well told, and the moral so good, that we decidedly like and commend it."—*Pacific Baptist, San Francisco.*

Lightning Source UK Ltd.
Milton Keynes UK
UKHW020613221218
334394UK00003B/161/P

9 780341 858898